Best of the Best from

Oregon

Cookbook

Selected Recipes from Oregon's
FAVORITE COOKBOOKS

Majestic Mt. Hood, overlooking Trillium Lake, is Oregon's best known and tallest mountain, standing at 11,240 feet. Located 50 miles east of Portland, it is now considered a dormant volcano; its last eruption was in 1907.

Best of the Best from
Oregon
Cookbook

Selected Recipes from Oregon's
FAVORITE COOKBOOKS

EDITED BY
Gwen McKee
AND
Barbara Moseley

Illustrated by Tupper England

QUAIL RIDGE PRESS
Preserving America's Food Heritage

Library of Congress Cataloging-in-Publication Data

Best of the best from Oregon : selected recipes from Oregon's favorite cookbooks /
    edited by Gwen McKee and Barbara Moseley ; illustrated by Tupper England.
    p. cm.
    ISBN-10: 1-893062-34-1
    ISBN-13: 978-1-893062-34-4
        1. Cookery, American 2. Cookery—Oregon. I. McKee, Gwen. II. Moseley, Barbara.

TX715.B4856418 2002
641.59795—dc21   2002019770

ISBN-10: 1-893062-34-1 • ISBN-13: 978-1-893062-34-4

First printing, June 2002 • Second, February 2003 • Third, February 2006 • Fourth, May 2008
Fifth, October 2010

QUAIL RIDGE PRESS
P. O. Box 123 • Brandon, MS 39043 • 1-800-343-1583
e-mail: info@quailridge.com • www.quailridge.com

Contents

Cascade Head, north of Lincoln City, rises 1200 feet above the Pacific surf. Beyond its cliffs, the 270-acre preserve hosts rare plants and animals in its unique environmental system of grasslands, groves, and rain forest.

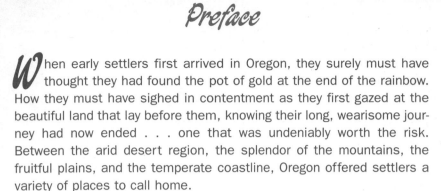

Preface

*W*hen early settlers first arrived in Oregon, they surely must have thought they had found the pot of gold at the end of the rainbow. How they must have sighed in contentment as they first gazed at the beautiful land that lay before them, knowing their long, wearisome journey had now ended . . . one that was undeniably worth the risk. Between the arid desert region, the splendor of the mountains, the fruitful plains, and the temperate coastline, Oregon offered settlers a variety of places to call home.

Home in the mountains, home on the plains. . . . Stretching majestically across the state's north/south expanse, the Cascade Mountains create two separate regions, offering a dramatic topographical diversity to the state's landscape. East of the Cascades are highly productive farmlands overflowing with potatoes, onions, carrots, etc. Here you will also find rolling wheat fields and a vast array of wild game and fish from abundant lakes. To the west, lush, rich lands yield hazelnuts, berries, fruits, and vegetables. Glistening streams overflow with salmon and trout, and the Pacific Ocean offers an abundance of crab, shrimp, scallops and oysters.

While the offerings of the land and sea dictate what goes into the cook pot, the people were (and are) just as instrumental in molding the character of Oregon's culinary history. Most notably, the skillful Native Americans introduced savory smoked salmon; the enterprising Pioneers brought with them their local foods and traditions; and immigrants from all corners of the world shared their native cuisine. We discovered all this and more in the 79 Oregon cookbooks that contributed some of their favorite Oregon recipes to this collection.

From Cracked Dungeness Crab with Herb Mayonnaise to Huckleberry-Cherry Pie, Oregon serves it up fresh, and the *Best of the Best from Oregon Cookbook* offers a taste of its incredible bounty, including such delicious recipes as Grilled Citrus Salmon, Oregon Crab Quiche, Pacific Stewpot, Zucchini and Three Pepper Stir-Fry, Blueberry-Raspberry Upside Down Cake, Snow White Bunnies or Chocolate Brown Bears. . . . We've also included photographs and quips about Oregon history and food to give you a better overall taste of the state. Following each recipe is the name of the contributing cookbook. A special Catalog of Contributing Cookbooks Section in the back of this book contains a picture of each book's cover, as well as a description of the

book and ordering information. This section is particularly popular with cookbook collectors.

We appreciate each and every person who contributed to this book, especially the people who so generously offered the recipes from their cookbooks. We thank all the food editors and the bookstore and gift shop managers who directed us to the state's most popular cook-books. Thanks also to Oregon's tourism department for providing his-toric and informative data about their state, and to many Chambers of Commerce who sent information as well as pictures. Thank you, too, Tupper England, for your charming illustrations that capture the true spirit of the state.

From all over Oregon, we are pleased and proud to present this col-lection, a true cornucopia of superb recipes. Enjoy your journey—by way of your taste buds—through this beautiful state. We hope you will find, like the settlers did, a delicious Oregon pot o' gold!

Contributing Cookbooks

Albertina's Exceptional Recipes
All About Crab
Begged, Borrowed and Stöllen Recipes
"Cate"ring to Shrimp
Caveman Classic Cuisine
Christian Bakers Cookbook
Christmastime Treats
Clam Dishes and Rock Fishes
Coastal Flavors
Collection Extraordinaire
Cookin' with Capital Press
Cooking from the Coast to the Cascades
Cooking Italian
Cooking with Love
Dilley Family Favorites
Dungeness Crabs and Blackberry Cobblers
Favorite Recipes Cookbook
Favorite Recipes from Ruralite Readers
Favorite Recipes from the Kitchen of Alma Irey
Favorite Recipes, Second Edition
Feasting in the Forest
Fiddlin' in the Kitchen
Flavor It Greek!
Fresh-Water Fish Cookbook
From Portland's Palate
The Fruit Loop Cookbook
Gems from the Kitchen
Get Cookin' with Sound Construction
Glorious Soups and Breads!
Grade A Recipes
Grandma Jean's Rainy Day Recipes
Great Recipes from Redeemer's Fellowship
Hazelnuts & More Cookbook
Heavenly Temptations
The 'Hole Cake Doughnut Book
Huckleberries and Crabmeat
King Estate New American Cuisine Pinot Gris Cookbook
The Lighter Side of Italy
Look What's Cooking
Manna by the Sea

Contributing Cookbooks

The Miller Cookbook
Multnomah Falls Lodge Cook Book
The New American Diet Cookbook
The New Complete Coffee Book
The New Tea Book
Oregon Cook Book
Oregon Farmers' Markets Cookbook and Guide
Oregon: The Other Side
Oregon Trail Cooking
Our Favorite Recipes
"Pacific"ally Salmon
Pig Out
Potluck and Patchwork
Quick & Healthy Recipes and Ideas (ScaleDown)
Quick & Healthy Volume II (ScaleDown)
Rainy Day Treats and Sunny Temptations
Recipes and Remembering
Recipes for the Weekend Gourmet
Recipes from the Kitchens of Family & Friends
Recipes, Recipes, Recipes!
Rogue River Rendezvous
Sagebrush Surprises Cookbook
Savor the Flavor
Savor the Flavor of Oregon
Scallops and Sole Food
Seasoned with Words
Serving Up Oregon
Summertime Treats
A Taste of Oregon
A Taste of Tillamook
Tastefully Oregon
Then 'til Now
Thyme and the River
Thyme & the River, Too
Treasured Recipes
West Coast Seafood Recipes
What's Cooking??
What's Cooking in Sisters
What's for Dinner?

Beverages and Appetizers

Crater Lake was formed after the violent eruption of an ancient volcano 7,700 years ago. The top 5,000 feet collapsed and subsequent lava flows sealed the bottom, creating the deepest lake (with depths up to 2,000 feet) in the U.S., and seventh deepest in the world.

Spiced Drink

2 cups apple juice
2 cups cranberry juice
1 small piece whole ginger
½ cup raisins

5 whole cloves
1 (2-inch) piece whole cinnamon
½ cup blanched whole almonds

Combine apple juice, cranberry juice, ginger, raisins, cloves, and cinnamon in heavy saucepan. Bring to boil and simmer 20 minutes. Add almonds and serve hot. Makes about 8 servings.

Savor the Flavor

Hot Spiced Wine

½ gallon burgundy wine
½ gallon apple cider
½ cup lemon juice
1 cup sugar (or to taste)

6 (3-inch) sticks cinnamon
1 tablespoon whole cloves
1 tablespoon allspice berries
Lemon slices (optional)

Heat all ingredients except lemon slices in microwave or on top of stove, stirring occasionally until sugar is dissolved and mixture is hot, not boiling. Transfer to a crockpot to keep at serving temperature. (Mixture can be started in a crockpot, but it will take much longer.) Add optional lemon slices.

Seasoned with Words

Orange Julius

This popular breakfast drink can also serve as a delicious after-school snack.

8 ounces nonfat plain yogurt	**2½ cups skim milk**
1 (6-ounce) can frozen orange juice concentrate	**1 teaspoon vanilla extract**

Blend all ingredients until smooth. Yields about 4½ cups or 6 servings.

Serving size: ¾ cup; Calories 115; Carbo. 22g; Prot. 7g; Fat 0g; Exchanges ½ milk, 1 fruit.

Quick & Healthy Recipes and Ideas (ScaleDown)

Banana Smoothie

When my kids were young, they voted me "Number 1 Mom" at a family reunion because I let them have shakes for breakfast. See what fresh juices or fruits are available at the grocery store or farmers' market and have fun experimenting with different flavors.

1 small ripe banana, cut into chunks	**½ cup plain yogurt**
½ cup fresh orange juice	**1 tablespoon sugar or honey to taste**
½ cup canned unsweetened pineapple juice	**Protein powder to taste (optional)**
	½ cup small or coarsely crushed ice cubes

In a blender, combine banana, orange juice, pineapple juice, yogurt, sugar, protein powder, and ice. Mix at high speed until smooth. Pour into 2 tall, frosty glasses.

Note: If crushing ice cubes is a problem for your blender, eliminate ice cubes, and freeze fruit and yogurt.

Summertime Treats

In Oregon, it's not just the pure mountain water that makes for the excellent-tasting beer produced by its renowned microbrewery industry—it's the hops. More than a dozen varieties grow in the Willamette Valley alone, including the Cascade hop, often considered the finest in the world.

Catalina Citrus Sun Tea

½–¾ cup black tea leaves, or 9–12 tea bags	2 cups fresh orange juice
4 cups (1 quart) cold water	Juice of 1 lemon
3 tablespoons sugar	1 peeled (membrane removed), seeded orange, cut thin
1 (6-inch) sprig fresh mint	Orange slices, mint leaves for garnish

In a glass jar, combine tea, water, sugar, and mint. Screw on cap and shake gently. Place jar in a warm, sunny location for 3 hours.

Blend orange juice and lemon juice into tea mixture. If desired, strain mixture through a sieve. Add orange pieces and refrigerate for several hours. Garnish with orange slices and mint leaves. Serves 6–8.

Variations:

Early Mint Sun Tea: For a quick, thirst-quenching sun tea, replace black tea with 2 tablespoons Earl Grey tea and omit orange and lemon juice.

Raspberry Fizz: Follow recipe for Catalina Citrus Sun Tea. Place 1–2 table-spoons raspberry syrup in a 10-ounce glass. Fill glass ⅓–½ full of chilled tea, and top with your favorite sparkling water. For a subtler taste, omit syrup and add your favorite raspberry-flavored sparkling water. Garnish with a wooden skewer threaded with the tip of a mint sprig and fresh raspberries.

Hollywood Spritzer: Follow recipe for Catalina Citrus Sun Tea. Place 1 table-spoon Cointreau in the bottom of a chilled glass or champagne flute. Fill glass ½ full of chilled tea and top with an inexpensive champagne.

The New Tea Book

Smoked Salmon Mousse

12 ounces hard smoked salmon,
  skinned (not lox)
1 tablespoon plus 2 teaspoons
  strained, fresh lemon juice
2 tablespoons chopped green onions
  (white part only)

1 teaspoon dried dill weed (or 2
  teaspoons chopped fresh)
3/4 cup melted butter, cooled
1 cup sour cream
Capers for garnish (optional)
Fresh dill weed for garnish (optional)

Break up salmon to feel for bone or skin; remove. Put in food processor with chopping blade. Add lemon juice, onions, and dill. Process until smooth. With machine running, slowly pour in cooled, melted butter until it's incorporated. Using rubber spatula, put smoked salmon mixture in a medium-size bowl. Slowly fold in sour cream till completely incorporated. Put in serving dish.

Can be served as spread on crackers, piped with decorative tip on toast rounds, or topped with tiny dollop of whipped cream with caper or sprig of dill.

Note: If using moist smoked salmon, decrease butter and sour cream to 1/2 cup each.

Coastal Flavors

Smoked Salmon Ball

1 (1-pound) can boneless, skinless
  smoked salmon
1 (8-ounce) package cream cheese,
  softened
1 teaspoon horseradish
2 teaspoons grated onion

1/2 teaspoon liquid smoke
1 tablespoon lemon juice
1/4 teaspoon salt
1/2 cup chopped pecans
3 tablespoons chopped parsley

Drain salmon. Blend with all other ingredients except pecans and parsley, then shape into a ball. Roll ball in chopped nuts and chopped parsley. Chill for several hours and serve with crackers.

Grandma Jean's Rainy Day Recipes

Salmon Pâté

This recipe was developed when we had a mound of leftover grilled salmon. Everyone fights over this pâté, including our grandchildren.

1¾ cups cooked salmon or
   1 (15-ounce) can red salmon,
   drained
1 tablespoon nonfat mayonnaise
½ cup nonfat plain yogurt
2 cloves garlic, minced
¼ teaspoon Tabasco sauce

1–2 teaspoons dried dillweed
¼ teaspoon (or less) Lite Salt
   (omit if using canned salmon)
¼ cup chopped green onions
2 teaspoons freshly squeezed lemon
   juice
1 tablespoon chopped fresh parsley

Remove skin and bones from salmon. Combine all ingredients and mix thoroughly with a fork (not a food processor). Cover and chill in refrigerator. Serve with low-fat crackers or thinly sliced French bread. Makes 2 cups.

Per ¼ cup: Calories 71; Sod. 101mg; Fiber Trace; Total Fat 3g; Sat Fat. 1g; Chol. 23mg; Chol-saturated Fat Index 2.

The New American Diet Cookbook

Gamberetti All'olio e Limone
(Marinated Shrimp)

Prepare the marinade and the shrimp separately and combine them just before serving. A stunning focal point for your antipasto!

1 pound frozen baby shrimp
   (already cooked, peeled and
   deveined)
½ cup extra virgin olive oil

2 tablespoons fresh lemon juice
1 clove garlic, minced
¼ teaspoon salt
½ teaspoon oregano

Defrost the shrimp by placing them in a colander, and running cold water over them. Drain well and place in a covered plastic container in the refrigerator. Meanwhile, in a small bowl, whisk together the remaining ingredients, and put that mixture in a separate plastic container. About 30 minutes before serving, combine the shrimp and the marinade, and serve. Serves 6.

Note: Resist the temptation to combine the shrimp with the marinade ahead of time—it will make the shrimp tough!

Feasting in the Forest

Dungeness Crab Puffs

6 ounces Dungeness crab
1 cup mayonnaise
1 cup grated Swiss cheese
1/2 cup finely chopped onion

1 package frozen puff pastry
  (2 sheets), defrosted
1 whole egg beaten with 1 teaspoon
  water

Preheat oven to 400°. Combine crab, mayonnaise, Swiss cheese, and onion in a medium bowl, blending well. Flatten sheets of puff pastry and lightly roll them out. Cut each of the sheets into thirds lengthwise, and then into fourths along the short side, making a total of 12 squares per sheet. Brush lightly with beaten egg and water. Put a teaspoon of filling in center of each square. Fold squares in half diagonally, and seal by pressing tines of a fork around the edges. Brush tops with more of the beaten egg mixture. Place puffs on a baking sheet lined with baking parchment (or a non-stick baking sheet) and bake for 10–12 minutes, or until puffed and golden brown. Let cool for 4 minutes or so before serving. Makes 24 appetizers.

Serving Size: 1 puff; Calories 210; Total Fat 19g; Sat. Fat 3g; Chol. 20mg; Sod. 140mg; Carbo. 10g; Fiber 0g; Sugars 1g; Prot. 5g.

All About Crab

Crabmeat Mornay

This is great served as an hors d'oeuvre in a chafing dish with melba rounds or in patty shells.

1 stick butter
1 small bunch green onions,
  chopped
1/2 cup finely-chopped parsley
2 tablespoons flour
3/4 pint half-and-half

3/4 pound grated Swiss cheese
Red pepper to taste
Tabasco to taste
Salt to taste
1 pound fresh lump crabmeat
1 tablespoon dry sherry

In a heavy saucepan, melt butter and sauté onions and parsley. Blend in flour, half-and-half, and cheese until cheese melts. Add red pepper, Tabasco, and salt to taste. Gently fold in crabmeat. It is important to continually stir to keep from scorching. Just before serving, blend in dry sherry.

What's Cooking??

Knock-Your-Socks-Off Hot Crab Dip

½ cup dry white wine
4 ounces cream cheese, room
  temperature
1 (16-ounce) can water-packed
  artichoke hearts, drained and
  finely chopped
1 cup mayonnaise

1 egg
1 pound fresh crab or 2 (8-ounce)
  cans crabmeat
2 ounces blue cheese, finely
  crumbled
Sliced black olives for garnish
  (optional)

Preheat oven to 350°. In a saucepan over low heat, combine white wine and cream cheese and simmer until cheese is creamy. Remove from heat and blend thoroughly with wire whisk. Stir in artichoke hearts, mayonnaise, egg, crabmeat, and blue cheese. Pour into 8x8-inch oven-proof baking dish and bake for 30 minutes at 350°. Garnish with black olives, if desired. Serve with crackers. Yields 10–12 servings.

From Portland's Palate

Crunchy Vegetable Dip

1 (8-ounce) package cream
  cheese, softened
1 tablespoon mayonnaise
1 tablespoon lemon juice
½ teaspoon salt
⅛ teaspoon pepper

¾ cup grated carrots
½ cup diced celery
½ cup diced cucumber
½ cup diced green pepper
⅓ cup diced green onions
Crackers or bread

In a mixing bowl, beat cream cheese, mayonnaise, lemon juice, salt and pepper until smooth. Stir in vegetables. Cover and refrigerate for 2–3 hours. Serve with crackers or use as a sandwich spread. Makes 2 cups.

Dilley Family Favorites

Spanish Avocado Dip

3 medium ripe avocados
2 tablespoons lemon juice
½ teaspoon salt
¼ teaspoon pepper
1 cup (8 ounces) sour cream
½ cup mayonnaise
1 package taco seasoning mix
2 cans bean dip

1 large bunch green onions, chopped
3 medium tomatoes, chopped
2 (3½-ounce) cans black olives,
    drained and chopped
8 ounces sharp Cheddar cheese,
    shredded
Tortilla chips

Mash avocados with lemon juice, salt and pepper. Combine sour cream, mayonnaise, and taco seasoning mix. Spread bean dip on large platter. Top with avocado mixture. Layer with sour cream and taco mixture. Top with onions, tomatoes, and olives. Cover with shredded cheese. Serve with large tortilla chips.

Note: May use 2 large pie plates or a 9x13-inch pan.

Favorite Recipes, Second Edition

Chili Cheese Dip

This dip is popular at parties. Watch your portion size as the calories can easily add up. We have chosen the light cream cheese instead of the nonfat because we think it has a better flavor in this recipe. However, many find the flavor of the non-fat cream cheese acceptable.

1 (15-ounce) can reduced-fat
    turkey chili with beans

½ cup light cream cheese

Mix together in a microwave-safe bowl. Cover and cook on HIGH until hot (about 1 minute), stirring several times during cooking. Yields 2 cups.

Serving size: 2 tablespoons; Calories 40; Carbo. 3g; Prot. 3g; Fat 2g; Exchanges ⅓ starch, ⅓ lean meat.

Quick & Healthy Volume II (ScaleDown)

Nurtured by up to 72 inches of rain per year, Tillamook's lush grasses sustain the herds of Oregon's dairy industry. Coincidentally, Tillamook is the home of Oregon's largest cheese factory where much of the county's annual milk production of 25 million gallons is made into cheese.

Brie with Mushrooms

½ pound sliced mushrooms
½ stick butter, melted
1 teaspoon Lawry's Garlic Blend

½–1 teaspoon brandy
1 large round of Brie

Sauté mushrooms in melted butter; season with garlic blend. Add brandy. Pour over Brie. Melt in microwave for 2 minutes or until soft. Serve with crackers.

Treasured Recipes

Warm Brie

Delicious yet simple to prepare.

1 (8-ounce) round Brie cheese
¼ cup margarine or butter
¼ cup packed brown sugar

¼ cup chopped nuts
1 tablespoon honey

Place round of Brie in a shallow baking dish or pie plate. Bake in a 350° oven for 10 minutes. Meanwhile, in a small saucepan, combine margarine or butter, brown sugar, nuts, and honey. Bring mixture to boiling over medium heat, stirring constantly. Pour sauce over Brie. Cut into wedges to serve. Serve with crackers. Makes 8 yummy appetizer servings.

Get Cookin' with Sound Construction

Mexican Caviar

**2 (4½-ounce) cans chopped
   ripe olives**
**2 (4-ounce) cans chopped green
   chiles**
2 tomatoes, peeled and chopped
3 green onions, chopped

2 garlic cloves, mashed
3 teaspoons olive oil
3 teaspoons red wine vinegar
1 teaspoon pepper
A dash of seasoning salt

Combine all ingredients and chill overnight. Serve with Fritos Scoops Corn Chips. Serves 8–10.

Treasured Recipes

Jalapeño Roll-Ups

This mixture works well for a dip with crackers, chips or veggies.

1 (8-ounce) package cream cheese, softened
1 cup sour cream
1 (4-ounce) can jalapeño peppers, diced
1 (6-ounce) can black olives, drained and finely chopped

2 cups grated Cheddar cheese
3/4 cup finely chopped onions
1 tablespoon Worcestershire sauce
Seasoned salt to taste
1 teaspoon garlic salt
1/2–1 teaspoon Tabasco sauce
6–8 burrito-size tortilla shells

Mix together softened cream cheese and sour cream. Add remaining ingredients except tortilla shells; mix well. Spread onto tortilla shells. (It should be spread thin.) Roll shells tightly. Wrap each in plastic wrap and let set at least 5 hours or overnight. Slice and serve with choice of salsa.

Pig Out

Egg Rolls

EGG SKINS:
12 eggs
2 tablespoons cornstarch

2 teaspoons salt
1 1/2 cups water

Beat eggs, add cornstarch and salt, and beat in water. Heat oil in bottom of wok or 8-inch frying pan and pour 1/2 cupful of batter into pan. Fry lightly, then turn and fry on other side. Reserve remaining batter. Makes 16 Egg Skins.

FILLING:
4 cups bean sprouts
1 cup shredded bamboo shoots
2 cups shredded water chestnuts
3 cups slivered cooked chicken
1 1/2 cups finely cut scallops

1/2 cup finely chopped parsley
1 cup finely chopped mushrooms
1/2 cup finely chopped green onions
1 teaspoon salt
3 tablespoons cooking oil

Mix all Filling ingredients together and cook in a little oil for 8–10 minutes, stirring occasionally to prevent sticking. Let mixture cool, then spoon onto Egg Skins, using about half a cup for each skin. Fold in the ends and completely seal. Dip in thin batter and fry in hot oil for 5 minutes, turning carefully to brown on both sides. When done, slice diagonally in 1-inch slices and serve hot.

Scallops and Sole Food

Cocktail Pizzas

A family favorite!

1/8 cup salad oil
1/2 onion, chopped
3 tablespoons vinegar
1 (4-ounce) can chile peppers,
  chopped

1 (4 1/2-ounce) can ripe olives,
  chopped
1 pound Cheddar cheese, grated
Cocktail rye bread rounds

Mix all ingredients except bread. Spread on cocktail rye bread slices.
Place under broiler until cheese melts, about 5 minutes.

Gems from the Kitchen

Pear Slices with Oregon Blue Cheese and Prosciutto

The major winter pear varieties include the Anjou, Bosc, Comice, Nelis, Forelle, and Seckel pears and, of the national harvest, 95 percent are grown in Oregon and Washington. Pears have a sweet, buttery flesh which makes them a perfect counterbalance to the saltiness of the prosciutto and cheese used in this recipe.

4 butter lettuce leaves
6 ounces thinly sliced prosciutto
1 ripe pear, cored and sliced into
  1/2-inch-thick wedges

1/2 pound blue cheese, broken into
  bite-size pieces

Line a plate with lettuce leaves. Separate the pieces of prosciutto and lay them on a cutting board. Cut each piece in half, lengthwise, into approximately 12 (3x5-inch) pieces. Slice each wedge of pear in half, or into a bite-size piece, and put each piece in the center of a piece of prosciutto. Put 1/2–1 teaspoon of blue cheese on top of the pear and wrap the prosciutto over the pear and cheese. Place seam-side-down on the lettuce-lined serving plate and chill until served. Serves 4.

Dungeness Crabs and Blackberry Cobblers

Bread and Breakfast

A favorite of photographers, the spectacular Painted Hills, part of John Day Fossil Beds, feature nature's watercolors at their best. The unusual stripes of color are actually layers of weathering volcanic ash deposited up to 40 million years ago.

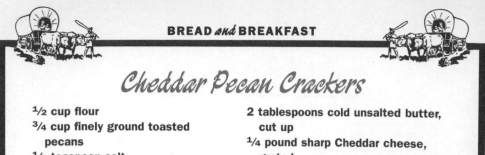
Cheddar Pecan Crackers

½ cup flour	2 tablespoons cold unsalted butter,
¾ cup finely ground toasted	cut up
pecans	¼ pound sharp Cheddar cheese,
½ teaspoon salt	grated
¼ teaspoon ground black pepper	2 tablespoons cold water
¼ teaspoon cayenne	Kosher salt for sprinkling (optional)

Heat oven to 350°. In food processor, pulse flour, pecans, ½ teaspoon salt, black pepper, and cayenne. Add butter; pulse until mixture resembles coarse meal. Add grated cheese; pulse until pieces are no longer visible. With machine running, gradually add cold water; process until dough comes together.

Transfer to a lightly floured surface; divide dough into 2 equal parts. Roll out each into a ¼-inch thickness. Sprinkle very lightly with kosher salt (optional). Cut dough into 2½-inch rounds or other desired shape; transfer to ungreased baking sheet. Bake for 15 minutes until centers are firm to touch. Do not overbake. Cool on wire rack. Store in airtight containers. Makes 16.

Great Recipes from Redeemer's Fellowship

Zingy Cheddar Butter

6 ounces shredded extra sharp	1 cup butter, room temperature
Cheddar cheese, room	2 teaspoons horseradish
temperature	

Combine all ingredients in the work bowl of a food processor fitted with a steel blade. Process on medium speed for 60 seconds, scraping down the sides as needed. Store in an air-tight plastic container in the refrigerator. Let stand at room temperature for 30 minutes before serving. Makes 1½ cups.

Serving Size: 1 tablespoon; Calories 96.4; Total Fat 10g (92%); Sat. Fat 6.3g; Chol. 28.2mg; Sod. 123mg; Carbo. Less than 1g.

Glorious Soups and Breads!

Focaccia
(Italian Snack Bread)

2½–3 cups flour, divided
1 package rapid-rise yeast
½ teaspoon salt
2 tablespoons sugar

1 cup warm water (120°–130°)
2 tablespoons olive oil
1 egg

In large bowl, combine 1 cup flour, yeast, salt, and sugar. Combine warm water and olive oil; add to flour mixture. Beat until smooth. Add egg and mix well. Then add enough flour to form a soft dough. Turn onto a floured surface; knead until smooth and elastic, about 6–8 minutes. Pat out evenly to fit a 12-inch pizza pan that has been greased with olive oil.

TOPPING:
¼ cup butter
½ cup white or brown sugar

2 teaspoons cinnamon
½ cup chopped walnuts

Melt butter, spread evenly on dough and sprinkle with mixture of sugar, cinnamon, and nuts. Let dough rise for 15–20 minutes. Bake at 350° for 25–30 minutes.

Potluck and Patchwork

Bruschetta

1 cup pitted ripe olives
2 teaspoons balsamic vinegar
1 teaspoon capers, drained
1 teaspoon olive oil
2 cloves garlic, minced
1 cup chopped red and/or yellow
   tomatoes
⅓ cup thinly sliced green onions
1 tablespoon olive oil

1 tablespoon fresh snipped basil or
   1 teaspoon dried oregano, crushed
Pepper to taste
1 (8-ounce) baguette, sliced
   ½ inch wide
2 tablespoons olive oil (optional)
½ cup Parmesan cheese, grated or
   shredded

In blender, combine first 5 ingredients and blend until smooth to make an olive paste (paste can be covered and chilled for up to 2 days). In separate bowl, stir next 5 ingredients together (this mixture can also be covered and chilled for up to 2 days). Brush bread slices lightly with olive oil, if desired. Place on baking sheet and bake, turning once, at 425°, until crisp and lightly browned (cooled bread slices can be stored, covered, at room temperature for 1 day). Spread each toast with a thin layer of olive paste. Top with 2 tablespoons tomato mixture. Sprinkle with Parmesan. Place on cookie sheet and bake at 425° for 2–3 minutes. Serve warm.

What's Cooking??

North Beach Bruschetta

⅔ cup part-skim ricotta cheese
¼ cup shredded carrot
¼ cup dried currants
2 tablespoons chopped green onion
1 tablespoon Dijon mustard, or
   more for garnish
½ teaspoon dried basil leaves

1 (½ pound) loaf crusty bread
   such as Italian ciabatta or
   French bread
½–¾ pound very thinly sliced
   pastrami
⅓ cup shredded mozzarella
Parsley sprigs

In a bowl, combine ricotta, carrot, currants, onion, mustard, and basil. Cut bread in half horizontally. Turn with crust down; if needed, trim from cut side to make pieces about 1 inch thick. Trim crust so bread sits steadily. Cut each piece in half crosswise. Spread cut sides of bread with ricotta mixture. Loosely pleat pastrami onto ricotta, covering bread, then sprinkle meat with mozzarella. Place bread on a 12x15-inch baking sheet. Bake in 400° oven until mozzarella melts, 7–10 minutes. Garnish with parsley and accompany with mustard. Serves 4.

Recipes, Recipes, Recipes!

Salmon Pasties

(Pass-tees)

1 (½-pound) can salmon
1 cup shredded Cheddar cheese
¼ cup chopped celery
1 tablespoon chopped parsley
⅓ cup sour cream

1 (10-count) package refrigerated
   biscuits
1 tablespoon butter or margarine,
   melted

Combine salmon, cheese, celery, parsley, and sour cream. Roll each biscuit into a 4-inch oval. Place ⅓ cup salmon mixture on each of 5 biscuits. Top with remaining biscuits; seal edges with a fork. Brush tops with melted butter. Let stand for 15 minutes. Place pasties on a cookie sheet. Bake at 400° for 15–18 minutes.

"Pacific"ally Salmon

The Chinook salmon Is Oregon's official state fish.

Tailgate Sandwich

Inspired by the annual "Civil War" football game between the University of Oregon and Oregon State University.

1 loaf focaccia	¼ pound turkey, sliced
Olive oil	¼ pound prosciutto, sliced
Salt and other desired dried herbs	1 red onion, thinly sliced
6–8 tablespoons butter, room temperature	¼ pound provolone cheese, sliced
	1 small tomato, thinly sliced
4–6 tablespoons mayonnaise	1 cup shredded fresh spinach
4–6 tablespoons Dijon mustard	

Preheat oven to 300°. Season bread by brushing top of loaf with olive oil and sprinkling with salt and other seasonings. Place on lightly greased cookie sheet and bake for 15–20 minutes in 300° oven. Remove and cool.

Slice cooled focaccia in half horizontally, and spread both halves with butter, mayonnaise, and mustard. Layer ingredients on bottom half of bread in the following order: turkey, prosciutto, onion, provolone, tomato slices, and spinach. Place second half on top of layered ingredients. Wrap sandwich tightly with plastic wrap, then wrap in aluminum foil. Refrigerate at least 8 hours, or overnight. Cut into wedges to serve. Yields 4–6 servings.

From Portland's Palate

Salad Buns

1 pound American cheese, grated	½ small can green chiles, chopped
6 green onions, chopped	1 small can ripe olives, chopped
2 cloves garlic, chopped	1 (15-ounce) can tomato sauce
3 boiled eggs, chopped	½ cup oil (optional)
½ tablespoon salt	18–24 English muffin halves

Mix all ingredients together. Spread on English muffins. Broil until brown and bubbly. Makes about 20 muffins.

Savor the Flavor

One Hour Dinner Rolls Italiano

3½–4 cups flour, divided
2 packages yeast
2 tablespoons sugar
2 teaspoons garlic salt
1 teaspoon Italian seasoning
1 cup milk

½ cup water
4 tablespoons butter, divided
1 egg
¾ cup Parmesan cheese (canned),
  divided

In a large mixing bowl, combine 1½ cups flour, yeast, sugar, garlic salt, and seasoning; mix well. In saucepan, heat milk, water, and 2 tablespoons butter; add to flour mixture. Add egg. Blend at low speed until moist; beat 3 minutes at medium speed. By hand, gradually stir in ½ cup cheese and remaining flour to make a stiff dough. Knead 3–5 minutes. Place in greased bowl; grease top of dough. Place in warm oven (turn on oven at lowest setting for one minute, then turn off) for 15 minutes. Punch down dough and divide into 16 pieces. Form into balls. Melt 2 tablespoons butter; dip tops of rolls into melted butter and remaining ¼ cup Parmesan cheese. Place in greased 9x13-inch pan or 2 (8-inch) round pans; cover and let rise in warm oven for 10 minutes. Bake at 375° for 20–25 minutes. Remove from pan and cool. Makes 16 rolls.

Rainy Day Treats and Sunny Temptations

Angel Biscuits

5 cups self-rising flour (sift, then
  measure)
⅓ cup sugar
1 teaspoon soda

1 cup shortening
2 cups buttermilk, room temperature
2 packages yeast, dissolved in ¼
  cup warm water (105°–115°)

Sift flour, sugar, and soda together. Add shortening and buttermilk. Add yeast mixture. Mix as for biscuits. Store in plastic bowl with tight-fitting lid in refrigerator and use as needed up to 2 weeks. Roll out on floured board, using self-rising flour, and cut. Let rise 1–2 hours. Bake at 425°–450° for 10–12 minutes. Yields 3 dozen.

Look What's Cooking

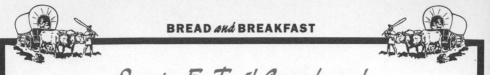
Santa Fe Trail Cornbread

Even those who don't like cornbread enjoy this.

1 cup butter or margarine
1 cup granulated sugar
4 eggs
1 (4-ounce) can green chiles, seeded and chopped (optional)
1 (16-ounce) can cream-style corn

½ cup shredded mild Cheddar cheese
1 cup sifted flour
1 cup sifted yellow cornmeal
4 teaspoons baking powder
½ teaspoon salt

Cream butter and sugar. Mixing well, add eggs, one at a time. Add chiles, corn, and cheese and mix well. Sift flour and cornmeal together with baking powder and salt. Add to corn mixture. Blend well. Pour into greased and floured 9x13-inch baking dish. Place pan in pre-heated 350° oven and immediately reduce heat to 300°. Bake for 1 hour and serve warm.

Recipes and Remembering

Yachats Indian Cornbread

1 (½-pound) can salmon, drained (reserve liquid)
1 cup flour, sifted
1 cup cornmeal
4 teaspoons baking powder
¼ cup sugar

½ teaspoon salt
1 egg, beaten
Salmon liquid plus enough milk to equal 1 cup
¼ cup butter or margarine, melted

Flake salmon. Sift together flour, cornmeal, baking powder, sugar, and salt. Combine egg, salmon liquid/milk mixture, and butter. Add to dry ingredients and mix just enough to moisten. Fold in flaked salmon. Place in well-greased, 8x8-inch baking dish and bake at 425° for 25 minutes.

"Pacific"ally Salmon

Overnight Hobo Bread

2 cups raisins
4 teaspoons baking soda
2¹/₂ cups boiling water
³/₄ cup brown sugar

1 cup sugar
4 tablespoons vegetable oil
1 teaspoon salt
4 cups flour

Put raisins, baking soda, and boiling water in a large bowl and soak overnight. The next day, combine brown sugar, sugar, oil, salt, and flour. Add to raisin mixture and mix well. Pour into 3 greased and floured 9x5-inch loaf pans. Bake at 350° for 50 minutes to 1 hour. Yields 3 loaves.

Savor the Flavor of Oregon

Cranberry-Orange-Banana Bread

2 cups flour
1 cup sugar
¹/₂ teaspoon soda
1 teaspoon salt
¹/₄ cup shortening
1 tablespoon finely grated orange peel

¹/₃ cup orange juice
1 egg, well beaten
¹/₂ cup mashed banana or 1 large banana
¹/₂ can whole cranberry sauce
¹/₂ cup chopped nuts (optional)

Combine flour, sugar, soda, salt, and shortening in a bowl until mixture resembles coarse cornmeal. Add orange peel, juice, well beaten egg, banana, cranberry sauce, and nuts. Mix only until flour is moistened and you don't see any white flour. Bake at 350° in 9x5x3-inch greased and floured pan about 1 hour or until toothpick tests clean. Can bake in 3 soup cans (sprayed with cooking spray) and bake 40–45 minutes.

Savor the Flavor

The river that flows from Steens Mountain to Malheur Lake was left with a rather unusual name. In 1864, Colonel George B. Currey, remembering his German lessons, called it the "Dunder und Blitzen" because of the thunder and lightning he encountered while crossing it. But when less cosmopolitan folks moved in, the "Dunder" part got changed. Now the Donner und Blitzen River sounds like it was named for some flying reindeer. A remote, scenic river, it is best known for its redband rainbow trout fishing.

Triple Chocolate Quick Bread

1/2 cup butter or margarine, softened
2/3 cup packed brown sugar
2 eggs
1 cup (6 ounces) miniature semisweet chocolate chips, melted
1 1/2 cups applesauce

2 teaspoons vanilla
2 1/2 cups flour
1 teaspoon baking soda
1 teaspoon baking powder
1 teaspoon salt
1/2 cup miniature semisweet chocolate chips

In a mixing bowl, cream butter and sugar. Add eggs and melted chocolate; mix well. Add applesauce and vanilla. Set aside. Combine dry ingredients and add to creamed mixture; mix well. Stir in chocolate chips. Spoon batter into 4 greased 5 1/2 x 3 x 2-inch loaf pans. Bake at 350° for 35–40 minutes or until they test done. Cool in pans 10 minutes before removing to a wire rack and cool completely. Drizzle Glaze over warm bread. Makes 4 mini-loaves.

GLAZE:

1/2 cup miniature semisweet chocolate chips
1 tablespoon butter or margarine
2–3 tablespoons half-and-half

1/2 cup powdered sugar
1/4 teaspoon vanilla
Pinch of salt

Melt chocolate chips and butter in saucepan; stir in half-and-half. Remove from heat; stir in sugar, vanilla, and salt.

Note: An acceptable substitute for butter or margarine is 7/8 cup of shortening plus 1/2 teaspoon salt.

Then 'til Now

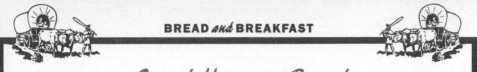

Grand Marnier Bread

Try it toasted, with Grand Marnier-flavored butter!

2 tablespoons active dry yeast
8–8½ cups all-purpose white
  flour, divided
2 teaspoons salt
¼ cup sugar
2 tablespoons honey
2 large whole eggs
¼ cup butter, melted

2 tablespoons grated orange zest
½ cup frozen orange juice
  concentrate, room temperature
2 tablespoons Grand Marnier liqueur
2 cups hot water (115°)
½ cup orange marmalade
1 egg white beaten with 2
  teaspoons water, for glaze

Combine yeast, 5 cups flour, salt, sugar, honey, eggs, melted butter, orange zest, orange juice concentrate, and Grand Marnier in a large mixing bowl. Mix lightly. Add hot water all at once, stirring well to combine. Beat with an electric mixer for 2–3 minutes. Add 3 more cups of flour and lightly work it in by hand. Turn the dough out onto a clean, dry, countertop and knead for 10 minutes, or until smooth and elastic, adding enough additional flour to keep the dough from sticking. Place dough in a warm, buttered bowl, turning to coat all sides. Cover with a clean, dry towel, and let rise in a warm, draft-free location until doubled (about 1½ hours). Punch dough down, and knead lightly.

Melt marmalade in a small saucepan over low heat. Set aside to cool slightly. Divide dough into 2 equal portions. Roll out each portion to a 9x12-inch rectangle. Using a pastry brush, spread ¼ cup marmalade on each portion, and roll up jellyroll-style, starting with the 9-inch side. Place loaves in buttered 5x9-inch bread pans. Cover with towels, and let rise in a warm place until they double again (about 1½ hours).

Preheat oven to 375°. Gently brush tops of loaves with egg white glaze and bake loaves for 30–35 minutes, or until they are a deep golden brown on top, and sound hollow when tapped. Cool in the pans for 10 minutes. Then remove loaves from pans and let cool completely on a rack. Makes 2 loaves.

Serving Size: 1 slice (¹⁄₁₆ of loaf); Calories 158; Total Fat 1.4g (8%); Sat. Fat .1g; Chol. 15.2mg; Sod. 149mg; Carbo. 31.8g.

Glorious Soups and Breads!

Toasted Hazelnut Grand Marnier Star

The dough for this pastry is quite soft, so it should be very cold when handled. Refrigerate any dough you are not using. It is also helpful to refrigerate the bottom round while working on the top. The recipe makes two pastries. Serve one and freeze the other.

FILLING:

6 ounces (1 cup) dried apricots
1 cup brown sugar
1 (8-ounce) package cream cheese, softened

2 tablespoons Grand Marnier liqueur
1/2 cup plus 1 tablespoon finely chopped, toasted hazelnuts

Soak apricots in boiling water to cover until softened, about 5 minutes. Drain, and chop in food processor. Mix in brown sugar, softened cream cheese, Grand Marnier liqueur, and toasted hazelnuts.

EGG YOLK GLAZE:

1 egg yolk
1 tablespoon cold water

Pinch salt

Whisk ingredients together and refrigerate.

ORANGE GLAZE:

1 cup sifted powdered sugar
1 teaspoon butter, melted
1 teaspoon orange zest

1 tablespoon Grand Marnier liqueur
Milk

Mix sugar, butter, orange zest, and Grand Marnier together. Add enough milk to make a thin glaze.

PASTRY:

1 1/2 tablespoons or 1 1/2
(1/4-ounce) packages active
dry yeast
1 cup warm water (105°–115°)
1/4 cup sugar, divided
1/2 cup butter, softened

1/4 cup nonfat dry milk
3 large eggs
1 teaspoon salt
4 cups unbleached white flour, divided

Stir yeast, warm water, and 2 tablespoons sugar together in a large mixing bowl. Let stand until foamy, about 3 minutes. Mix in butter, dry milk, eggs, salt, and the remaining sugar. Add 1 1/2 cups flour and beat with electric mixer until the consistency of thick cake batter, about 2 minutes. Gradually mix in remaining flour. With a heavy duty mixer, or by hand, knead until the dough is smooth and elastic.

Place in greased bowl, turn to coat entire ball, cover with dampened kitchen towel, and refrigerate overnight, or for about 6 hours. Punch down, turn out onto lightly floured surface, and divide into 4 equal

(continued)

(Toasted Hazelnut Grand Marnier Star continued)

parts. Refrigerate dough that is not being used. Roll one piece of dough into a 11½-inch circle. Place in the center of a greased 12-inch pizza-type pan.

Spread half the Filling on the pastry to within ½ inch of the outer edge. Lightly brush edge with cold water.

Roll another piece of dough into a 11½-inch circle and place on top of Filling. Gently press edges together. Using a 2-inch biscuit cutter, make an outline of the circle in the center of the dough. With scissors, make 6 snips to form a 6 pointed star, starting in the center of the pastry and cutting to the outline of the circle. Lay the points open to expose the filling. Sprinkle one tablespoon chopped toasted hazelnuts over the exposed Filling.

With knife or pizza cutter, cut pie-shaped wedges, starting one inch from edge of exposed Filling, cutting to the outer edge of the pastry. Wedges should be ½ inch wide at the center and 1½ inches wide at the outside edge. Give each wedge a double twist, forming a starburst pattern. Repeat with remaining dough, making 2 pastries. Cover with an oiled plastic wrap and let rise until a slight indention remains when lightly pressed with fingertip, about 45 minutes. Shortly before baking, position a baking rack in the center of the oven and heat the oven to 350°. Brush loaves with Egg Yolk Glaze and bake on the center rack of a 350° oven until golden, about 20–25 minutes. Cool on rack and drizzle with Orange Glaze.

Hazelnuts & More Cookbook

The United States imported most of its hazelnuts from Italy, Spain, France, and Turkey until the 1940's. They are now grown in Oregon and Washington. Oregon is the only state that has an official state nut—the hazelnut. Almost all of the hazelnuts grown in the United States are from the rich soil of the Willamette Valley in Oregon. These hazelnuts, also known as filberts, are considered to be the best in the world. Dorris Ranch in Springfield became the first commercial filbert orchard in the state.

Cranberry Muffins

1 cup raw, chopped cranberries	3/4 teaspoon baking soda
3/4 cup sugar, divided	1 egg, beaten
2 cups flour	3/4 cup sour milk or buttermilk
1/4 teaspoon salt	1/4 cup melted shortening

Combine cranberries and 1/2 cup sugar. Sift flour, salt, soda, and 1/4 cup sugar together. Mix egg, milk, and shortening; add to dry ingredients; then add cranberries, mixing slightly. Fill greased muffin pan 2/3 full. Bake at 400° for 20 minutes. Makes 1 dozen.

Gems from the Kitchen

Raspberry Lemon Streusel Muffins

Although these muffins require a lot of prep time, they are scrumptious and definitely worth it. Don't let the raspberries thaw, they will begin to run into the batter.

STREUSEL TOPPING:

1/4 cup butter or margarine, melted	1 1/2 teaspoons finely shredded
1/2 cup flour	lemon peel
2 tablespoons sugar	

Stir all ingredients together to form soft, crumbly dough. Set aside.

MUFFINS:

2 1/2 cups flour	1 cup buttermilk
2 teaspoons baking powder	1/2 cup butter or margarine, melted
1 teaspoon baking soda	1 tablespoon lemon juice
1 1/3 cups sugar	1 1/2 cups (about 6 ounces) whole
1 tablespoon finely shredded	frozen raspberries (do not thaw)
lemon peel	Flour (to coat raspberries)
1 egg	

Whisk dry muffin ingredients and lemon peel together. In a separate bowl, combine all liquid ingredients, including egg. Add in dry ingredients and stir until almost fully incorporated. Roll frozen raspberries in flour to coat, then fold into dough. Using paper muffin cup liners, fill each cup within 1/4-inch from top. Crumble Streusel Topping over each. Bake for 15 minutes, then reduce heat to 350° and bake for another 10 minutes, or until lightly browned, and muffin springs back when pressed lightly with fingertip. Makes 24 muffins.

Serving Up Oregon

Cream Cheese Swirls

DOUGH:

1 cup sour cream	2 packages yeast (dry)
½ cup butter, melted	½ cup warm water
½ cup sugar	2 eggs, beaten
1 teaspoon salt	4 cups flour

Combine sour cream, butter, sugar, and salt. Mix well. Dissolve yeast in warm water in large bowl. Stir in sour cream mixture, then eggs. Add flour 1 cup at a time, mixing well. Dough will be soft. Cover and chill overnight.

FILLING:

1 (8-ounce) package cream cheese, softened	2 teaspoons vanilla
¾ cup sugar	⅛ teaspoon nutmeg
1 egg	½ teaspoon salt

Divide Dough into 2 equal portions. Knead each on lightly floured board 4–5 times and roll into 10x16-inch rectangle. Beat Filling ingredients together and spread ½ (approximately 1 cup) on each rectangle. Roll up, jellyroll-fashion, seal ends, and cut into 1½-inch-thick slices. Place 2 inches apart on greased baking sheets. Cover and let rise in warm place until doubled. Bake at 375° for 12 minutes, until golden brown.

GLAZE:

2 cups powdered sugar	2 teaspoons vanilla
¼ cup milk	Dash of nutmeg

Mix Glaze ingredients and drizzle over rolls.

Great Recipes from Redeemer's Fellowship

Sour Cream Rollups

As anyone who visits the Steamboat Inn knows, this dish is our "House Breakfast Special"—we couldn't remove them from the menu even if we wanted to without having a battle on our hands!

1 cup white flour
1 cup whole wheat flour
1/2 teaspoon salt
1 1/2 teaspoons baking powder
1 1/2 teaspoons sugar
1 1/2 teaspoons baking soda
2 cups buttermilk

2 eggs
2 1/2 tablespoons oil
2 cups sour cream
1 cup preserves, homemade or
**   purchased**
Powdered sugar

Combine dry ingredients. Combine buttermilk, eggs, and oil together and add to dry ingredients, beating just until all is incorporated.

To cook on a griddle: Ladle out a 12-inch strip of batter, using 1/2 cup of batter. Cook until batter starts to bubble and firm up. Flip over to cook other side.

To cook in a skillet: Pour batter in a round pancake shape and cook as above. When pancake is finished cooking, remove from pan.

Spoon 1/3 cup sour cream along the pancake and top with 3 table-spoons preserves. Roll up in jellyroll fashion and top with a dollop of sour cream and jam. Dust with powdered sugar.

Thyme & the River, Too

Wonders

3 eggs
3 tablespoons sugar
½ teaspoon salt

3 tablespoons melted shortening
2 cups flour

Beat eggs very light; add sugar and salt, then shortening and flour to make a batter stiff enough to roll. Roll very thinly on a floured surface; cut in 3-inch squares. Make several slits to form "fingers" in each square to ½ inch of edge. Fry in deep hot fat (375° to 385°) until golden brown. Drain on paper towels. When cool, dust with powdered sugar.

The 'Hole Cake Doughnut Book

Bohemian Nut Slices

1 envelope yeast
¼ cup warm water (about 95°)
1 teaspoon plud ½ cup sugar, divided
¾ cup margarine
2 cups flour

½ teaspoon salt
2 eggs, separated
1 teaspoon vanilla
¼ cup chopped nuts
Powdered sugar

Soften yeast in water and sugar. Cut margarine into flour and salt. Add egg yolks and yeast mixture to flour mixture to form smooth ball. Divide dough in half. Roll out on floured surface to 9x13 inches. Spread with meringue made of egg whites, ½ cup sugar, and vanilla, beaten until stiff peaks form.

Sprinkle nuts over meringue; roll up as for jellyroll. Place on greased baking sheet. Make a ½-inch-deep cut down center of roll. (Repeat with other half of dough.) Bake at 375° for 22 minutes. Sprinkle with powdered sugar. Cool and cut into 26 slices.

What's Cooking??

Cherry Cream Cheese Coffee Cake

If you love cheesecake, you now can have it for breakfast, too. The crunchy hazelnuts add a nice contrast to the smooth, creamy filling.

CREAM CHEESE FILLING:

1 (8-ounce) package cream cheese, softened
⅓ cup sugar
2 large eggs
1 tablespoon fresh lemon juice
1 teaspoon lemon zest

In food processor, or with electric mixer, beat cream cheese, sugar, eggs, lemon juice, and lemon zest. Transfer to small bowl and set aside.

COFFEE CAKE:

2¼ cups all-purpose flour
¾ cup sugar
2 teaspoons baking powder
½ teaspoon baking soda
¼ teaspoon salt
¾ cup cold butter, cut in ½-inch pieces
1 cup finely chopped, toasted hazelnuts, divided
¾ cup sour cream
1 egg, slightly beaten
1 cup prepared cherry pie filling

Position a baking rack in the bottom third of the oven and heat oven to 350°. Grease a 9-inch springform pan with solid shortening.

Place flour, sugar, baking powder, baking soda, and salt in a food processor bowl fitted with a metal blade. Pulse several times to blend. Add butter and ½ cup finely chopped hazelnuts and process until mixture is crumbly, about 20 seconds. Remove one cup of the mixture and reserve. Add sour cream and egg and process just until evenly moistened. Do not overprocess. Spread batter evenly over bottom and 2 inches up the sides of the prepared pan, taking care that the batter is not too thick around the edges. Pour reserved cream cheese filling over batter. Spoon cherry filling over cream cheese and sprinkle with reserved crumbs and remaining ½ cup finely chopped hazelnuts.

Bake in the bottom third of a 350° oven for 60 minutes or until the center is set. Let stand for about 15 minutes and loosen the ring from the pan. Cool to room temperature before removing the bottom of the pan. Yields 10–12 servings.

Note: Sour cream can vary a great deal in thickness, so if the batter is very thick, several tablespoons of milk may be added to make it easier to handle. The batter should be about like soft biscuit dough.

Leftovers may be frozen. Reheat very gently in the microwave so that the Cream Cheese Filling does not get too hot.

Hazelnuts & More Cookbook

Blueberry Streusel Coffee Cake

CAKE:

2¾ cups flour
1½ teaspoons baking powder
1½ teaspoons baking soda
½ teaspoon salt
¾ cup butter or margarine,
    softened

1 cup sugar
3 eggs
1 pint sour cream (may use plain
    yogurt)
2 teaspoons vanilla extract

Grease and flour a 10-inch tube pan. Combine flour, baking powder, baking soda, and salt. Set aside. In a large bowl, cream butter or margarine and sugar until light and fluffy. Add eggs one at a time, beating well after each addition. Add flour mixture alternately with sour cream and vanilla to batter.

STREUSEL:

¾ cup brown sugar
¾ cup chopped walnuts
1 teaspoon cinnamon

2–2½ cups blueberries (if frozen,
    drain before using)

Combine Streusel ingredients except blueberries. Set aside ½ cup for topping. Toss remaining Streusel with berries. Spread ⅓ of the batter in prepared pan; sprinkle with ½ of the berry mixture. Spread ⅓ of the batter over that and sprinkle with remaining berry mixture. Top with remaining batter and reserved Streusel. Bake at 375° for 60–65 minutes or until toothpick inserted in center comes out clean. Cool in pan on wire rack for 10 minutes. Remove from pan and serve. Serves 16.

Savor the Flavor of Oregon

Orange Scones with Sun-Dried Cherries or Cranberries

Dried cherries and cranberries are available in specialty stores. They lend a unique flavor that is different than their fresh counterparts and with less moisture.

3 cups all-purpose flour
¾ cup sugar
½ teaspoon baking powder
1 teaspoon baking soda
2 teaspoons grated orange peel
½ cup butter or margarine, cold

¾ cup sun-dried cherries or cranberries
¾ cup buttermilk
Sugar for topping

Preheat oven to 400°. In large mixing bowl, stir together flour, sugar, baking powder, baking soda, and orange peel. Cut in butter or margarine using pastry blender or fingers until butter is worked into flour to fine crumb consistency. Toss cherries or cranberries in flour mixture. Add buttermilk until mixture holds together and is evenly moist. Add more if necessary. Knead about 10 times on a lightly floured surface.

On greased cookie sheet, pat dough into a 9-inch round, mounding slightly in center. Sprinkle with granulated sugar. Bake until evenly browned and toothpick comes out clean, about 40 minutes. Cover with foil during last part of baking to prevent overbrowning. Serve cut into wedges with butter, honey butter, or orange butter. Yields 1 (9-inch) round.

Rogue River Rendezvous

Oregon Cherry Growers cooperative members are busy tending their orchards, paying attention to the details that make Oregon's cherries the finest in the world. It has been a way of life since 1847 when the first "rooting" stocks were brought to the area by covered wagon.

Apricot-Pecan Scones

No collection of brunch recipes would be complete without scones! These are quick to assemble, delicate in texture and full flavored.

1 cup flour	**¹/₂ cup snipped apricots**
1 cup whole wheat pastry flour	**¹/₂ cup chopped pecans**
1 tablespoon baking powder	**2 eggs**
6 tablespoons sugar	**¹/₄ cup half-and-half**
6 tablespoons cold butter	

Preheat oven to 375°. Combine flours, baking powder, and sugar. Cut in the butter. Stir apricots and pecans into flour mixture. Beat eggs and half-and-half together. Stir into flour mixture. Gather into a ball and turn out onto a lightly floured counter. Knead gently a few times. Roll out to ¹/₂ to ³/₄ inch thick and cut with biscuit cutter. Place scones on a lightly buttered (or parchment covered) baking sheet and bake for 12–15 minutes in the preheated oven. Serve warm from oven with butter and honey. Makes 8–10 scones.

Note: For an alternative shape, drop by spoonful onto lightly buttered baking sheet. Bake as directed.

Thyme & the River, Too

Miss Maple Oatis

Miss Maple Oatis is a light, but hearty pastry. It keeps well and tastes great at room temperature.

FILLING:

1 cup walnuts	1/3 cup honey
1 cup butter	3/4 teaspoon cinnamon
1/3 cup maple syrup	

Put nuts in food processor and "womp" until fine. Add other ingredients. Womp until well blended. Can be made ahead of time.

DOUGH:

2 tablespoons yeast	2 cups oats
1 cup warm water	1 cup boiling water
1 cup margarine	2 eggs
1/2 cup sugar	5–5 1/2 cups flour
1 1/2 teaspoons salt	Chopped walnuts (optional)

In large mixing bowl, proof* yeast with water. In another bowl, combine margarine, sugar, salt, and oats; pour boiling water over. Let mixture cool, then combine with yeast mixture. Mix in eggs. Stir in flour. Dough should be slightly sticky. Cover and refrigerate overnight.

In the morning, remove from refrigerator and let Dough set at room temperature for approximately 1/2 hour. Flour a surface and roll Dough out into a large circle; Dough should be approximately 1/4 inch or less thick. Spread Dough with Filling; cut into 16 triangles. Roll triangles croissant-style—start at wide end and roll towards point. Place on tray and let set until about 1/2 size larger.

Bake at 275° (convection oven) or 350° (conventional oven) until lightly browned. Remove and drizzle with Drizzle! Garnish with chopped walnuts, if desired.

DRIZZLE:

1 cup powdered sugar	Mini pinch of salt
1/2 teaspoon vanilla	2–4 tablespoons heavy cream
1 teaspoon maple extract	

Combine all ingredients; Drizzle should fall in a stream off the end of a whisk.

Note: Don't be nervous about the margarine! It works best in this recipe.

*To proof yeast, dissolve in a warm liquid (usually water) and set it aside in a warm place for 5–10 minutes until it swells and becomes bubbly.

Coastal Flavors

Angel Food Doughnuts

3 cups flour
1/2 teaspoon baking powder
1/2 teaspoon baking soda
1/4 teaspoon salt
1/2 cup sour cream

1/2 cup sour milk
1 cup sugar
3 eggs
1 teaspoon vanilla

Sift flour with baking powder, soda, and salt; set aside. Beat cream and milk together until foamy; add sugar and beat again. Beat in eggs one at a time; add vanilla. Stir in flour mixture. (Up to 1/2 cup more flour can be added to make a soft dough that can be handled.) Chill dough. Knead lightly on floured board. Roll 1/3 inch thick. Cut with floured doughnut cutter. Fry in deep hot fat until golden brown, turning once. Drain on paper towels. Dust with powdered sugar, if desired.

The 'Hole Cake Doughnut Book

Banana Doughnuts

5 cups sifted flour
4 teaspoons baking powder
1 teaspoon baking soda
2 teaspoons salt
1/2 teaspoon cinnamon
1 teaspoon nutmeg

1/4 cup butter, softened
1 cup sugar
3 eggs, beaten
1 cup mashed ripe bananas
1/2 cup sour milk or buttermilk

Sift together flour, baking powder, soda, salt, cinnamon, and nutmeg; set aside. Cream butter and sugar. Stir in eggs, bananas, and milk. Stir in dry ingredients. Chill. Roll dough out on a lightly floured board. Cut with floured doughnut cutter. Fry in deep fat (365°) until golden brown, turning once. Drain on absorbent paper.

The 'Hole Cake Doughnut Book

Honey Coconut Doughnuts

2½ cups flour	½ cup honey
2 teaspoons baking powder	½ cup sour cream
½ teaspoon baking soda	1 tablespoon margarine
1 teaspoon salt	½ cup fine unsweetened coconut
2 eggs	1 teaspoon vanilla

Sift together flour, baking powder, baking soda, and salt; set aside. Beat eggs and honey together until light and lemon colored. Add sour cream and margarine and beat well. Stir dry ingredients into egg mixture until blended. Stir in coconut and vanilla. Roll out ⅓-inch thick and cut with floured doughnut cutter. Fry in deep hot fat (360°) until brown, turning once. Drain on paper towels. Dust with sugar.

The 'Hole Cake Doughnut Book

Miniature Orange Doughnuts

4 cups sifted flour	2 tablespoons butter, melted
2 teaspoons baking powder	1 tablespoon grated orange rind
1 teaspoon baking soda	1 (6-ounce) can undiluted frozen
1 teaspoon salt	orange juice, defrosted
2 eggs	¼ cup sour milk
1¼ cups sugar	

Sift together flour, baking powder, soda, and salt; set aside. Beat eggs until light. Add sugar gradually, beating constantly. Blend in butter, orange rind, defrosted orange juice, and sour milk. Stir in sifted dry ingredients. Chill thoroughly. Using ⅓ of the dough at a time, roll out on a lightly floured board to ¼-inch thickness. Cut doughnuts with frozen juice can; cut out centers with a thimble. (These must be cut small.) Fry in deep hot fat (375°) until well browned on both sides. Drain on absorbent paper. Dust with powdered sugar or frost with a powdered sugar frosting and sprinkle with grated orange rind. Makes 4 dozen.

The 'Hole Cake Doughnut Book

Apple French Toast

1 cup packed brown sugar	12–14 slices French bread
1/2 cup butter	5 eggs
2 tablespoons water	1 1/2 cups milk
2 green apples, peeled and sliced	1 tablespoon vanilla
1/4 teaspoon cinnamon	

In a saucepan, heat brown sugar and butter until butter is melted. Add water, apples, and cinnamon and continue cooking until apples are slightly soft and sauce is foamy. Pour mixture into a 9x13-inch pan and let cool. Cover with bread slices. Combine eggs, milk, and vanilla. Pour over bread. Cover and refrigerate overnight. Uncover and bake at 350° for 45 minutes to 1 hour, depending on the thickness of the bread. Serves 12.

Collection Extraordinaire

Nutty French Toast

12 slices French bread (1 inch thick)	1/2 teaspoon ground cinnamon
8 eggs	3/4 cup butter, softened
2 cups milk	1 1/3 cups packed brown sugar
2 teaspoons vanilla extract	3 tablespoons dark corn syrup
	1 cup chopped walnuts

Place bread in a greased 9x13x2-inch baking dish. In a large bowl, beat eggs, milk, vanilla, and cinnamon; pour over bread. Cover and refrigerate for 30 minutes before baking.

Meanwhile, in a mixing bowl, cream butter, brown sugar, and corn syrup until smooth; spread over bread. Sprinkle with nuts. Bake, uncovered, at 350° for 1 hour or until golden brown. Serves 6–8.

Treasured Recipes

In 1876, the University of Oregon opened in Eugene. Deady Hall was the first building on campus and still exists.

Deluxe French Toast

4 eggs	**1 cup crushed cornflakes**
¼ cup heavy cream	**½ cup slivered almonds**
⅛ cup orange juice	**¼ cup sugar**
1 tablespoon vanilla	**6 slices thick egg bread**
1 tablespoon plus 1 teaspoon	**Butter**
cinnamon, divided	**Hot maple-flavored syrup or jam**

In mixing bowl, whip together eggs, cream, orange juice, vanilla, and 1 teaspoon cinnamon until blended. Preheat well-greased grill or skillet. In small bowl, mix together cornflake crumbs, almonds, sugar, and 1 tablespoon cinnamon. Turn into shallow pan and set aside. Dip bread quickly into egg batter, and dip into crumb mixture to coat (you may need to spoon some on top and pat into bread). Cook until golden brown; turn over and cook other side. Serve with butter and syrup or jam.

Oregon Cook Book

Sticky Orange Rolls

Refrigerator biscuits (whatever is	**Orange juice**
on sale)	**Sugar cubes**

Place biscuits side by side in baking pan with edges. Pour orange juice into shallow bowl. For each biscuit, dip a sugar cube into the orange juice, holding it down briefly so it will absorb some juice, then push it lightly but firmly into the dough. Bake according to package directions or until rolls are nicely browned.

Seasoned with Words

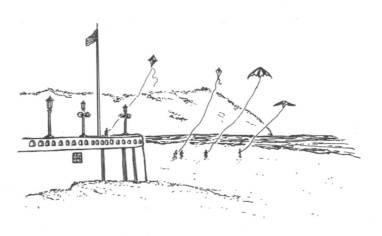

Hazelnut Buttermilk Pancakes with Blackberry Butter

These wonderfully dense pancakes, loaded with bits of roasted hazelnuts, are served with warm Blackberry Butter. The Blackberry Butter can be made days ahead and the pancake batter the night before. Blackberry Butter makes a great gift, too, tucked into a basket of homemade biscuits.

PANCAKES:

1 package active dry yeast
$^1/_2$ cup warm water
$2^1/_2$ cups buttermilk
3 eggs
2 cups all-purpose flour

3 tablespoons sugar
1 tablespoon baking soda
1 teaspoon salt
$^1/_4$ cup finely ground, toasted
 hazelnuts

In a large bowl dissolve yeast in warm water. Add buttermilk and remaining ingredients and mix well. Cover and place in refrigerator overnight. In the morning stir in more buttermilk if batter seems too thick. Heat a lightly greased griddle and cook pancakes on one side until bubbles rise to the surface and pop. Turn pancakes over and cook for 2–3 more minutes. Serve with Blackberry Butter. Serves 4.

BLACKBERRY BUTTER:

8 tablespoons ($^1/_2$ cup) unsalted
 butter
1 cup sugar

2 cups fresh blackberries (or 1
 pound frozen and thawed, puréed
 and seeded)

Melt butter and stir in sugar and blackberries. Remove from heat and stir until sugar is dissolved. Taste for sweetness. More sugar may need to be added depending on sugar content of blackberries. Store in refrigerator (good for up to 2 weeks). Makes 2 cups.

Variations: May substitute raspberries or strawberries for blackberries.

Dungeness Crabs and Blackberry Cobblers

Lincoln City is named the "Kite Capital of the World" because of it's two kite festivals held every Spring and Fall on the reliably windy beach.

Ginger Pancakes with Cinnamon Apples

PANCAKES:

1⅓ cups flour	½ teaspoon ginger
1 cup whole wheat flour	1 cup light sour cream
⅓ cup powdered sugar	2 tablespoons butter, melted
1½ teaspoons baking soda	1 cup apple cider or apple juice
1 teaspoon baking powder	¼ cup milk
1 teaspoon cinnamon	2 eggs

In large bowl, stir together first 7 ingredients. In small bowl, stir together all remaining pancake ingredients until smooth. Stir into flour mixture until well blended. Heat lightly-greased griddle to 350°, or until drops of water sizzle. For each pancake, pour ¼ cup batter on the hot griddle and cook until bubbles form. Turn pancake and continue cooking 1–2 minutes. Keep warm in 200° oven until ready to serve.

APPLE TOPPING:

¼ cup butter	3 medium red apples, cored,
1 tablespoon cornstarch	sliced
2 tablespoons cold water	1 cup light sour cream
⅔ cup firmly packed brown sugar	2 tablespoons powdered sugar
1 teaspoon cinnamon	Cinnamon for garnish

In 10-inch skillet, melt butter. In small bowl, stir together cornstarch and water, adding brown sugar and cinnamon. Stir into melted butter and cook over medium heat, stirring constantly, until sugar dissolves and mixture bubbles and thickens. Stir in apples. Continue stirring constantly, cooking until apples are evenly coated and crisply tender (4–7 minutes). In small bowl, stir together sour cream and powdered sugar. Serve Apple Topping over hot Pancakes; dollop with sour cream mixture and sprinkle with cinnamon.

Oregon Cook Book

Eggs Newport

1 can cream of mushroom soup
1/2 cup milk
1/2 cup mayonnaise
1/4 cup chopped onion

1/4 cup chopped pimentos
8 strips cooked, crumbled bacon
Salt and pepper to taste
6–8 hard-boiled eggs

Mix all ingredients except eggs. Grease casserole dish and layer the liquid with the sliced eggs. Bake, covered, at 350° for 25 minutes. Serve over toasted, buttered English muffins. Serves 4.

Recipes for the Weekend Gourmet

Caveman Scrambles

1 tablespoon vegetable oil
6–8 corn tortillas
12 eggs
Garlic powder to taste
Salt and pepper to taste

1 (4-ounce) can green chiles,
  chopped
4 green onions, chopped
Cheddar cheese
Monterey Jack cheese

Pour vegetable oil in medium-size skillet over medium heat. Tear tortillas into bite-size pieces and cook until brown and crisp on both sides, then remove from pan and drain. Pour all but 1 teaspoon oil from pan and let cool briefly. Replace chips in pan. Crack eggs in medium bowl and slightly beat, then pour over tortillas in pan, cooking at low heat, stirring frequently. Add garlic powder, salt and pepper to taste. Add chiles and cook to desired consistency. Top with green onions and grated cheeses. Cook until cheese melts. Tee-off this scramble with hot tortillas. Serves 3 hungry golfers.

Caveman Classic Cuisine

Not far from Cave Junction in Takilma, the nation's only treehouse resort welcomes families and romantics who like to slumber among the branches of mighty oaks. You can stay in the Peacock Perch, the Treezebo, the Serendipitree, the Treeplex...or if you're just curious, you can take the high-rise Mountain View Treeway tour.

Salmon Scramble Supreme

⅓ cup chopped dry-roasted
  peanuts
½ cup chopped green onions
¾ cup shredded Cheddar cheese
8 eggs

1 tablespoon water
½ teaspoon salt
¼ teaspoon pepper
3 tablespoons butter or margarine
1 (½-pound) can salmon

Combine peanuts, onions, and cheese; set aside. Beat together eggs, water, salt and pepper. Melt butter in a large frying pan over medium heat; add eggs, then chunks of salmon. Cook slowly, gently lifting the cooked portion from the bottom to allow the uncooked egg to flow underneath. Cook just until set. Transfer to serving platter and sprinkle with cheese mixture. Serves 4.

"Pacific"ally Salmon

Ham and Potato Omelet

¼ cup butter or margarine
2 cups diced, uncooked potatoes
¼ cup chopped onion
1 cup diced ham
6 eggs

1 tablespoon dried parsley flakes
½ teaspoon salt
Dash pepper
2 tablespoons water
½ cup shredded Cheddar cheese

Melt butter in 9- or 10-inch nonstick frying pan. Add potatoes and onion; cover and cook over medium-high heat, stirring occasionally to brown evenly, for about 20 minutes or until potatoes are tender and golden. Add ham and cook a few minutes longer until lightly browned. Reduce heat.

Beat together eggs, parsley flakes, salt, pepper, and water until well blended. Pour egg mixture over potatoes and ham. Cover and cook until eggs are almost set (about 10 minutes), slipping spatula around edge of pan occasionally to allow egg mixture to run down. Sprinkle with cheese and cover again until cheese melts. Cut in wedges to serve. Makes 4–6 servings.

Oregon: The Other Side

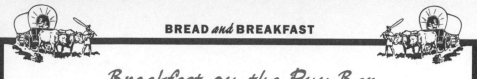
Breakfast-on-the-Run Bar

Great with a hot drink of your choice.

1 egg, slightly beaten
1/2 cup peanut butter
1/4 cup honey
2 tablespoons molasses

1/3 cup instant nonfat dry milk
3 cups whole wheat and bran cereal
    with raisins, apples and almonds

Combine egg, peanut butter, honey, and molasses; mix well. Add dry milk and mix until well blended. Add cereal and mix until evenly coated. Press firmly into greased 8-inch-square pan. Bake at 325° for 20 minutes. Cool; cut into 6 bars.

Variation: Can use egg substitute and plain cereal with bits of dried fruit and nuts of choice.

Pig Out

Paradise Fruit Pizza

2 cups biscuit mix
2 tablespoons sugar
1/4 cup butter or margarine, melted
1/2 cup milk
1 (8-ounce) can crushed pineapple
1 1/2 cups canned sliced peaches
   (plus 1/2 cup syrup)
3 tablespoons maraschino cherries,
   halved (plus 2 tablespoons syrup)

1/4 teaspoon cinnamon
1/8 teaspoon nutmeg
1/8 teaspoon allspice
1 tablespoon butter or margarine
2 teaspoons lemon juice
1/4 cup chopped nuts
1/4 cup coconut flakes
Cool Whip for garnish

Combine biscuit mix and sugar. Stir in melted butter and milk. Spread dough on the bottom of a 12-inch pizza pan. Drain pineapple, reserving syrup in a small saucepan. Drain peaches, adding 1/2 cup peach syrup and 2 tablespoons cherry syrup to saucepan. Stir in cinnamon, nutmeg, and allspice. Cook until clear then add 1 tablespoon butter and lemon juice. Arrange pineapple, peaches, cherries, nuts, and coconut on pizza dough. Pour sauce over pizza. Bake at 450° for 12–15 minutes. Serve warm topped with Cool Whip.

Grandma Jean's Rainy Day Recipes

Soups, Chilies and Stews

The Three Sisters of the Cascade Mountains were originally named Faith, Hope, and Charity by early pioneers, but are now called South Sister, Middle Sister, and North Sister (pictured above).

Salmon Chowder

1 cup chopped fresh onion
¾ cup sliced celery
2 tablespoons butter
8 cups chicken broth
½ cup chopped fresh parsley
1 (14½-ounce) can peeled and
  diced tomatoes, drained
2 cups fresh or frozen corn
2 cups peeled and diced russet
  potatoes

1 teaspoon dried thyme
¼ teaspoon ground white pepper
1 teaspoon salt
1 cup heavy whipping cream
2 tablespoons flour
1–1½ pounds fresh salmon
  fillets, rinsed
2 tablespoons lemon juice
Chopped fresh parsley for garnish

In a large stockpot over medium-high heat, sauté onion and celery in butter until limp—about 5 minutes. Add chicken broth, chopped parsley, tomatoes, corn, potatoes, thyme, pepper, and salt. Bring soup back to a boil, then reduce heat and simmer, uncovered, for 30 minutes. In a small bowl, whisk together cream and flour—then stir into soup. Cut salmon fillets into 1-inch cubes, making sure to remove all bones. Add salmon and lemon juice to soup and simmer for 15–20 minutes, stirring occasionally. Serve hot, garnished with chopped parsley. Makes 4½ quarts.

Serving Size: 8 ounces; Calories 184; Total Fat 11.1g (54%); Sat. Fat 5.0g; Chol. 46.6mg; Sod. 546mg; Carbo. 9.9g.

Glorious Soups and Breads!

Blaine Freer's Ultimate Seafood Chowder

I've never actually measured anything while making this chowder, but it always comes out fine. The following proportions are only suggestions to use as a guide. Should you put a little more of this, or a little less of that, it'll no doubt turn out great.

4 slices bacon, diced
1 cup diced onion
1 cup diced celery
1 cup diced potato
1 (10-ounce) jar oysters
1 (6½-ounce) can clams
½ pound shrimp

½ pound crabmeat (imitation okay)
2 cups milk (more or less)
1 can cream of potato soup
½ stick margarine
Salt, pepper, seafood seasoning to
   your taste
3 tablespoons cornstarch

In a kettle or Dutch oven, fry bacon. Retain fat, as desired, and sauté onion, celery, and potato until tender. Add oysters, whole or chopped, clams, shrimp, and crabmeat. Stir in milk, soup, margarine, and seasonings. Add cornstarch dissolved in a bit of milk; stir to just short of boiling and simmer for maybe half an hour.

West Coast Seafood Recipes

Oregon Coast Clam Chowder

4 slices bacon, diced
1 tablespoon pan drippings
1½ cups chopped onion
¼ cup flour
¼ cup grated carrot
¼ cup chopped celery

3 cups peeled, diced potatoes
1 teaspoon salt
⅛ teaspoon pepper
2 (8-ounce) cans chopped clams,
   drained (reserve liquid)
1 cup evaporated milk

In large saucepan, cook diced bacon until lightly browned; drain, reserving 1 tablespoon. In reserved drippings, sauté onions until translucent. Stir in flour; add bacon, carrot, celery, potatoes, and seasonings. To reserved clam liquid, add enough water to make 3 cups. Stir into vegetable mixture, bring to boil. Reduce heat and boil gently, uncovered, 20 minutes, stirring occasionally. Add clams; cook 5 minutes longer. Stir in milk; reheat. Makes 7½ cups.

Oregon Cook Book

Fresh Corn and Crab Chowder

12 ears fresh corn, husks and silk
  removed
4 ounces salt pork, rind removed
  and cut into 2 pieces
1 tablespoon butter
1 cup chopped onion
2 teaspoons minced fresh garlic
6 cups chicken broth
3 cups (about 1 pound) diced red
  potatoes, skins on

½ teaspoon dried thyme leaves
Dash cayenne pepper
2 tablespoons minced fresh parsley
2 cups (1 pint) heavy whipping
  cream
1 teaspoon salt, or to taste
¼ teaspoon ground white pepper
Enough flour to thicken as desired
1 pound Dungeness crabmeat
Chopped fresh parsley for garnish

Using a chef's knife, cut the kernels from 4 ears of corn by standing them on end, and cutting with a downward motion. You should get about 3 cups of corn. Set aside. Next, using a box grater, grate the corn from the remaining ears and place in a separate bowl. Then with the back of the knife, scrape the cobs to remove the "milk," adding it to the grated corn.

In a large stockpot over medium-high heat, sauté the salt pork until it is crisp and golden, using tongs to turn it, pushing down to render the fat. Reduce heat and add butter, onion, and garlic and sauté until onion is soft. Remove salt pork and discard. Next, add chicken broth, grated corn with its "milk," diced potatoes, thyme, cayenne, and parsley. Bring to a boil, then reduce heat and simmer until potatoes are tender, 8–10 minutes. Stir in heavy whipping cream and return to a simmer. Add corn kernels, salt, and white pepper and return once again to a simmer. Add flour and allow it to thicken the chowder, as desired. Finally, add crabmeat and heat through. Serve hot, garnished with a little chopped fresh parsley. Serves 8.

Serving Size: 1½ cups; Cal 270; Total Fat 17g; Sat Fat 10g; Chol. 85mg; Sod. 460mg; Carbo. 18g; Fiber 1g; Sugar 3g; Prot. 12g.

All About Crab

Oregon and New Jersey are the only states without self-service gas stations.

Shrimp and Sweet Corn Chowder

1 cup chopped onions
2 tablespoons butter
8 cups chicken broth
3 cups peeled and diced russet
  potatoes
1 teaspoon salt
1/4 teaspoon ground white pepper

1 cup whipping cream
1/2 pound large green (raw)
  shrimp, peeled and deveined
2 cups fresh sweet corn, cut from
  the cob
3 ounces grated sharp Cheddar
  cheese

In a stockpot over medium heat, sauté onions in butter until limp. Add chicken broth, potatoes, salt, white pepper, and whipping cream. Bring to a boil. Reduce heat and simmer, uncovered, for 30 minutes. Add shrimp and sweet corn. Return to a simmer; cook for 10 minutes, or until shrimp are firm but tender. Remove soup from heat and stir in cheese. Stir well. Serve immediately. Makes 3 1/2 quarts.

Serving Size: 8 ounces; Calories 185; Total Fat 11.2g (54%); Sat. Fat 6.5g; Chol. 65.7mg; Sod. 698mg; Carbo. 12.4g.

Glorious Soups and Breads!

Northwest Cioppino

1 1/2 pounds halibut, lingcod,
  rockfish, or sea bass (fresh or
  frozen)
2 cups sliced onions
2 cloves garlic, finely minced
1/4 cup oil (olive or canola)
1 can (1 pound 12 ounces) Italian
  stewed tomatoes, undrained
1 cup (8 ounces) tomato sauce

1 cup water
1/4 cup chopped parsley
2 teaspoons salt
1 teaspoon basil
1/2 teaspoon oregano
1/4 teaspoon pepper
1 dozen clams (in shells), washed
1 cup cooked, peeled shrimp

Cut fish into 1 1/2-inch chunks. Cook onions and garlic in oil till onion is tender but not brown. Add tomatoes, sauce, water, and all spices. Cover and simmer 30 minutes. Add fish chunks; cover and simmer 10-20 minutes. Add clams in shell and shrimp; cover and cook 10 minutes longer or until fish flakes easily when tested with a fork. Yields 6–8 servings.

Coastal Flavors

Andalusian Gazpacho

An authentic version of the Spanish classic!

½ cup diced green bell pepper
½ cup diced sweet red bell pepper
1 cup chopped onion
2 (14½-ounce) cans peeled and diced tomatoes (with juice)
2 cups peeled and chopped cucumbers
4 teaspoons minced garlic
1 cup diced French bread cubes, without the crust
2 tablespoons tomato paste

2 cups Spicy Hot V8 vegetable juice
2 tablespoons extra virgin olive oil
¼ cup red wine vinegar
1 tablespoon paprika
1 teaspoon salt
¼ teaspoon ground cumin
½ cup each for garnish: sliced green onion tops; red, green, and yellow bell pepper; peeled and chopped cucumber; and diced fresh tomato

In the work bowl of a food processor fitted with a steel blade, purée the first 7 ingredients. Place them in a large bowl, and stir in the next 7 ingredients. Cover and refrigerate for several hours before serving. Taste and add extra salt, if desired. To serve, ladle soup into chilled bowls. Place the garnishes in several small bowls on the table and let your guests garnish the soup in their own fashion. A little Tabasco sauce can add some extra zing! Your guests might like you to pass the bottle! Makes 2½ quarts.

Serving Size: 8 ounces; Calories 100; Total Fat 3.5g (29%); Sat. Fat Less than 1g; Chol. 0mg; Sod. 608mg; Carbo. 16.3g.

Glorious Soups and Breads!

Celia's Gazpacho

This is really fine in hot weather.

1 (16-ounce) can tomato sauce
1 can condensed consommé
¼ cup vinegar
⅓ cup (or less) salad oil
¼ teaspoon Tabasco
Salt and pepper to taste

8 green onions
2 medium cucumbers
2 medium tomatoes
½ green pepper
1 clove garlic

Mix the liquids and the seasonings together. Finely chop the onions, cucumbers, tomatoes, and green pepper and add to liquid. Slice several times into but not through the garlic clove, impale it on a toothpick and drop it into soup. Refrigerate several hours before serving. Remove garlic clove before serving in bowls with an ice cube in each.

Begged, Borrowed and Stöllen Recipes

Crab Bisque

¼ cup butter
1 large onion, chopped
1 cup chopped celery
6 potatoes, pared and cut in cubes
½ teaspoon salt
¼ teaspoon pepper

1 bay leaf
1 quart chicken broth
1 quart milk
1 pound crabmeat
3 tablespoons cornstarch
¼ cup cold water

In large soup pot, melt butter over medium heat. Add onion and celery; cook until onion is tender, stirring occasionally. Add potatoes, salt, pepper, bay leaf, and chicken broth. Cover and cook until potatoes are tender. Stir in milk; cover and cook until soup is hot but not boiling. Stir in crabmeat. Blend cornstarch and water, and add to soup. Over medium heat, bring to a slow boil until soup thickens. Remove bay leaf before serving. Serves 8.

Grade A Recipes

Seafood Bisque

This is the best seafood bisque ever!

2 sticks butter (no substitute)
⅓ cup finely chopped celery
⅓ cup finely chopped onion
½ bay leaf
Pinch of Italian seasoning
½ pinch tarragon
4 drops Tabasco sauce

3 tablespoons clam juice
⅓ cup flour
2 tablespoons sherry
1 quart half-and-half
1 pound seafood chunks (shrimp,
    crab, scallops, white fish)
1½ teaspoons salt

Melt butter in skillet; add celery, onion, and bay leaf. Sauté until tender. Add Italian seasoning, tarragon, Tabasco sauce, clam juice, and flour. Stir to make a roux (remove bay leaf). Remove from heat; add sherry and set aside.

In top of double boiler, heat the half-and-half. Stir in roux and heat (stirring) until thickened, 7–10 minutes. Add mixed seafood (raw ones before cooked or covered ones). Heat until seafood is cooked through, 10 minutes. Add extra clam juice if it gets too thick. Salt to taste.

Manna by the Sea

Hot and Sour Crab Soup

8–10 dried shiitake mushrooms, or about 6 ounces fresh

1 cup matchstick carrots

1 cup matchstick leeks

6 cups chicken stock

1 tablespoon fresh ginger root juice

¼ cup rice vinegar

1 tablespoon white vinegar

1 tablespoon sesame oil

1 teaspoon freshly ground black pepper

½ cup thinly sliced green onions (white and green portions)

1 stalk lemon grass cut into 2-inch pieces (or 1 teaspoon grated lemon zest)

3 tablespoons cornstarch mixed with 3 tablespoons cold water

½ pound Dungeness crabmeat

½ teaspoon hot pepper flakes

2 whole eggs, beaten well

Remove mushroom stems and discard them. Thinly slice caps and set aside with carrots and leeks. Bring stock to a boil, and add mushrooms, carrots, leeks, ginger juice, rice vinegar, and white vinegar. Return to a boil and add sesame oil, pepper, green onions, and lemon grass (or lemon peel). Remove 1 cup of stock from pot and stir it into the cornstarch/water mixture. Stir until blended, then return it to the pot. Add crabmeat and hot pepper flakes and stir thoroughly, returning again to a slow boil. Turn off heat and drizzle beaten eggs into the soup in a thin stream. Let stand for 5 minutes. Remove the lemon grass stalks before serving. Serve hot. Serves 6–8.

Note: If using dried shiitake mushrooms, place them in a small bowl and pour 3 cups boiling water over them. Let stand for about 20–30 minutes, or until soft. Discard water; rinse mushrooms thoroughly before proceeding. To cut carrots into "matchstick" pieces, simply make thin, diagonal slices of a peeled carrot. Then, stacking a few slices at a time, cut them into thin shreds. For leeks, cut the white portion into 2-inch pieces, then cut those in half lengthwise, and then into shreds. Ginger root juice can be made by grating 1 (2–3 inch) piece fresh ginger root and then squeezing out the juice.

Serving Size: 1½ cups; Calories 100; Total Fat 2.5g; Sat Fat 0g; Chol. 20mg; Sod. 420mg; Carbo. 10g; Fiber 1g; Sugars 2g; Prot. 8g.

All About Crab

Crab Soup

1 tablespoon butter	½ pound crabmeat
1 tablespoon flour	3 teaspoons sherry
1 can cream of celery soup	Salt and pepper to taste
1 cup milk	1 generous teaspoon grated lemon
1 cup cream	peel
2 eggs, hard-boiled, separated	1 teaspoon chopped parsley

Melt butter, stir in flour, and add soup, milk, cream, and crumbled egg yolks. Heat (do not boil), then add crabmeat and cook slowly for 10 minutes. Add sherry, slivered egg whites, salt, pepper, lemon peel, and parsley.

Favorite Recipes from Ruralite Readers

Colony Chicken Soup

An old favorite—the sauerkraut makes it special.

2½ pounds chicken pieces	¼ cup butter, melted
6 cups water	¼ cup flour
4 teaspoons chicken base, or	1½ cups half-and-half or milk
4 chicken bouillon cubes	¼ teaspoon white pepper
1 cup chopped celery	2 cups sauerkraut, rinsed, drained,
1 cup grated carrots	and chopped
1 cup chopped onions	

In a large kettle, simmer chicken in water to which chicken base or bouillon cubes have been added, being careful not to boil. When chicken is cooked through and tender, about 30–45 minutes, remove chicken. When cool, skin, debone, and cut into bite-size pieces and set aside to add later. Degrease broth.

Add celery, carrots, and onions to chicken broth. Simmer about 12 minutes or until tender. Mix melted butter and flour. Gradually add to broth, stirring well. Add half-and-half and white pepper. Stir frequently until soup is very hot and slightly thickened. Add sauerkraut and chicken pieces. Simmer on very low heat for a few minutes before serving. The flavor of this delicious soup becomes even better when served the second day. Serves 8–10.

Albertina's Exceptional Recipes

Tomato Florentine Soup

1 cup chopped onion
5–6 cloves garlic, minced
8 cups chicken broth, divided
1½ teaspoons oregano leaves
1 teaspoon thyme leaves
1½ teaspoons basil leaves
½ teaspoon black pepper
¼ cup red wine
2 (14½-ounce) cans chopped
   tomatoes, undrained

1 (12-ounce) can unsalted tomato
   paste
½ cup water
1 (10-ounce) package frozen
   chopped spinach, thawed
1 tablespoon balsamic vinegar
2 tablespoons grated Parmesan
   cheese

Spray a large soup pot with nonstick spray and warm over medium heat. Add onion, garlic, and ¼ cup broth. Stir and cook until onions are limp. Stir in oregano, thyme, basil, pepper, and red wine. Add remaining broth, chopped tomatoes, tomato paste, water, and thawed spinach which has been drained and squeezed dry. Mix and bring soup to a simmer; cook for about 10 minutes. Add balsamic vinegar and serve immediately after adding vinegar. Spoon grated Parmesan cheese on top of each bowl when serving. Serves 14.

Note: Use lower sodium chicken broth and no-salt-added canned tomatoes, if desired.

Nutritional analysis per serving: Serving size 1 cup; Cal 70; Fat 1g; Chol. trace mg; Prot. 3g; Carbo. 11g; Sod. 420Mg.

Tastefully Oregon

Pioneer Place, in the heart of downtown Portland, is an open courtyard surrounded by shops and restaurants. It serves as a gathering place for political speeches, musical performances and the lighting of the city Christmas tree. It is also the home of the Weather Machine, which plays a fanfare everyday at high noon, then displays a symbol of the predicted weather for the day. A Sun will forecast sunshine, a Heron speaks of rain showers, and the Dragon warns of thunderstorms.

Winter Soup

1 cup dried lentils, washed
2 quarts water
¼ cup tomato sauce
2 teaspoons salt
1 teaspoon oregano
½–1 teaspoon basil
½ teaspoon thyme
Fresh ground pepper
1 clove garlic, minced
2 stalks celery, sliced
1 onion, sliced
3 carrots, sliced

6 mushrooms, sliced
1 baking potato, unpeeled and cut in
   chunks
⅓ cup fresh parsley
1–2 (16-ounce) cans tomatoes,
   drained
4 ounces pork sausage, browned
   and well drained
1 tablespoon butter
Lots of grated fresh Parmesan
   cheese

Combine all ingredients except tomatoes, sausage, butter, and Parmesan cheese. Cover and simmer for 1 hour. Add tomatoes and browned sausage; simmer 15–30 minutes longer. Add butter, blending into soup. Sprinkle each serving with Parmesan cheese. Serves 5–6.

Optional: May use liquid drained from tomatoes as part of required 2 quarts of water.

A Taste of Oregon

Taco Soup with Toppings

2–3 (16-ounce) cans beans
   (kidney, black, chili, vegetarian
   or refried)
2 (15-ounce) cans Mexican stewed
   tomatoes
1 (16-ounce) can tomato sauce

½ cup V-8 juice
3 cups water
1 package taco seasoning mix
1 (15-ounce) can whole-kernel corn
   (optional)

Mix all ingredients in a large pan. Heat and simmer at least 15 minutes. Serve with your choice of Toppings.

TOPPINGS:
Black olives
Sour cream
Tortilla chips

Guacamole
Shredded cheese

Place each in a separate bowl on a lazy susan or tray.

Savor the Flavor

Tuscan Bread Soup

1 medium onion, coarsely chopped
2 tablespoons olive oil
2 ribs celery, diced
1 carrot, finely diced
6 cloves garlic, minced (2 tablespoons)
2 small russet potatoes, peeled, coarsely chopped
1 (16-ounce) can tomatoes, undrained
6 cups chicken or vegetable broth
1 bunch spinach, coarsely chopped
1/4 cup fresh parsley, chopped
1 tablespoon basil
1/2 teaspoon thyme
1/2 teaspoon rosemary
Pinch of granulated sugar
Salt and pepper
Pinch of dried red pepper flakes
1 (16-ounce) can white beans
4 slices cracked wheat sourdough bread, day old or lightly toasted, in bite-size pieces
1/4 cup grated Parmesan cheese

Sauté onion in oil. Add celery, carrot, garlic, and potatoes and cook until onion begins to caramelize and mixture begins to brown. Add tomatoes, broth, spinach, parsley, basil, thyme, and rosemary. Bring to boil; reduce heat and simmer, partially covered, for 15 minutes. Season to taste with sugar, salt and pepper, and red pepper flakes. Stir in beans. Fold in bread chunks. Cover and refrigerate at least 2 hours, preferably overnight. To serve, reheat and sprinkle with grated Parmesan.

Cooking with Love

A Bit O' Emerald Soup

For a change-of-pace way to serve cabbage on St. Patrick's Day, begin the meal with this creamy green soup.

3 tablespoons butter or margarine, divided
1 medium-size onion, chopped
1 clove garlic, minced or pressed
3½ cups regular-strength chicken broth
1 small head (about 1 pound) cabbage

½ pound (about 1 small bunch) spinach, thoroughly washed with stems removed
2 cups milk
¼ cup dry sherry (optional)

In a 5- to 6-quart kettle, combine 2 tablespoons butter, onions, and garlic. Cook over medium heat, stirring until onion is limp. Add broth, cover, and bring to a boil. Meanwhile, cut cabbage in half and core. With a sharp knife, finely shred cabbage and spinach. Add cabbage and about half of the spinach to broth. Cook, uncovered, just until cabbage is tender to bite. Whirl soup, a portion at a time, in a blender on low speed until smooth. Return to pan. Add milk and remaining spinach and return to a boil. Stir in sherry (if used) and remaining butter. Makes 8 servings. Top serving with teaspoon of butter.

Recipes, Recipes, Recipes!

Cabbage Patch Soup

4–5 stalks celery
1 medium onion
2–3 carrots
½ head cabbage
1½ pounds hamburger
28 ounces stewed tomatoes

1 can beef broth
30 ounces kidney beans
15 or 16 ounces tomato sauce
Dash of pepper
1 tablespoon chili powder

Chop celery, onion, carrots, and cabbage. Brown hamburger, celery, and onion together. Place mixture in crockpot. Add all other ingredients except cabbage, and cook on HIGH for about 4–5 hours. Add cabbage half through the cooking time.

Favorite Recipes from the Kitchen of Alma Irey

Baked Potato Soup

A make-ahead recipe.

4 large baking potatoes
1/2 cup margarine
1/2 cup flour
1 teaspoon garlic salt
1/2 teaspoon pepper
1/2 teaspoon onion powder

6 cups 1% low-fat milk
1 cup grated Cheddar cheese
1/3 pound bacon, cooked and
   crumbled
2 green onions, chopped

Bake potatoes at 400° for 1 hour. Cool. Peel and cut into cubes. Freeze in Ziploc bag.

Thaw potatoes. Melt margarine in a saucepan and add flour, garlic salt, pepper, and onion powder. Add milk and stir constantly until soup comes to a boil and begins to thicken. Add potato cubes and simmer on low heat for at least 30 minutes, longer if desired. Serve topped with cheese, bacon, and green onions. Serves 6.

Note: Amount of milk may vary according to your liking. As the soup simmers, it will thicken, and you may need to add more milk before serving.

What's for Dinner?

Italian Sausage and Bean Soup

Treat your family to the heavenly aroma of this hearty soup on a cold, rainy day.

1 pound navy or small white beans
5–6 cups water
1 pound mild Italian sausage
1 tablespoon vegetable oil
2 medium onions, chopped
2 cloves garlic, minced
4 stalks celery, sliced thin

2 carrots, sliced
1 1/2 quarts beef broth
1 (15-ounce) can stewed tomatoes
1 teaspoon basil
1 teaspoon oregano
3–4 small zucchini, sliced (optional)

In a Dutch oven, place beans in water. Bring to a boil, reduce heat and simmer 1 1/2–2 hours or until just tender. Slice sausage into 1/4-inch-thick slices. In a 10-inch skillet, brown sausage in oil. Remove from skillet; drain well. Add onions, garlic, and celery to oil in skillet. Add more oil if necessary. Sauté until onions are transparent.

In very large kettle, combine sausage and sautéed vegetables, carrots, and beans. Add broth and tomatoes; stir in basil and oregano and simmer 30 minutes. Skim off any fat. If desired, add zucchini in the last 10 minutes of cooking time. Serve hot. Yields 10–12 servings.

Rogue River Rendezvous

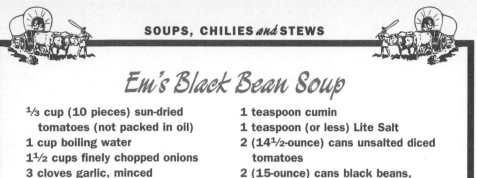

Em's Black Bean Soup

⅓ cup (10 pieces) sun-dried
   tomatoes (not packed in oil)
1 cup boiling water
1½ cups finely chopped onions
3 cloves garlic, minced
¼–½ teaspoon cayenne pepper
   or 1 teaspoon Tabasco sauce
   or to taste
1 tablespoon vegetable oil

1 teaspoon cumin
1 teaspoon (or less) Lite Salt
2 (14½-ounce) cans unsalted diced
   tomatoes
2 (15-ounce) cans black beans,
   undrained
¼ cup chopped fresh cilantro
Nonfat yogurt or nonfat sour
   cream for garnish

In a small bowl, cover sun-dried tomatoes with 1 cup boiling water and set aside. In a soup pot, sauté onions, garlic, and cayenne in oil for 5 minutes, stirring frequently until onions are translucent. Add cumin, Lite Salt, tomatoes (including the liquid), and black beans. Bring to a boil; reduce heat to low and cover. Simmer 20 minutes, stirring occasionally to prevent sticking.

Drain and chop the softened sun-dried tomatoes. Add them to soup and cook 10 minutes. Stir in cilantro and remove soup from heat. Purée half of the soup in a blender or food processor and return to pot. If soup is too thick, add water. Heat soup and serve with a dollop of yogurt or sour cream. Makes 8 cups.

Per Cup: Cal 208; Sod 186mg; Fiber 10gm; Total fat 3g; Sat fat Trace; Chol 0mg; Chol-saturated fat Index Trace.

The New American Diet Cookbook

The Rogue River draws white water enthusiasts from all over the world to challenge the Class III-V rapids. Tales of shooting Blossom Bar, Wildcat, Devil's Stairs and the infamous Coffee Pot of Mule Creek Canyon are swapped at the end of the wild run.

Hearty Split Pea, Bean and Barley Soup

This soup is wonderful reheated and will keep for 4–5 days refrigerated.

15 cups water
1 meaty ham bone, or 2 large pork hocks (about 2 pounds total)
2 cups (1 pound) dry green split peas, picked over and rinsed
1/2 cup pearl barley
1/2 cup dry black-eyed peas, picked over and rinsed
1/2 cup dry navy beans, picked over and rinsed
3 bay leaves

2 beef bouillon cubes (or up to 5 as needed)
2 large onions, coarsely chopped
2 large carrots, thinly sliced
2 large celery stalks, including leaves, thinly sliced
2 garlic cloves, minced
1/2 teaspoon (generous) dried thyme
1/2 teaspoon ground celery seed
1/2 teaspoon black pepper
Salt to taste

In a large, heavy soup pot, combine water, ham bone, split peas, barley, black-eyed peas, and beans. Bring to a boil over high heat. Add bay leaves, 2 bouillon cubes, onions, carrots, celery, garlic, thyme, celery seed, and pepper. Cover and lower heat. Simmer, stirring occasionally, until beans are tender and split peas have thickened the soup, about 2–2 1/2 hours.

As soup thickens, lower heat and stir more frequently to prevent split peas from sticking to bottom of pot. Taste the soup. If more bouillon cubes are needed, add them, along with salt, if desired.

When beans are tender, remove ham bone or pork hocks. If pork hocks have been used, discard them. If a ham bone has been used, reserve and cool slightly. Meanwhile, remove soup from heat and skim fat off top and discard. Then, if ham bone has been used, cut meat into bite-size pieces and return it to soup. Bring soup to a boil again. Stir well before serving. Serves 12–14.

Get Cookin' with Sound Construction

Minestra de Fagioli

(White Bean Soup with Tomatoes and Garlic)

1 pound dried canellini (white
  beans)
6 cups boiling water
6 slices pancetta (or bacon)
1 cup coarsely chopped onion
1 cup thinly sliced celery
3 teaspoons minced garlic
2 cups peeled, seeded, and diced
  tomatoes

1/2 teaspoon salt
1/4 teaspoon freshly ground black
  pepper
4 large, fresh sage leaves (or 1
  teaspoon dried)
1 teaspoon grated Parmesan cheese
  per serving

Place beans in a large stockpot and cover with boiling water. Bring beans back to a boil—cover and remove from heat. Let stand for 1 hour to soften the beans. Meanwhile, cut the pancetta (bacon) into small slivers and sauté in a large skillet. As it begins to brown, add onion, then celery and garlic. Sauté until vegetables are limp. Set aside. After beans have soaked, add contents of skillet and remaining ingredients (except Parmesan). Bring soup to a boil. Reduce heat and simmer, covered, for 1 1/2–2 hours, or until beans are very tender. Serve hot, garnished with Parmesan. Yields 12 servings.

Note: Keep well covered, in the refrigerator for up to a week—in the freezer for up to 3 months.

Nutritional Analysis: Serving Size: 1 cup; Calories 128; % of Calories from Fat 18%; Total Fat 2.68g; Sat. Fat 1.06g; Prot. 7.64g; Carbo. 19.3g; Sod. 183mg; Chol. 4.34mg.

The Lighter Side of Italy

Minestrone Hamburger Soup

1 pound ground beef	¼ cup rice
1 cup chopped onions	1 small bay leaf
1 cup cubed, raw potatoes	½ teaspoon dried thyme leaves
1 cup sliced, raw carrots	½ teaspoon dried basil leaves
½ cup diced celery	5 teaspoons salt
½ cup shredded cabbage	½ teaspoon pepper
1 (20-ounce) can tomatoes (2½ cups)	1½ quarts water
	Grated Cheddar cheese

Cook beef with onions until slightly browned; add potatoes, carrots, celery, cabbage, and tomatoes. Bring to a boil. Sprinkle in rice; add bay leaf, thyme, basil, salt, pepper, and water. Cover and simmer 1 hour. To serve, sprinkle with cheese. Makes 5 servings.

Oregon: The Other Side

Deer or Beef Chili

Here is a recipe for the best chili I have ever eaten. The more it is reheated, the better it is.

½ pound pinto beans	2 cloves garlic, crushed
5 cups canned tomatoes	½ cup chopped parsley
1½ teaspoons cumin seed	½ cup butter
2 tablespoons salt	2½ pounds deer meat (or lean beef), chopped
1½ teaspoons pepper	
1 pound green peppers, chopped	1 pound ground lean pork (or sausage)
1½ tablespoons salad oil	
1½ pounds onions, chopped	½ cup chili powder

Wash beans and soak overnight in a big pot in water 2 inches above beans. Cook in same water until done. Do not drain. Add tomatoes and simmer for 5 minutes. Remove from heat. Add cumin, salt and pepper. Sauté green peppers in salad oil 5 minutes, in cast-iron skillet. Add onions and cook until tender, stirring often. Add garlic and parsley. Let simmer on low for 5 minutes.

In another large skillet, melt butter and sauté deer meat and pork for 15–20 minutes. Add meat to onion mixture and stir in chili powder. Cook 20 minutes. Add all this to beans and other spices. Simmer covered for 1 hour; cook uncovered for an additional 30 minutes.

Favorite Recipes from Ruralite Readers

Spud's Chili

1 (1-pound) bag dried pinto or red beans	1 or 2 (according to taste) jalapeño peppers, seeded and finely chopped
1 pound coarse ground extra lean beef	2 tablespoons ground cumin seed
1 large onion, coarsely diced	2 tablespoons chili powder
3–4 cloves garlic, finely minced	1 teaspoon salt
1 (4-ounce) can diced green chiles	1 (28-ounce) can chopped tomatoes

Put beans in a large cooking pan and cover with water. Lightly salt water and let soak overnight (or for a quick soak, bring to a boil, remove from heat, and let stand for 1 hour). Cook beans until soft, adding enough water to keep covered if necessary.

In a large stockpot, brown the ground beef until medium rare, then drain off fat. Add onion, garlic, green chiles, and jalapeños. Simmer until onions are tender. Add cumin, chili powder, and salt, and simmer for about 2–3 minutes to allow flavors to meld. Add tomatoes and continue to simmer for 15–20 minutes, stirring often. Add beans with about half of the cooking water. Continue to simmer for about 30 minutes. Taste and correct seasonings. Serve with garnish of shredded Cheddar cheese and chopped onions, if desired.

Seasoned with Words

Chicken Chili

Chili lovers will enjoy this thick chili. It is so simple and tasty.

1/2 pound skinless, boneless chicken breasts	1 (16-ounce) can diced tomatoes, not drained
1 medium onion, chopped	1/2 cup water
2 teaspoons chopped garlic	1 tablespoon dried cilantro
2 (15¼-ounce) cans kidney beans, drained	2 teaspoons chili powder
1 (4-ounce) can diced green chiles	1/2 teaspoon cumin

Cut chicken in bite-size pieces. Brown chicken in a saucepan that has been sprayed with nonstick cooking spray. Add remaining ingredients. Cover and simmer for 30 minutes or until chicken is tender. Yields 6 cups.

Serving size: 1½ cups; Calories 296; Carbo. 42g; Prot. 26g; Fat 3g; Exchanges 2 starch, 2½ very lean meat, 2 vegetable.

Quick & Healthy Volume II (ScaleDown)

No Peek Stew

A family favorite. I come home at noon and put this in the oven if I am having week-day company, and serve it with cornbread or baking powder biscuits.

2 pounds stew meat
8–10 carrots, cubed
5–8 potatoes, cubed
2–3 stalks celery, cubed
2 medium onions, cubed
1 large can tomatoes (or 1 quart home canned)
2 cans string beans (or 1 quart home canned)
1 tablespoon salt
1 teaspoon pepper
4–6 tablespoons tapioca

Put raw stew meat and all vegetables in a roaster with lid. Mix in salt, pepper, and tapioca. Cover and bake at 250° for $4^{1}/_{2}$–$5^{1}/_{2}$ hours. Do not peek!

Favorite Recipes, Second Edition

Beef Stew Bourguignonne

2 pounds beef stew meat, cut in 1-inch cubes
2 tablespoons oil
1 ($10^{3}/_{4}$-ounce) can condensed golden mushroom soup
$^{1}/_{2}$ cup chopped onion
$^{1}/_{2}$ cup shredded carrots
$^{1}/_{3}$ cup dry red wine
1 (3-ounce) can chopped mushrooms, drained
$^{1}/_{4}$ teaspoon crushed, dried oregano
$^{1}/_{4}$ teaspoon Worcestershire sauce
$^{1}/_{4}$ cup all-purpose flour
Hot cooked noodles

In skillet, brown meat in hot oil; drain. Transfer meat to crockery slow cooker. Stir in soup, onion, carrots, wine, mushrooms, oregano, and Worcestershire. Cover; cook on LOW heat setting for 12 hours. Turn cooker to HIGH heat setting. Blend $^{1}/_{2}$ cup cold water slowly into flour; stir into beef mixture. Cook and stir until thickened and bubbly. Serve beef mixture over noodles. Serves 6.

Recipes from the Kitchens of Family & Friends

Oregon Venison Stew

Settlers of the West survived on wild game during their first years. Wild meat often was stewed with vegetables. Emigrants hunted rabbits, raccoons, squirrels, and deer. The meat from deer is called venison.

1 large onion
2 pounds venison or stew beef
1 tablespoon vegetable oil
4 1/3 cups water, divided
3 beef bouillon cubes
1 1/2 teaspoons dried marjoram
1/8 teaspoon salt

1/8 teaspoon pepper
2 medium carrots
1 medium parsnip
1 medium potato
1 cup chopped cabbage
1/3 cup all-purpose flour

Remove skin from onion. Chop into small pieces. Cut meat into 1-inch chunks. Heat oil in Dutch oven or large saucepan over medium-high heat. Cook meat and onions in oil until meat is browned, stirring occasionally. Stir in 4 cups water, bouillon cubes, marjoram, salt and pepper. Cook 40 minutes over low heat, partially covered.

While mixture cooks, peel and slice carrots, 1/2 inch thick. Peel parsnip; chop into small pieces. Cut potato into 3/4-inch cubes. Chop cabbage. Stir in carrots, parsnip, potato, and cabbage. Cook 1 hour or until meat and vegetables are tender.

In small bowl, mix 1/3 cup flour and 1/3 cup water until smooth. Stir into stew. Cook stew 5 minutes or until thickened, stirring occasionally. Makes 7–8 servings.

Oregon Trail Cooking

Tualatin Crayfish Stew

3 tablespoons vegetable oil
2 small onions, chopped
1/2 green pepper, chopped
2 stalks celery, chopped
1/2 clove garlic, minced
2 tablespoons flour

1/2 cup tomato sauce
1/4 teaspoon pepper sauce
1 tablespoon Worcestershire sauce
Salt and pepper to taste
1 1/2 cups water
2 pounds crayfish tails

Heat oil in cooking pot. Add onions, green pepper, celery, and garlic. Sauté until clear. Add flour, tomato sauce, seasonings, water, and crayfish tails; simmer over low heat for 30 minutes. Serve on hot rice, if desired. Yields 8 servings.

Fresh-Water Fish Cookbook

Pacific Stewpot

12 slices bacon, diced
1 cup chopped onion
1 cup chopped celery
1/2 lemon, thinly sliced
1 clove garlic, minced
1 quart water
2 (29-ounce) cans tomatoes,
  about 7 cups
1/4 cup ketchup

1/4 teaspoon curry powder
2 teaspoons salt
1/4 teaspoon Tabasco sauce
1 tablespoon Worcestershire sauce
1 pound scallops
1 pound rockfish, cut in chunks
1 pound Pacific shrimp, cleaned
1/2 cup sherry
4 tablespoons butter

In a large kettle, sauté bacon until golden brown. Add onion and celery; cook for 5 minutes. Add lemon slices, garlic, water, tomatoes, ketchup, curry powder, salt, Tabasco and Worcestershire sauces; cook slowly for 30 minutes. If scallops are large, cut in half. Add scallops, fish, and shrimp along with the wine and butter. Cook 10 minutes, or until fish flakes when tested with a fork. Serve with thick slices of garlic bread.

Clam Dishes and Rock Fishes

Salads

These tulips grown near Woodburn are just one of the many products grown throughout the state. Oregon is host to many farms, vineyards, and orchards in the fertile Willamette and Hood River valleys.

Broccoli and Flank Steak Salad

This salad makes a hearty first course. It stands alone as a main luncheon course when served on a bed of fresh spinach or romaine.

SOY DRESSING:

⅓ cup rice wine vinegar

⅓ cup vegetable oil

3 tablespoons soy sauce

1 large clove garlic, minced

2 teaspoons minced fresh
  gingerroot

Combine ingredients and mix well. Makes about ¾ cup dressing.

SALAD:

1 pound broccoli, cut into spears
  and peeled (reserve stem ends
  for another use)

8 ounces (½ pound) cooked flank
  steak or beef tenderloin

½–¾ cup Soy Dressing

1 cup thinly sliced red cabbage

2 tablespoons toasted sesame seeds
  (optional)

Lightly blanch broccoli in salted water. Drain and immerse in ice water to stop the cooking process. (The broccoli should be very green and crisp.) Drain, lay out on a towel, and set aside. Slice cooked meat across the grain into ¼-inch strips and cut the strips into 1½-inch pieces. Toss with some of the dressing and set aside.

In another bowl, toss sliced cabbage with some of the dressing. Arrange broccoli, marinated flank steak, and marinated cabbage in an interesting pattern on serving plates. Garnish with toasted sesame seeds, if desired. Makes 3–4 luncheon or 8 first course servings.

Thyme and the River

Taco Salad

1 pound lean hamburger
¼ teaspoon garlic powder
1 teaspoon seasoned salt
¼ teaspoon black pepper
1 small head lettuce, shredded

2 tomatoes, diced
1 cup shredded Cheddar cheese
1 small bag taco chips
Thousand Island Salad Dressing

Fry hamburger. Drain. Add garlic powder, seasoned salt, and pepper. Cool slightly. Mix shredded lettuce, diced tomatoes, and shredded cheese. Add cooled hamburger mixture. Crumble taco chips. Add half the chips to the meat and vegetable mixture. Cover and chill to allow flavors to blend. Before serving, add remaining taco chips. Serve with Thousand Island Salad Dressing. Serves 6.

Christian Bakers Cookbook

Salad Bowl Puff

A favorite!

PASTRY:
⅔ cup water
¼ cup margarine

1 cup biscuit mix
4 eggs

Heat oven to 400° and grease a pie plate. Heat water and margarine to boil in a 2-quart saucepan. Add biscuit mix and stir over low heat until it forms a ball. Remove from heat; beat in eggs, one at a time. Spread into pie plate (not up sides). Bake until puffed and dry in center, 35–40 minutes; cool.

FILLING:
1 (10-ounce) package frozen peas
2 cups cubed ham
1 cup shredded Cheddar cheese

2 tablespoons chopped onions
¾ cup mayonnaise
1½ teaspoons prepared mustard

Rinse peas, drain, and mix with remaining ingredients. Fill pastry and cover. Refrigerate at least 2 hours. Cut in wedges to serve.

Gems from the Kitchen

Turkey Cranberry Salad

Extraordinary!

CREAM CHEESE DRESSING:

3 ounces cream cheese

2 tablespoons cider vinegar

2 tablespoons sugar

1/8 teaspoon garlic salt

1/4 teaspoon salt

1/8 teaspoon white pepper

1 tablespoon prepared mustard

2 tablespoons salad oil

2 tablespoons milk

Mix all dressing ingredients in a food processor until well blended. Refrigerate. If dressing is too thick to mix well when adding to turkey salad, thin with 1–2 tablespoons more milk.

SALAD:

1/2 cup orange juice, warmed

1/2 cup dried cranberries

4 cups cooked, diced turkey breast (3/4-inch chunks)

1 1/2 cups sliced water chestnuts

1 1/2 cups thinly sliced celery

3/4 cup golden raisins

3/4 cup coarsely chopped walnuts, divided

8 lettuce leaves

Orange twists and parsley (optional)

Pour warmed orange juice over dried cranberries. Cover and let set for 1–2 hours. Drain cranberries before using.

In a large mixing bowl, combine turkey, cranberries, water chestnuts, celery, and raisins. Add Cream Cheese Dressing and mix well. Cover and refrigerate.

At serving time, set aside 1/4 cup walnuts (for garnish) and stir remaining nuts into salad. Serve on a lettuce leaf and sprinkle remaining walnuts on top. Garnish with orange twist and parsley sprig. Serve with Cranberry Orange Relish.

CRANBERRY ORANGE RELISH:

1/2 medium orange

1 cup canned cranberry sauce (whole berries)

Cut orange half into 4 pieces (do not peel). Place in food processor and pulse until orange is finely chopped, with no large pieces of rind. Add cranberry sauce and blend well. Serve in small individual cups or pass in a relish dish.

Albertina's Exceptional Recipes

Curried Turkey and Grapes

2¼ cups cooked turkey, cut in
 ½-inch cubes
1 cup thinly sliced celery
1 cup red seedless grapes
1 (8-ounce) can pineapple chunks,
 drained
1 cup chopped cashews or almonds
1½ teaspoons lemon juice

½ cup mayonnaise
½ teaspoon curry powder
½ teaspoon dry mustard
4 red lettuce leaves
4 cups small pieces of salad greens
4 tablespoons chopped cashews or
 almonds
4 small bunches grapes for garnish

Combine turkey, celery, grapes, pineapple, and nuts. In another bowl, combine lemon juice, mayonnaise, curry, and dry mustard. Combine the two mixtures and mix well. Line 4 plates with red lettuce leaves and divide salad greens evenly. Mound the turkey mixture evenly on each of the 4 plates. Sprinkle with chopped nuts and garnish with bunches of grapes. Serves 4.

Savor the Flavor of Oregon

Haystack Rock at Cannon Beach is 235 feet high and is the third largest coastal monolith in the world. Climbing "The Rock" is prohibited because it is a sanctuary harboring four types of birds. The surrounding tide pools and marine life are also protected.

Cold Chicken Salad

2 cups boneless, cooked chicken, cut in chunks
2 cups frozen petite peas
1/2 cup green onions, chopped
1 (8-ounce) can sliced water chestnuts, drained
1 1/2 cups slivered almonds (save 1/2 cup for garnish)
3 cups chow mein noodles
Mayonnaise
Lettuce

Combine chicken, uncooked peas, onions, water chestnuts, almonds, and noodles. When ready to serve (and not before or noodles will become soft), add enough mayonnaise to bind all ingredients together. Serve on a bed of lettuce. Sprinkle with remaining almonds.

A Taste of Tillamook

Tortellini Chicken Salad

1 (9-ounce) package uncooked cheese tortellini
2 boneless chicken breasts, cooked and cut into thin strips
2 cups torn spinach leaves
1 (12-ounce) can green beans
1/4 cup black olives
1/4 cup minced onion
1 large tomato, diced
1 (6-ounce) jar artichoke hearts, drained
1 bottle Caesar salad dressing

Cook tortellini according to package directions. Cool. Mix all ingredients, except dressing, in salad bowl. Top with dressing and serve. Serves 4.

Recipes for the Weekend Gourmet

The Denny's restaurant at Exit 191 in Eugene is not your basic run-of-the-mill Denny's. In fact, it was here that Jack Nicholson's famous "Chicken-Salad-Sandwich-Between-the-Knees" scene was shot for the 1970 film, "Five Easy Pieces."

Exotic Chicken Salad

4 cups chopped cooked chicken
2 (5-ounce) cans water chestnuts,
  sliced
1 cup finely chopped celery
1 pound fresh seedless grapes
1 cup toasted slivered almonds

1 cup mayonnaise
1½ teaspoons curry powder
1 tablespoon soy sauce
1 tablespoon lemon juice
Lettuce leaves
1 (16-ounce) can pineapple chunks

Combine chicken, water chestnuts, celery, grapes, and almonds. Mix mayonnaise, curry powder, soy sauce, and lemon juice. Add seasoned mayonnaise to chicken mixture and chill for several hours. Serve on a lettuce leaf and top with pineapple chunks. Serves 10–12.

Cooking with Love

Judy's Fabulous Crab Salad

This is the best crab salad, from a lifetime resident of the coast.

1 loaf white sandwich bread
Butter (for bread slices)
1 medium onion, chopped very fine
4 hard-boiled eggs, chopped very
  fine

2 cans salad shrimp
1 can (or ½ pound) crabmeat
1 cup chopped celery
3 cups mayonnaise

Cut crust off bread; butter slices lightly on both sides. Cut into cubes and return to bread sack with onion and eggs. Refrigerate overnight. Place in bowl with shrimp, crab, celery, and mayonnaise. Mix well. Refrigerate at least 3 hours before serving.

Coastal Flavors

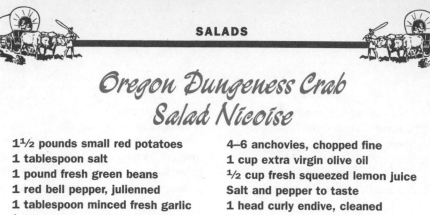

Oregon Dungeness Crab Salad Nicoise

1½ pounds small red potatoes
1 tablespoon salt
1 pound fresh green beans
1 red bell pepper, julienned
1 tablespoon minced fresh garlic
½ cup mixed chopped fresh herbs:
   rosemary, thyme, tarragon, basil
3 tablespoons Dijon-style mustard
½ teaspoon crushed red pepper

4–6 anchovies, chopped fine
1 cup extra virgin olive oil
½ cup fresh squeezed lemon juice
Salt and pepper to taste
1 head curly endive, cleaned
1 head radicchio, cleaned
1 pound Dungeness crabmeat
¼ cup capers
½ cup pitted black Kalamata olives

Quarter the potatoes and place in a nonreactive saucepan covered with 1 inch of cold water. Add salt to water and bring potatoes to a simmer over medium heat, taking care to not allow them to come to a boil. Stir gently and cook until just tender, about 10–15 minutes. Drain potatoes and spread on a cookie sheet to dry.

Blanch green beans and red bell pepper quickly in boiling water and refresh them in cold tap water. Drain. Pat dry with towel and combine with dry potatoes in mixing bowl.

In a small bowl, mix garlic, herbs, mustard, red pepper, and chopped anchovies. Gradually whisk in olive oil until lightly emulsified. Then gradually whisk in lemon juice and adjust the seasoning with salt and pepper to taste. Moisten the potatos, beans, and peppers with dressing. Arrange this mixture on a bed of curly endive and radicchio. Top with Dungeness crab and a garnish of capers and olives. Serve with additional dressing on the side.

Cookin' with Capital Press

Oregon's capitol building is located in Salem. Earlier capitols were in Oregon City and Corvallis.

Tex-Mex Pasta Salad

12 ounces corkscrew pasta
1 cup mayonnaise
1/2 cup Italian dressing
1 teaspoon chili powder
1 teaspoon cumin
1 (16-ounce) can red kidney
  beans

1 small green pepper, chopped
1/2 cup chopped celery
1 (4-ounce) can chopped green
  chiles
1 large tomato, chopped
1 (8-ounce) can corn, drained
2 tablespoons minced fresh parsley

Cook pasta as package directs. Drain and rinse with cold water until completely cool. In large salad bowl, blend mayonnaise, dressing, and spices. Toss with beans, pepper, celery, green chiles, tomato, corn, and parsley. Chill and serve.

Savor the Flavor

Mediterranean Pasta Salad

A great choice for picnics and potlucks, since it is meant to be served at room temperature!

1 (1-pound) package rotini-style
  pasta
2/3 cup olive oil
3 tablespoons red wine vinegar
2 tablespoons basil
2 tablespoons chopped green onion
2 tablespoons Parmesan cheese,
  fresh grated
Salt and pepper to taste

1 small red bell pepper
1 small yellow bell pepper
1 small green bell pepper
1 tomato
1 small can sliced ripe olives (or
  use Greek-style olives)
6 ounces feta cheese, cubed and
  rolled in basil
1 teaspoon oregano

Cook pasta according to package directions; drain. Combine oil, vinegar, basil, onion, Parmesan cheese, salt and pepper. Pour over cooked pasta and toss to mix.

Cut bell peppers and tomato in strips and add to salad. Add olives and cubes of feta cheese. Sprinkle with oregano. Serve at room temperature. Can be made in advance; I usually add the vegetables right before serving. Serves 8–10.

Rainy Day Treats and Sunny Temptations

Broccoli Noodle Salad

6 ounces Japanese soba noodles or
angel hair pasta
3 tablespoons sesame oil, divided
1 bunch broccoli, flowerets and
stems
1 cup thinly sliced red cabbage
1 cup packed coarsely grated
carrots

$\frac{1}{2}$ cup thinly sliced green onion
$\frac{1}{2}$ cup sliced almonds, toasted
$\frac{1}{4}$ cup vegetable oil
$\frac{1}{3}$ cup rice vinegar
3 tablespoons soy sauce
2 teaspoons minced fresh ginger
1 clove garlic, minced
Few drops hot chili oil

Cook noodles or pasta per package instructions. Drain, rinse, and toss with 1 tablespoon of the sesame oil. Set aside. Cut broccoli into flowerets. Lightly blanch flowerets in boiling salted water. Drain, then run under cool water to stop cooking process. Drain again. Peel and slice broccoli stems. Combine broccoli stems, blanched flowerets, red cabbage, carrots, green onion, and almonds in a nonreactive container.

Combine vegetable oil, rice vinegar, remaining sesame oil, soy sauce, fresh ginger, garlic, and chili oil. Mix well. Add noodles and dressing to the vegetable mixture, mixing well. Taste and adjust seasonings. Serves 6–8.

Thyme & the River, Too

Broccoli-Peanut Salad

SALAD:

1 bunch broccoli
1 cup chopped celery
8 strips bacon, crisped and crumbled

¾ cup raisins
¼ cup peanuts

Break broccoli into small flowerets. Mix broccoli, celery, and bacon. Add raisins and peanuts.

DRESSING:

1 cup mayonnaise
2 tablespoons vinegar

¼ cup sugar

Mix Dressing ingredients thoroughly. Combine with Salad. Refrigerate. This salad keeps nicely for several days. You may want to adjust the amount of Dressing.

Treasured Recipes

Black-Eyed Pea and Rice Salad

¼ cup cider vinegar
1 teaspoon each: cumin, black
    pepper, minced garlic
1½ teaspoons salt
⅓ cup olive oil
2 cups chopped celery
½ cup finely chopped red onion

½ cup chopped fresh cilantro
1 small can minced green chiles
3 cups cooked long grain white rice
2 cans black-eyed peas, drained, or
    1 bag frozen black-eyed peas,
    cooked
10 ounces (or more) frozen corn

Combine all ingredients and stir together well. Cover and refrigerate up to 24 hours. Serves 12 as a side dish.

Get Cookin' with Sound Construction

The Columbia River forms most of the northern border between Oregon and Washington. The Snake River forms over half of the eastern boundary with Idaho.

Wild Rice Salad

A wonderful picnic or potluck dish!

1 cup wild rice, rinsed
8 cups chicken broth, divided
1 cup white, red, or brown rice
1 cup chopped apricots
¾ cup yellow raisins
⅓–½ cup sun-dried tomatoes
   (in oil, drained on paper once)
3 cloves garlic, squeezed (less if
   desired)

1 cup julienne smoked turkey
1 small jar artichokes, drained and
   halved
6 green onions, diced (including
   green tops) or 1 small red onion,
   chopped
¾ cup chopped toasted pecans for
   garnish

Cook wild rice in 4 cups chicken broth until tender. Drain and cool. Cook other rice separately in remaining 4 cups broth. Drain and cool. When both are cool, mix and fluff with fork. Toss together all but onions and pecans; chill until ready to serve. When ready to serve, add onions, toss with Dressing, and garnish with toasted pecans. Can be prepared the night before, but do not mix in onions or dressing until the next day. Serves 8–10.

DRESSING:

1 small lemon, squeezed
1–2 tablespoons pure olive oil

2–3 tablespoons Japanese vinegar
Fresh ground pepper

Combine lemon juice, olive oil, vinegar, and pepper. Set aside until ready to toss with Salad.

Variations: Add baby shrimp; walla walla onions; currants instead of raisins; mandarin oranges; fresh chopped tomatoes; fresh chopped green (or red) pepper; chopped filberts instead of pecans—use your imagination.

Rainy Day Treats and Sunny Temptations

 The Hood to Coast Relay is the world's largest and longest relay race, covering 195 miles from Timberline Lodge to Seaside. About 900 twelve-person teams begin the jaunt on a Friday in late August and finish the following day. The fastest time ever is just under 15 hours and 45 minutes.

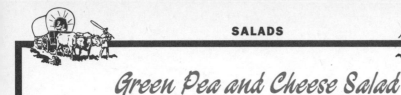

Green Pea and Cheese Salad

1 (10-ounce) package frozen peas
1 cup cubed Cheddar cheese
½ cup diced celery
¼ cup sliced radishes

2 tablespoons chopped onion
3 tablespoons sweet pickles
3 hard-boiled eggs, chopped
⅓ cup mayonnaise or salad dressing

Cook peas slightly; drain and chill. Add remaining ingredients. Chill at least 1 hour before serving—overnight is better.

The Miller Cookbook

Green Bean Tossed Salad

Buck and Judy Lovett of Mountain Spring Farms in Myrtle Creek saw a need for a farmers' market in their area, so they started the Douglas County Farmers' Market in 1994 in addition to their community supported agriculture (CSA) project based on their farm. For the ultimate salad, use young, tender green beans.

DRESSING:
2 cloves garlic, minced
½ cup chopped and packed
  fresh basil
2 tablespoons white wine vinegar

1 tablespoon grated Parmesan
  cheese
Salt and pepper to taste

Mix Dressing ingredients together and set aside.

SALAD:
1½ pounds fresh green beans,
  blanched
8 sun-dried tomatoes, sliced with
  some of the oil

½ cup pine nuts, toasted (toast
  on cookie sheet at 300° for 5
  minutes)

Mix Salad ingredients and toss with Dressing. Serve on chilled plates.

Oregon Farmers' Markets Cookbook and Guide

Radicchio, Curly Endive, Fennel and Apple Salad

1 tablespoon Dijon mustard
3 tablespoons sherry wine vinegar
3/4 cup olive oil
Salt
Freshly ground pepper
2 tart green apples, cored and
thinly sliced

1/2 medium head curly endive, torn
into bite-size pieces
1 large head radicchio, quartered,
cored and thinly sliced
1 fennel bulb, trimmed, halved, and
cut into strips

Combine mustard and vinegar in small bowl. Gradually whisk in oil. Season with salt and pepper. Mix in apples. Combine endive, radicchio, and fennel in large bowl. Add apples and dressing mixture and toss. Serves 6.

Collection Extraordinaire

Tomatoes Lutece

This is always a hit. Great for potlucks.

8 firm ripe tomatoes
1/4 cup chopped parsley
1 clove garlic, crushed
1 teaspoon salt
1 teaspoon sugar

1/4 teaspoon pepper
1/4 cup olive oil or salad oil
2 tablespoons tarragon or cider
vinegar
2 teaspoons prepared mustard

Slice tomatoes and place on a shallow serving dish. Combine all remaining ingredients in a small jar. Cover; shake well and pour over tomatoes. Cover lightly and let stand at room temperature at least 20 minutes before serving. If you have any leftovers, chill and serve the next day.

What's Cooking in Sisters

The state of Oregon has one city named Sisters and another called Brothers. Sisters got its name from a nearby trio of peaks in the Cascade Mountains known as the Three Sisters. Brothers was named as a counterpart to Sisters. Other amusing names of cities in Oregon are Beaver, Boring, Drain, Eureka, Half.com, Idiotville, Sodaville, Windmaster Corner, and Zig Zag.

Layered Green Salad

1 medium head lettuce (bite-size pieces)
½ cup thinly sliced green onions
½ cup thinly sliced celery
1 can water chestnuts, thinly sliced
1 package frozen green peas, uncooked
2 cups mayonnaise or Miracle Whip (or combination)

2 teaspoons sugar
1 teaspoon seasoned salt
¼ teaspoon garlic powder
½ cup Parmesan cheese or 1 cup shredded Cheddar cheese
Tomatoes
3 hard-boiled eggs
⅓ pound crisp bacon, crumbled

In large bowl, preferably glass, layer first 5 ingredients, beginning with lettuce and ending with peas. Mix together well, mayonnaise, sugar, seasoned salt, and garlic powder. Spread over top of salad. Cover bowl with plastic wrap and refrigerate overnight.

Before serving, layer cheese on top of the dressing. Thinly slice wedges of tomatoes and ring the outside, then next a ring of sliced hard-boiled eggs, filling the center with crumbled bacon.

Variation: Tomatoes and eggs can be chopped. Put a layer of tomatoes, a layer of eggs, then bacon, and cover with cheese. The first one is colorful, but in the second one, the ingredients mix better when dishing it up.

Recipes from the Kitchens of Family & Friends

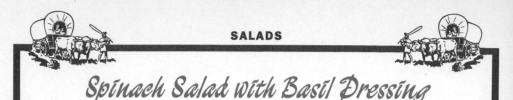

Spinach Salad with Basil Dressing

For feta cheese lovers everywhere!

SALAD:

1 bunch spinach, torn into pieces

1 small avocado, cubed

4 ounces (½ cup) feta cheese, crumbled

½ small red onion, thinly sliced

½ cup coarsely chopped walnuts or pecans

In a large bowl, combine spinach, avocado, feta, onion, and nuts.

BASIL DRESSING:

2 large garlic cloves, minced

¼ cup fresh basil leaves (packed) or 2 tablespoons dried

¼ cup red wine vinegar

2 teaspoons granulated sugar

½ cup olive oil

½ teaspoon freshly-ground black pepper

In food processor or blender, add garlic and pulse 4–5 times. Add basil, pulse to combine, then add vinegar and sugar. With processor running, drizzle in olive oil until emulsified. Season with pepper. Pour Dressing over Salad and toss well. Serve immediately. Yields 6–8 servings.

Note: A mixture of spinach and red leaf lettuce adds festive color. Consider jicama root as an addition also.

From Portland's Palate

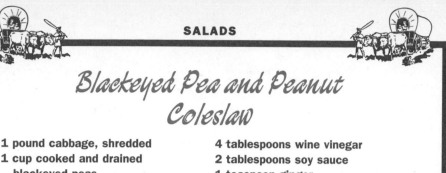

Blackeyed Pea and Peanut Coleslaw

1 pound cabbage, shredded
1 cup cooked and drained
   blackeyed peas
1/2 cup roasted peanuts, chopped
2 pickled jalapeño peppers,
   seeded, deveined, and chopped

4 tablespoons wine vinegar
2 tablespoons soy sauce
1 teaspoon ginger
2 tablespoons sesame seed oil
6 tablespoons peanut oil
Salt and pepper to taste

Combine cabbage, peas, peanuts, and peppers. Whisk other ingredients until combined. Toss and chill.

Caveman Classic Cuisine

Christine's Coleslaw

1 head cabbage, finely shredded
1/4 cup finely diced carrots
2 tablespoons finely diced onion
1/2 cup granulated sugar
1 teaspoon salt

1/2 cup Miracle Whip salad dressing
1/2 cup sour cream
3 tablespoons distilled white vinegar
2 tablespoons vegetable oil

In a large bowl, toss together cabbage, carrots, onion, sugar, and salt and set aside. In a small bowl, combine salad dressing, sour cream, vinegar, and oil; mix well. Toss the dressing with the cabbage mixture. Chill at least 1 hour before serving.

Dilley Family Favorites

The Portland Rose Festival, Oregon's premier civic celebration, has been a Northwest tradition for 95 years. This unique festival bursts into bloom each spring to celebrate the City of Roses with events, excitement and entertainment for all ages.

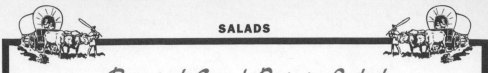

Roasted Greek Potato Salad

For an especially colorful presentation, serve on a platter or bowl lined with lettuce leaves.

3 pounds new potatoes, unpeeled, quartered, or halved

4 tablespoons olive oil, divided

1 red bell pepper, seeded and cut into ¾-inch squares

1 yellow bell pepper, seeded, and cut into ¾-inch squares

1 head garlic, cloves separated and peeled

2 teaspoons minced fresh oregano leaves

¼ cup fresh lemon juice

¼ cup chopped fresh parsley

⅓ cup Kalamata olives, pitted and halved lengthwise

Salt and ground black pepper to taste

¼ pound (about 1 cup) feta cheese, crumbled

Preheat broiler. Position rack 6 inches from broiler element. In a bowl, toss potatoes with 2 tablespoons olive oil. Place potatoes in roasting pan, then slip under broiler for 10 minutes. Remove from broiler, add red and yellow peppers, garlic cloves, and oregano; toss to coat with residual oil. Return to broiler and cook, tossing all the vegetables every 5 minutes, until nicely browned and tender, about 15 minutes longer.

Remove from broiler and transfer to salad bowl. Drizzle with remaining 2 tablespoons olive oil and lemon juice and toss well. Let cool to room temperature. Add parsley, olives, salt and pepper; toss again.

Just before serving, toss in the feta cheese. Leftovers can be covered and refrigerated for up to 4 days. To freshen the salad, squeeze lemon juice to taste over the top and toss well. Serves 6.

Summertime Treats

Greek Potato Salad
(Patatosalata)

2 pounds small potatoes	1 tablespoon chopped fresh dill
1 bunch green onions, chopped	1/2 cup olive oil
2 garlic cloves, chopped	2 tablespoons white vinegar
2 tablespoons chopped fresh parsley	Salt and pepper to taste

Boil potatoes in their skins in a stockpot until tender. Cool. Remove skins and cut potatoes into small cubes. Add onions, garlic, parsley, dill, oil, vinegar, salt and pepper. Toss gently. Serve at room temperature.

Flavor it Greek!

Salad Coquille

1 head lettuce, bite-size	1 red onion, sliced in thin rings
1 bunch leafy lettuce, bite-size	1/4 cup toasted slivered almonds
1 cup mandarin oranges, drained	

Layer lettuce, oranges, and onion in bowl. Toss with Dressing. Sprinkle with toasted almonds.

DRESSING:

2 1/2 tablespoons wine vinegar	1/3 cup sugar
1/2 tablespoon lemon juice	1/2 teaspoon grated onion
1/2 teaspoon dry mustard	1/2 cup salad oil
2 1/2 tablespoons honey	

Heat all ingredients, except oil, until sugar dissolves. Add oil. Chill before serving. Toss well.

What's Cooking??

Thanks to the Oregon Beach Bill passed in 1967, all 400 miles of the state's coast-line belong to the public. This landmark legislation means that no homeowner or hotel manager can prevent you from building a two-story sand castle that will block their million-dollar view.

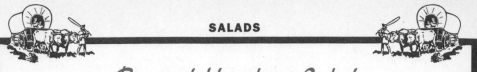

Roasted Hazelnut Salad

The warm smell of roasting hazelnuts will remind you of the cozy atmosphere in your grandmother's kitchen. Serve with salmon or steelhead.

SALAD:

½ cup Oregon hazelnuts, roasted
1 head romaine lettuce, torn into
   bite-size pieces
1 avocado, peeled and cubed

2 tomatoes, seeded and cubed
½ cup alfalfa sprouts
⅓ cup sliced green onions
½ cup shredded mozzarella cheese

To roast hazelnuts, place on a cookie sheet in a 275° oven for 20–30 minutes, until skins crack. To remove skins, rub warm nuts between your hands or in a towel. (Or microwave 3–4 minutes on FULL power.) Chop nuts, saving a few whole nuts for garnish.

In a large salad bowl toss romaine, avocado, tomatoes, nuts, sprouts, onions, and cheese.

DRESSING:

2 tablespoons white wine vinegar
1–2 tablespoons Dijon mustard

⅓ cup olive oil
Freshly ground pepper to taste

In a small bowl, whisk together vinegar and mustard. Gradually drizzle in olive oil. Whisk; add pepper. Chill and pour over Salad just before serving. Garnish with whole roasted hazelnuts. Yields 10 servings.

Rogue River Rendezvous

Blue Cheese–Pear Salad with Hazelnuts

DRESSING:

1½ tablespoons vegetable oil
2 tablespoons hazelnut oil (available at specialty shops)
2 tablespoons hazelnut liqueur
1 tablespoon white wine vinegar

1½ teaspoons lemon juice
¼ teaspoon Dijon mustard
Salt to taste
Pepper to taste

In a jar combine all ingredients and shake well to blend. Chill.

SALAD:

6 cups mixed greens, such as romaine, spinach, or leaf lettuce, torn into bite-size pieces
¼ cup (2 ounces) crumbled blue cheese

2 green onions, thinly sliced (optional)
2 pears
3 tablespoons hazelnuts, toasted, skin removed, and chopped

Prepare greens and add the blue cheese and green onion, if desired. Immediately before serving, core and dice pears, leaving skin on. Add to greens mixture along with Dressing. Sprinkle hazelnuts on top. Serves 6–8.

Collection Extraordinaire

Citrus Salad

This unusual salad is great with Mexican food. The addition of fruit gives this salad an interesting and refreshing taste.

1 grapefruit, peeled
1 orange, peeled
1½ quarts lettuce
1 small red onion, sliced thin
2 tablespoons cider vinegar
1 tablespoon lime juice

1 tablespoon salad oil
1 tablespoon water
¼ teaspoon pepper
¼ teaspoon cumin
⅛ teaspoon salt (optional)

Cut fruit in bite-size pieces. Toss with lettuce and onion. Mix remaining ingredients for dressing. Drizzle over salad and toss just before serving. Yields 8 cups.

Serving size: 1½ cups; Calories 96; Carbo. 14g; Prot. 2g; Fat 3g; Exchanges ½ fruit, 1 vegetable, ½ fat.

Quick & Healthy Volume II (ScaleDown)

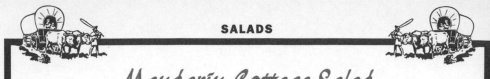

Mandarin Cottage Salad

This light dish has a refreshing taste and a pretty pastel orange color.

2 cups low-fat, small curd cottage cheese
1 (11-ounce) can mandarin orange sections, drained
1 (8-ounce) can crushed pineapple (packed in juice), drained

2 (0.3-ounce) packages sugar-free, orange flavored gelatin
1 cup light whipped topping
8 ounces vanilla nonfat yogurt, sweetened with artificial sweetener

Mix all ingredients. Cover and refrigerate until serving. Yields 5 cups.

Serving size: ¾ cup; Calories 131; Carbo. 14g; Prot. 13g; Fat 2g; Exchanges ½ milk, 1 lean meat, ½ fruit.

Quick & Healthy Volume II (ScaleDown)

Mandarin Salad

SWEET AND SOUR DRESSING:
¼ cup vegetable oil
2 tablespoons white sugar
2 tablespoons cider vinegar
1 tablespoon finely minced parsley

½ teaspoon salt
Dash pepper
Dash cayenne pepper

Shake all ingredients together in a bottle. Refrigerate before serving.

SALAD:
¼ cup sliced almonds
1 tablespoon plus 1 teaspoon white sugar
¼ head lettuce, torn
¼ head romaine, torn

2 stalks celery, sliced
2 green onions, chopped (tops included)
1 (7-ounce) can mandarin oranges, drained

Cook almonds and sugar in frying pan until sugar is melted and almonds are coated and very lightly browned. Watch carefully because almonds tend to get too brown. Cool on waxed paper and break apart. Can store at room temperature.

Place remaining ingredients in salad bowl. Add Sweet and Sour Dressing just before serving and top with prepared almonds. Serves 4–6.

What's Cooking in Sisters

Cranberry Salad

¹/₄ cup frozen cranberry juice
    cocktail concentrate, thawed
¹/₄ cup rice wine vinegar
1¹/₂ teaspoons Dijon mustard
¹/₄ teaspoon pepper
¹/₂ cup vegetable oil
1 bunch fresh spinach, rinsed well,
    dried

2 pears, cored, sliced
¹/₂ red onion, sliced
1 cup dried cranberries
¹/₂ cup feta cheese
1 avocado, peeled, pitted, sliced

Whisk cranberry juice cocktail, vinegar, mustard, pepper, and oil in small bowl. Cover and chill dressing. Combine spinach, pears, onion, cranberries, feta cheese, and avocado in large bowl. Add dressing and toss to mix. Yields 4–6 servings.

Cooking from the Coast to the Cascades

Frozen Fruit Salad

This is a nice make-ahead dish for a company dinner, or just make it and store it in the freezer for a few weeks in case you have unexpected guests.

1 (14-ounce) can sweetened
    condensed milk
1 (21-ounce) can peach or cherry
    pie filling
1 (15-ounce) can mandarin
    oranges, drained

1 (20-ounce) can crushed pineapple,
    drained
²/₃ cup chopped pecans or walnuts
1 (8-ounce) carton whipped topping

In a large bowl, combine milk and pie filling. Add fruits and nuts. Gently fold in whipped topping. Spread in 9x13x2-inch pan; cover and freeze. Remove from freezer 15 minutes before serving and cut into squares. Makes 12–15 servings.

Then 'til Now

Oregon is a shopper's paradise—there is no sales tax.

Fresh Cranberry Sauce

2 medium bags fresh or frozen   Zest from ¹/₂ orange
  cranberries   Juice from ¹/₂ orange
1 yellow apple   Sugar to taste
1 red apple

Finely chop cranberries and apples. Add orange zest and juice; add sugar to taste. Chill before serving.

Grade A Recipes

Apricot Balsamic Dressing

As owners of Luckiamute Bee, Ron and Judy Bennett's flavored honeys are a sought after treat at the Independence Farmers' market. Judy's sensational dressing is perfect over fresh garden greens, fruit salads, or as a marinade for chicken or rabbit.

¹/₂ cup pitted ripe apricots or   ¹/₂ teaspoon dried tarragon
  canned apricots, drained   ¹/₂ teaspoon dried parsley
¹/₃ cup balsamic vinegar   ¹/₄ teaspoon salt
¹/₄ cup honey   ¹/₄ teaspoon pepper
2 teaspoons Dijon mustard   1 tablespoon virgin olive oil
1 clove garlic, minced

Purée apricots in a blender; add everything except the oil and process until smooth. Slowly dribble in the oil until combined. Makes about 1 cup.

Oregon Farmers' Markets Cookbook and Guide

Million Dollar Relish

3 quarts finely chopped cucumbers   1 teaspoon celery seed
¹/₄ cup salt   3 cups vinegar
6 medium carrots, ground   4 cups sugar
2 medium green peppers, ground   1 teaspoon turmeric
4 medium onions, ground   1 teaspoon mustard seed

Soak the chopped cucumbers in salt for 2 hours and drain. Combine the remaining ingredients and boil for 20 minutes. Pack into hot sterile jars and seal. Makes about 4 pints.

Recipes and Remembering

Vegetables

Considered to be one of the nation's most photographed lighthouses, Heceta Head's light first shone in 1894. Still in use and seen 21 miles from land, it is rated as the strongest light on the Oregon coast.

Special Potatoes

12 medium potatoes
1 can mushroom soup
1 (8-ounce) carton sour cream
1 bunch green onions, sliced

Salt and seasoning to taste
¼ cup melted margarine
1 cup grated cheese

Scrub and boil potatoes until nearly done. Peel and grate. Add remaining ingredients. Mix and put in 9x13-inch casserole. Top with grated cheese. Bake at 350° for 30 minutes.

Savor the Flavor

Scalloped Potatoes

4 pounds potatoes, sliced
2 tablespoons minced onion
1 green pepper, chopped
2 cans cream of celery soup
1 (8-ounce) package cream cheese

1½ cups half-and-half
1 teaspoon salt
½ teaspoon pepper
½ pound bacon, cooked crisp,
  crumbled

Stir together potatoes, onion, and green pepper. Heat soup, cream cheese, half-and-half, salt and pepper. Mix with potato mixture and place all in a greased casserole. Bake at 350° for 1½ hours. About 15 minutes before removing from oven, sprinkle bacon bits over top and return to oven.

Our Favorite Recipes

Deluxe Hash Browns

1 large package frozen hash browns
1 can cream of potato soup
1 can cream of celery soup
Chopped onion to taste
Chopped green pepper to taste

1 (8-ounce) carton sour cream
Salt to taste
Pepper to taste
Parsley flakes
Paprika

Put everything but parsley and paprika into a large bowl. Allow potatoes to thaw, and mix well. Pour into a well-greased 9x13-inch pan. Sprinkle with parsley flakes and paprika. Bake, uncovered, in 300° oven for 1½–2 hours. Serves 12.

Manna by the Sea

Cheesy Hash Browns

Perfect for Sunday brunch! This dish can be prepared the night before then baked in the morning. Leftovers also taste great fried with a little oil until heated through and crunchy on both sides (like regular hash browns).

2 pounds frozen hash browns
1/4 cup melted butter or
   margarine
1/2 cup chopped onions
1 can cream of chicken soup

1 (10-ounce) package grated
   Cheddar cheese
1 pint sour cream
1 teaspoon salt
1/4 teaspoon pepper

Defrost hash browns on kitchen counter or in microwave. Combine butter and chopped onions in a skillet and sauté for 10 minutes. Combine cooked onions and remaining ingredients. Mix until well blended then spread evenly in a 9x13-inch casserole dish. Bake at 350° for 1 hour.

Grandma Jean's Rainy Day Recipes

Hash Brown Casserole

A make-ahead recipe.

2 cans cream of potato soup
1 cup light sour cream
1/2 teaspoon garlic salt
1 pound hash brown potatoes

2 cups grated Cheddar cheese
1/2 cup grated Parmesan cheese
1 1/2 cups diced ham

Combine soup, sour cream, and garlic salt. Add potatoes, cheeses, and diced ham. Mix well. Freeze in Ziploc bag.

   Thaw. Pour into 9x13-inch pan. Bake uncovered at 350° for 45–60 minutes until potatoes are tender and top is browned. Serves 8.

Per serving: Cal 380; Fat 24g; Cal from fat 57%.

What's for Dinner?

VEGETABLES

Low-Fat French Fries

This is a children's favorite that is so easy to prepare!

4 medium potatoes (5 ounces each) **Salt to taste (optional)**
1 tablespoon oil (canola or olive) **Malt vinegar to taste**

Preheat oven to 475°. Scrub potatoes but don't peel. Cut into ½-inch slices or strips. Place potato slices in a plastic bag with the oil and shake well to coat potatoes evenly. Spray baking sheet with a nonstick cooking spray. Arrange potatoes in a single layer and bake for 30 minutes, or until golden brown, turning potatoes every 10 minutes. Sprinkle with salt, if desired, and serve with malt vinegar. Yields 4 servings.

Serving size: ¼ recipe; Calories 185; Carbo. 35g; Prot. 3g; Fat 4g; Exchanges 2 starch, ½ fat.

Note: Temperature may be decreased to 450° and baking time increased to 40 minutes.

Quick & Healthy Recipes and Ideas (ScaleDown)

Rosemary-Blue Cheese Potatoes

1½ pounds red potatoes, cut in **1 teaspoon minced fresh rosemary**
½-inch cubes **2 tablespoons minced fresh parsley**
2 tablespoons butter **Dash salt, pepper, and cayenne**
2 tablespoons blue cheese

Cook potatoes 10 minutes in a pot of rapidly boiling salted water. Drain and set aside.

Melt butter and blue cheese; add rosemary. Combine partially cooked potatoes and butter mixture and place on an ungreased baking sheet. Bake in preheated 375° oven 20–25 minutes. Remove from oven and sprinkle with parsley, salt, pepper, and cayenne. Mix well. Serves 6.

Thyme and the River

 Eugene was the first city to have one-way streets.

Stuffed Zucchini

12 zucchini (medium size)
1 onion
1 bunch parsley
2 cloves garlic
1½ pounds ground chicken

3 eggs, beaten
2 cups bread crumbs
½ cup grated cheese
Salt
Pepper

Parboil zucchini. Half, lengthwise, and scoop out centers. Place halves in a jellyroll pan. Chop onion, parsley, zucchini centers, and garlic in food processor, then sauté with chicken, bread crumbs, grated cheese, salt and pepper. Add eggs and mix well. Fill zucchini halves and bake at 350° for 20–30 minutes or until centers are done.

Look What's Cooking

Zucchini Patties
(Kolokithokeftethes)

This recipe was created by my mother, Despina Carandanis. I embellished it a little and entered it in a James Beard cooking contest in the 1970s and to my surprise, it won an "honorable mention" award! These patties are delicious hot or cold and a wonderful picnic item.

2–3 medium zucchini, grated
¼ cup finely chopped fresh
    parsley
¼ cup chopped fresh mint, or
    1 teaspoon dried
½ teaspoon garlic powder
3 green onions, chopped
1 cup grated feta cheese

1 cup grated Cheddar cheese
¼ cup grated Parmesan or
    Romano cheese, or combination
    of both
1 cup flour
3 eggs, beaten
Salt and pepper
Vegetable oil

In a bowl, combine the above ingredients except oil. Heat oil in a large skillet and drop squash mixture by spoonfuls into hot oil. As they fry, shape them into round patties with a spoon. Brown to a golden brown on each side and remove with a slotted spoon. Serves 4.

Flavor it Greek!

Zucchini Fritters

½ pound zucchini, coarsely grated
2 tablespoons grated onion
1 teaspoon minced fresh basil, or
 ¼ teaspoon dried
¼ teaspoon salt
Pepper

1 tablespoon flour
1 egg, well beaten
2 teaspoons olive oil
Grated Cheddar or mozzarella
 cheese (optional)

Put grated zucchini and onion in mixing bowl and add basil, salt and pepper to taste. Add flour and toss. Stir in egg. Put oil in a 10-inch nonstick skillet and place over medium heat until oil ripples, then reduce heat to low. Drop zucchini batter by heaping tablespoons into pan to make 3 fritters at a time. Cook until golden brown on both sides, 5–6 minutes total. Serve hot and sprinkle with cheese, if desired.

Dilley Family Favorites

Zucchini and Three Pepper Stir-Fry

One couldn't ask for a brighter display of color! The simple seasonings allow the natural flavors of the vegetables to come through.

1 tablespoon olive oil
¾ cup thinly sliced red onion, divided
1 small garlic clove, minced, divided
½ large red pepper, seeded and cut into ¼-inch strips
½ large yellow pepper, seeded and cut into ¼-inch strips
½ large green pepper, seeded and cut into ¼-inch strips
1 tablespoon butter

1 pound zucchini, cut into ¼-inch diagonal slices
8 medium-sized mushrooms, stemmed, quartered (reserve stems for another use)
¼ cup dry white wine
2 tablespoons sugar
¼ teaspoon salt
Dash pepper
1½ teaspoons cornstarch, dissolved in 1 tablespoon cold water

Heat olive oil in a medium-sized skillet. Add ½ of the onion and garlic. Add sliced peppers and sauté 3–4 minutes, until peppers start to soften. Remove peppers from skillet and set on a heated platter. Melt butter in same skillet. Add remaining onion and garlic, the zucchini, mushrooms, and white wine. Cook 5 minutes and return the peppers to pan along with sugar, salt, and a sprinkling of pepper. Cook an additional 5 minutes.

Add dissolved cornstarch and cook until vegetables are glazed. Serve immediately. Serves 4.

Note: When using zucchini (or yellow squash) in stir-fries, we always remove the pithy interior. If left in, the pith will turn mushy and add a muddier look to your finished dish. We cut the zucchini lengthwise into fourths and scrape away (and discard) the very center, then slice the remainder.

Thyme and the River

It took approximately one year, and over 370,000 bricks to construct Oregon's tallest lighthouse, the Yaquina Head Lighthouse. The 93-foot tower, Oregon's tallest, is located on a narrow point of land jutting due west into the Pacific Ocean north of Newport, at Yaquina Head Outstanding Natural Area. Winds and rain have buffeted this lighthouse since its beginning in 1872.

Peperonata

(Peppers, Onions, Olives, and Tomatoes)

1 tablespoon extra virgin olive oil
1 cup sliced fresh onion
2 cups whole peeled tomatoes, diced, with juice
1/4 cup sliced ripe olives
2 tablespoons capers in brine
1 large sweet red bell pepper, cut into strips (about 1 cup)

1 large green bell pepper, cut into strips (about 1 cup)
2 teaspoons minced fresh garlic
1/4 cup chopped fresh basil (or 1 tablespoon, dried)
Salt and freshly ground black pepper to taste

Combine all ingredients (in order given), in a large skillet over medium heat. Simmer until vegetables are tender. Serve hot as a side dish, or cold as part of an antipasto plate. Yields 6 servings.

Note: Keeps well in refrigerator, covered, for up to a week.

Nutritional Analysis: Serving Size: 5 ounces; Calories 60.9; % of Calories from Fat 42%; Total Fat 3.13g; Sat. Fat .421g; Prot. 1.38g; Carbo. 8.31g; Sod. 143mg; Chol. 0.0mg.

The Lighter Side of Italy

Fresh Veggie Frittata

1/2 cup asparagus tips
1 medium zucchini, sliced and quartered
1 cup fresh sliced mushrooms
6 eggs
Egg substitute to equal 6 eggs

2 cups nonfat cottage cheese
2 cups grated low-fat mozzarella cheese
1/2 cup chopped green onions
1 teaspoon fresh dill

Preheat oven to 350°. Lightly sauté asparagus, zucchini, and mushrooms. Be careful not to over cook. Combine eggs and egg substitute and beat until light and fluffy. Mix in cottage cheese and mozzarella, then add green onions and sautéed veggies; add dill, mixing until well blended. Pour into 9x13-inch baking dish coated with nonstick cooking spray. Sprinkle with additional dill; bake in preheated oven at 350° for 1 hour or until knife inserted in center comes out clean. Garnish with sprigs of fresh dill. Serves 10–12.

Caveman Classic Cuisine

Frontier Hazelnut Vegetable Pie

1 cup chopped fresh broccoli*
1 cup sliced fresh cauliflower*
2 cups chopped fresh spinach*
1 small onion, diced
1/2 green pepper, diced
1 cup grated Cheddar cheese
1 cup coarsely chopped, roasted
   hazelnuts

1 1/2 cups milk
1 cup baking mix (Bisquick)
4 eggs
1 teaspoon garlic salt
1/2 teaspoon pepper

Pre-cook broccoli and cauliflower until almost tender (about 5 minutes). Drain well. Mix broccoli, cauliflower, spinach, onion, green pepper, and cheese and put into a well-greased 10-inch pie plate. Top with hazelnuts. Beat together the milk, Bisquick, eggs, garlic salt, and pepper; pour over hazelnuts and vegetables. Bake at 400° for 35-40 minutes; let pie stand 5 minutes before cutting and serving.

*Ten ounce packages of frozen chopped broccoli, cauliflower, and spinach may be substituted for fresh. Thaw and drain well. Do NOT pre-cook.

Cooking with Love

Verdure al Cartoccio
(Vegetables Baked in Parchment)

A delightful way to cook and serve vegetables! It not only steams them to tender perfection, but captures the nutrients in the parchment envelope.

2 (10-ounce) packages frozen vegetables (broccoli spears, asparagus spears, green beans, etc.)

6 tablespoons butter, melted
6 slices fresh lemon (approximately ¼ inch thick)
Salt to taste

Defrost vegetables to room temperature. Cut baking parchment into squares approximately 10x10-inches. On each square, place 3–4 ounces of the vegetables. Top with a tablespoon melted butter, a sprinkling of salt, and a lemon slice. Bringing the sides of the parchment up, seal the packet as tightly as you can, and tuck ends underneath. Place packets on a baking sheet, and bake in preheated 400° oven for 25 minutes. Serve by opening packet slightly to allow steam to escape and let the pretty colors of the lemon and vegetables tantalize your guests! Yields 4–6 servings.

Note: The packets can be made up several hours in advance, and stored in the refrigerator until just before serving time. Then, time the baking to coincide with the rest of your meal!

Feasting in the Forest

Savory Carrots with Hazelnuts

4 large carrots, peeled
¼ cup (½ stick) butter or margarine
2 tablespoons honey
¼ teaspoon nutmeg
½ teaspoon salt

¼ teaspoon pepper
3 tablespoons finely chopped fresh parsley
1 tablespoon apple juice
¼ cup toasted hazelnuts
¼ teaspoon garlic powder

Steam carrots until tender-crisp. Remove to a plate and let cool enough to handle. Grate the carrots into a bowl and set aside. Melt the butter in a saucepan over medium-low heat. Stir in honey, nutmeg, salt, pepper, parsley, apple juice, hazelnuts, and garlic powder. Add grated carrots and sauté until just heated through. Yields 6 servings.

Cooking from the Coast to the Cascades

Cooked Greens with Bacon and Vinegar

10 cups fresh greens (spinach, mustard greens, Swiss chard)
5 slices bacon
1 tablespoon vinegar or raspberry vinegar

Wash greens. Remove any tough stems. Tear greens into medium-size pieces. Toss together in bowl. Cut bacon into 1-inch pieces.

In Dutch oven or saucepan, cook bacon until crisp. Place bacon on paper towel to cool. Drain fat, reserving 2 tablespoons. Add greens; cook over medium heat 6–8 minutes or until greens have wilted and are tender. Sprinkle with bacon pieces and 1 tablespoon vinegar. Serve immediately. Makes 6 servings.

Oregon Trail Cooking

Green Beans with Mushrooms

2 cloves garlic, minced
¼ pound small fresh mushrooms, sliced
1 tablespoon butter
1 medium onion, cut in thin strips
1 pound fresh green beans, trimmed
Pepper to taste
1 teaspoon dill weed
2 tablespoons toasted almonds or pine nuts

Sauté garlic and mushrooms in butter until tender. Stir in onion; set aside. Steam or cook beans in small amount of water until crisp-tender. Drain. Combine beans with mushroom mixture; add pepper and dill. Garnish with nuts. Serve immediately. Serves 6.

Recipes from the Kitchens of Family & Friends

Fed by 17 mountain streams, Upper Klamath Lake is a virtual "nutrient trap"—the only place on earth that grows blue-green algae, which contains all the minerals and proteins needed to sustain human and animal life.

Good Green Beans

1 (16- to 17-ounce) can green
  beans, drained
1 (3½-ounce) can French fried
  onions
1 can cream of mushroom soup

¼ teaspoon salt
Dash of pepper
1 (4-ounce) can mushrooms
2 tablespoons toasted almonds
½ cup grated Tillamook cheese

Place beans and onions alternately in 1-quart casserole dish. Mix the rest of ingredients, except cheese, together and pour over beans. Sprinkle with cheese and bake at 375° for 30 minutes.

A Taste of Tillamook

Baked Beans

1 pound hamburger
1 pound bacon
3 (16-ounce) cans pork and beans
1 (16-ounce) can lima beans,
  drained and rinsed
1 (16-ounce) can kidney beans,
  drained and rinsed

3 large onions, chopped
1 cup ketchup
½ cup white sugar
¾ cup brown sugar
2 tablespoons vinegar
1 teaspoon dry mustard

Brown hamburger and bacon; drain. Combine all ingredients in large baking dish and bake at 350° for 1 hour, or put into 5-quart crockpot and cook on HIGH for 6 hours.

Sagebrush Surprises Cookbook

The International Museum of Carousel Art in Hood River contains the world's largest and most comprehensive collection of antique carousel animals, mechanisms, and decorative art. In addition, the city of Salem has carved a new chapter in carousel history by opening its new Riverfront Carousel. The project is based entirely on community involvement. Everything about it has been done by volunteers—from carving the horses, to constructing the building, to planning the opening!

Lenticchie e Sedona

(Lentils and Celery)

This dish has an excellent protein content. I like using Italian or French breads with this meal and a glass of good red table wine. A small green salad, some cheese and you have a good light, sufficient meal.

½ box (1 cup) lentils
Salt to taste
½ cup olive oil
1 clove garlic, minced

1¼ cups tomatoes
Parsley, chopped
1 celery stalk, chopped

Mom would soak the lentils for an hour in lukewarm water. She would then heat the water with the lentils to a boiling point and then drain the lentils. After that was done, she would add freshly boiled water to the lentils and salt and allow to boil slowly on a very low flame or heat for 1½ hours.

She would then boil mixture of oil, garlic, tomatoes, and parsley for 10 minutes. Then the lentils were added plus the celery, which had been boiled in a separate pan earlier. Be sure to use dark green cooking celery. Cook for about 15 minutes. Serves 4.

Cooking Italian

Spinach Casserole

2 packages frozen chopped spinach
3 large tomatoes
1/3 cup chopped onion
4 tablespoons melted butter or
  margarine
1/4 teaspoon salt
1/2 teaspoon garlic
2 eggs, beaten
1/2 teaspoon crumbled thyme
1/4 cup bread crumbs
1/3 cup grated Parmesan cheese

Cook and drain spinach. Peel and slice tomatoes into 10–12 thick slices. Lay them flat in baking dish. Mix spinach with remaining ingredients except bread crumbs and cheese. Spoon spinach mixture on top of tomatoes. Sprinkle with bread crumbs and cheese. Bake at 350° for 15 minutes. Serves 8.

Treasured Recipes

Spinach Dumplings

2 (10-ounce) packages frozen
  chopped spinach (or 1½
  pounds fresh)
Salt and pepper to taste
4 tablespoons butter
2 teaspoons grated onion
3/4 cup ricotta cheese
1 egg, slightly beaten
6 tablespoons flour
3/4 cup Parmesan cheese, grated
6 quarts water
1 tablespoon salt
Bisquick, for breading
Spaghetti sauce
Parmesan cheese, grated

Cook spinach thoroughly, seasoning with salt and pepper to taste. Squeeze spinach dry and chop fine. Melt butter in skillet over moderate heat and add spinach and onion. Cook, stirring constantly for 2 minutes, or until most of the moisture is absorbed. Add ricotta cheese and cook 3–4 minutes longer, mixing well. Remove from heat and cool. Mix cooled spinach mixture with egg, flour, cheese, salt and pepper to taste. Mix well, then refrigerate 45 minutes until firm. Bring salted water to a rapid boil. Shape spinach mixture into balls and roll in Bisquick. Drop into boiling water and cook, uncovered, 6–7 minutes; drain. Arrange on platter. Pour heated spaghetti sauce over dumplings and sprinkle with Parmesan cheese.

What's Cooking in Sisters

Scalloped Cabbage

1 (3-pound) head of cabbage
¼ cup chopped onion
½ cup chopped green pepper
¼ cup butter
¼ cup flour
½ teaspoon salt
¼ teaspoon pepper
2 cups milk
½ cup mayonnaise
¾ cup shredded Cheddar cheese
3 tablespoons chili sauce

Cut cabbage in pieces; steam for 25 minutes. Drain and place in baking dish. Sauté onion and pepper in butter. Stir in flour, salt and pepper. Gradually add milk; cook until thickened. Pour over cabbage and bake uncovered 15 minutes at 375°. Mix mayonnaise, cheese, and chili sauce and spoon over cabbage. Return to oven for 5 minutes or until cheese melts.

Potluck and Patchwork

Sweet Onion Pie

Ron Bennett of Luckiamute Bee raises honeybees and sells flavored honey such as blueberry, wild blackberry, raspberry, meadowfoam and mint at the Independence Farmers' market. Wonderful as a main dish or served on the side, this standout pie is bound to bring out the onion lover in us all.

1 (9-inch) pie crust
4 large sweet onions (Walla Walla
   or yellow Granex), chopped
1 tablespoon extra virgin olive oil
3 tablespoons butter
2 eggs
1 cup cream or half-and-half
2 tablespoons flour
1 teaspoon salt
⅛ teaspoon hot red pepper (or
   more to taste)
¼ teaspoon freshly ground black
   pepper
1 pinch nutmeg
2 ounces Swiss cheese, grated,
   divided
Fresh parsley, chopped

Prepare and partially bake a crust to fit a 9-inch pan using a basic pie dough recipe or purchased pie crust. Sauté onions in oil and butter over low heat until golden brown. Beat together eggs, cream (or half-and-half), flour, salt, peppers, and nutmeg, and then add the onions and half the grated cheese. Pour into crust and sprinkle remaining cheese on top. Bake at 375° for 25–30 minutes or until golden brown. Garnish with parsley. Serves 4.

Oregon Farmers' Markets Cookbook and Guide

Sweet and Sour Red Cabbage

At the west end of the Columbia Gorge situated on a high hill is Winters Farms, a family farm first begun in the 1940s by Howard and Ruth Winters. The Winters family grows an assortment of popular and unique berries along with many vegetables including green and wax beans, pickling and slicing cucumbers, sweet onions, beets, English peas, and sweet corn. Summer and winter squash, tomatoes, red and green cabbage and many herbs top the list. In addition to growing for the Beaverton and Portland Farmers' Markets, their wholesale customers and brokers remain an important part of their business. Their red cabbage is frequently requested at the market and so is this recipe.

4 cups red cabbage
1 tart apple
4 tablespoons butter
1 heaping tablespoon brown sugar
1 cup minced onions

6 tablespoons red wine vinegar
1 cup beef or chicken broth or water
1 teaspoon salt
1/2 cup red currant jelly

Wash, dry, and shred cabbage. Chop apple. Melt butter in a large frying pan and stir in brown sugar. Add apple and onions, cover, and cook over low heat for 4–5 minutes or until wilted. Stir in cabbage and vinegar, cover, and braise for 10 minutes.

Pour in broth or water and salt; cook, covered, over low heat for 2 hours (or bake in a preheated 300° oven for 2 1/2 hours). Stir in jelly before serving. Depending on the freshness of the cabbage, cooking time can be reduced. Start checking texture after 1 hour of cooking. Makes 6 cups.

Oregon Farmers' Markets Cookbook and Guide

Corn Scallop

1 (17-ounce) can cream corn
2 eggs, beaten
1/2 cup crushed Ritz Crackers
1/4 cup butter or margarine,
   melted
1/4 cup undiluted evaporated milk
1/4 cup finely shredded carrot

1/4 cup chopped green pepper
1 tablespoon chopped celery
1 teaspoon chopped onion
1/2 teaspoon sugar
1/2 teaspoon salt
1/2 cup shredded Cheddar cheese
Paprika

Combine corn and all remaining ingredients except cheese and paprika. Mix thoroughly and turn into a greased 8x8x2-inch baking dish. Top with cheese and sprinkle with paprika. Bake at 350° for 30 minutes or until mixture is set and top is golden brown. Makes about 8 servings.

Oregon: The Other Side

Nut Balls and Sauce

1 cup soda cracker crumbs
1 cup whole-wheat bread crumbs
   (dried)
1/2 cup finely chopped walnuts
5 eggs, slightly beaten

1 tablespoon soy sauce
1 teaspoon salt
1 teaspoon sage
1 medium onion, finely chopped

Mix all ingredients for Nut Balls together and form into balls. Place on a greased cookie sheet and bake in 350° oven for about 20 minutes.

SAUCE:
1/4 cup chopped onion
1 clove garlic, chopped
1/4 cup butter

1 (29-ounce) can tomatoes
1/2 teaspoon salt
1/4–1/2 cup chopped parsley

Sauté onion and garlic in butter; add tomatoes, salt, and chopped parsley. Arrange nut balls in a baking dish; pour Sauce over them and bake in 350° oven 35–40 minutes.

Savor the Flavor

Hot Fruit Casserole

1 (16-ounce) can pear halves
1 (16-ounce) can peach halves
1 (16-ounce) can apricot halves
1 (16-ounce) can sliced pineapple
1 (14-ounce) jar spiced apple rings

2 tablespoons flour
1/2 cup firmly packed brown
   sugar
3/4 cup butter or margarine
1 cup dry sherry

Drain all fruits and cut pineapple slices in half. In a large 18x28-inch baking dish, arrange fruits in alternating layers, using apple rings for top.

Combine flour, sugar, butter, and sherry in top of a double boiler over simmering water and cook, stirring until mixture is thickened and smooth, about 10 minutes. Pour mixture over fruit, cover with plastic wrap, and let stand overnight in refrigerator.

Preheat oven to 350°. Place casserole in oven and bake until bubbly hot and slightly glazed on top, 20–30 minutes. Makes 12–14 servings.

Then 'til Now

Pasta, Rice, Etc.

At 7,800 feet deep, Hells Canyon is North America's deepest river-carved gorge—one-third of a mile deeper than the Grand Canyon and five miles narrower. Walls of the canyon are like a museum displaying 3,000-year-old pictographs and petroglyphs, evidence of the Indians' early settlements.

Angel Hair Pasta with Tomatoes and Basil

This is a perfect side dish with baked salmon and makes a wonderful light entrée. If you reheat this dish, first add a little wine or water.

8 ounces angel hair pasta
1 teaspoon olive oil
2 cloves garlic, minced
1/2 cup dry white wine
2 tablespoons freshly squeezed
   lemon juice

2 cups chopped Roma tomatoes
1/2 cup chopped fresh basil, or 2
   tablespoons dried basil leaves
1/2 teaspoon (or less) Lite Salt
1/4 teaspoon pepper
1/4 cup grated Parmesan cheese

Cook pasta in unsalted water according to package directions. Meanwhile, heat olive oil and sauté garlic until golden brown. Add wine and cook 2 minutes. Stir in lemon juice and tomatoes. When pasta is done, drain and put into serving bowl. Add tomato mixture, basil, Lite Salt, and pepper. Toss. Sprinkle with Parmesan cheese just before serving. Makes 4 servings (1^{1}/$_{2}$ cups each).

Per Serving: Calories 309; Sod. 252mg; Fiber 3g; Total Fat 4g; Sat. Fat 2g; Chol. 5mg; Chol-saturated Fat Index 2.

The New American Diet Cookbook

Cavitelli con Broccoli
(Pasta with Broccoli)

Broccoli is a vegetable which most people feel must be cooked alone or maybe with a small onion or two. But never with anything but another vegetable.

1 clove garlic, chopped
6 tablespoons olive oil
1/2 teaspoon salt

Crushed red pepper to taste
1/2 pound broccoli
1/2 pound cavitelli

Brown garlic in olive oil. Remove garlic and add salt and red pepper. Cook broccoli and pasta in two separate saucepans until tender. When they are cooked, add to the olive oil and simmer together slowly until all flavors are combined. Serves 4.

Note: Cavitelli are tube pasta about 2 inches long and 1/8 or 1/4 inch in diameter. May substitute perciatelli or small rigatoni.

Cooking Italian

Pasta with Garden Vegetables

1½ cups thinly sliced carrots
1 cup chopped green onions
1 large red onion, coarsely chopped
¾ cup thinly sliced radishes
½ cup coarsely chopped Italian
  parsely
¼ cup fresh chopped basil, or
  1½ tablespoons dried leaves
5 cloves garlic, minced
3 cups chopped tomatoes
3 cups diced zucchini
1 large green bell pepper, diced

1½ cups dry white wine or water
1½ teaspoons Lite Salt
¾ teaspoon black pepper
1 teaspoon sugar
1 tablespoon margarine
1 tablespoon flour
1 cup nonfat milk
1 (16-ounce) can tomato paste
1½ pounds shell-shaped pasta
½ cup fresh grated Parmesan
  cheese

Spray large cooking pot with nonstick cooking spray. Add carrots, green and red onions, radishes, parsley, basil, and garlic. Add a very small amount of water to prevent sticking. Sauté the vegetables, stirring often, until they begin to color, about 20 minutes. Reduce heat, cover saucepan, and simmer vegetables for about 15 minutes. Add tomatoes, zucchini, bell pepper, wine or water, Lite Salt, pepper, and sugar. Simmer the sauce, uncovered, for about 45 minutes to 1 hour.

In a small saucepan, melt margarine. Stir in flour until a smooth paste develops. Slowly add milk, stirring it into the paste with a wire whisk. Add tomato paste and whisk mixture again until it is very smooth. Stir it into the vegetables. Continue simmering sauce over low heat, stirring often, until it is thickened.

Cook pasta in a large kettle of unsalted boiling water until al denté (barely cooked), drain, and pour into a large serving dish. Add vegetable sauce, toss, and sprinkle grated Parmesan over the top. Serve immediately. Serves 8.

Nutritional analysis per serving: Serving size 2 cups; Calories 432; Fat 5g; Chol. 5mg; Prot. 16g; Carbo. 74g; Sod. 562mg.

Tastefully Oregon

Oregon has been a big-hearted state since Day One—it became a state on Valentine's Day, February 14, 1859.

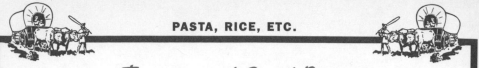

Tomato and Basil Pasta

Fresh tomatoes and basil add a wonderful flavor to this light dish.

2 large tomatoes, diced (2 cups)
1 teaspoon dried basil
1 teaspoon chopped garlic
1/2 teaspoon salt (optional)

1/8 teaspoon pepper
6 ounces angel hair pasta
Parmesan cheese (optional)

Mix first 5 ingredients and let set at room temperature at least 1 hour. Cook angel hair pasta according to package directions, omitting oil and salt. Drain pasta and add tomato mixture. Serve immediately and top with Parmesan cheese, if desired. Yields about 4 cups.

Serving size: 1 cup; Calories 170; Carbo. 34g; Prot. 6g; Fat 1g; Exchanges 2 starch, 1 vegetable.

Quick & Healthy Recipes and Ideas (ScaleDown)

Pasta with Chicken and Tomato

A make-ahead recipe.

1 pound frozen chicken breast
  tenders
12 ounces linguini
2 cups frozen broccoli
3 tablespoons olive oil, divided
4 teaspoons minced garlic, divided
1 1/2 tablespoons red wine vinegar

3 tablespoons basil
2 scallions, chopped
1/2 teaspoon salt
1/8 teaspoon pepper
3 cups diced tomatoes
1/2 cup grated Parmesan cheese

Thaw chicken. Boil noodles and broccoli together, just until tender. Drain well and transfer to a large bowl. Sauté chicken pieces in 1 tablespoon olive oil and 1 teaspoon garlic. Cook until tender and slightly browned, breaking up into small chunks as you cook. Mix together red wine vinegar, remaining garlic and oil, basil, scallions, salt and pepper. Toss with noodles, tomatoes, chicken, and broccoli. Serve sprinkled with grated Parmesan. Serves 6.

Note: Cooked carrots can easily be substituted for the broccoli in this recipe. Try bow tie or shell pasta for a fun change.

Per serving: Cal 415; Fat 10g; Cal from fat 22%.

What's for Dinner?

Mexican Lasagna

1 pound lean ground beef
1 (16-ounce) can refried beans
2 teaspoons dried oregano
1 teaspoon ground cumin
¾ teaspoon garlic powder
12 lasagna noodles, uncooked
2¼ cups water

2½ cups picante sauce
2 cups (16 ounces) sour cream
¾ cup finely sliced green onions
1 (2.2-ounce) can sliced black
  olives, drained
1 cup (4 ounces) shredded
  Monterey Jack cheese

Combine beef, beans, oregano, cumin, and garlic powder. Place 4 lasagna noodles in bottom of 9x13x2-inch baking pan. Spread half beef mixture over noodles. Top with 4 more noodles and remaining beef mixture. Cover with remaining noodles. Combine water and picante sauce. Pour over all. Cover tightly with foil and bake at 350° for 1½ hours or until noodles are tender. Combine sour cream, onions, and olives. Spoon over casserole. Top with cheese. Bake, uncovered, until cheese melts, about 5 minutes.

A Taste of Tillamook

Crab Fettuccine

4 tablespoons butter
2 garlic cloves, minced
4 tablespoons flour
½ cup sherry or dry white wine
2 cups half-and-half
½ pound mushrooms, sliced

Butter for sautéing
⅓ cup Parmesan cheese
Salt and pepper
1 pound crabmeat
Cooked fettuccine

Melt 4 tablespoons butter in large skillet; add garlic and sauté until soft. Add flour and cook briefly. Gradually add sherry and half-and-half. Cook until sauce is smooth and thick; set aside. Sauté mushrooms in generous amount of butter. Add mushrooms and any juice to cream sauce. Stir in Parmesan cheese and add salt and pepper to taste. Gently fold in crabmeat. Heat through. Serve over freshly cooked fettuccine (your own or store bought). Serves 6.

A Taste of Oregon

Thai Chicken Fettuccine

A colorful warm summer day entrée. Serve with fruit and roll for a complete meal.

1 cup picante sauce
¼ cup peanut butter
2 tablespoons honey
¼ cup orange juice
1 teaspoon soy sauce
½ teaspoon ground ginger
12 ounces dry fettuccine, cooked
  and well drained

2 cups cooked chicken breast, cut
  in chunks (3 breasts)
Iceberg lettuce or savory cabbage
  leaves for garnish
¼ cup chopped cilantro
¼ cup chopped unsalted peanuts
¼ cup thinly sliced red bell pepper

Combine picante sauce, peanut butter, honey, orange juice, soy sauce, and ginger in small saucepan. Cook and stir over low heat until blended and smooth. Reserve ¼ cup picante sauce mixture; toss remaining mixture with hot cooked fettuccine. Mix reserved picante sauce mixture with cooked chicken pieces. Line large platter with lettuce leaves, if desired. Arrange fettuccine mixture over lettuce; top with chicken mixture. Sprinkle with cilantro, peanuts, and red bell pepper. Cool to room temperature before serving, or serve chilled. Serves 6.

Nutritional analysis per serving: Serving size 1 cup; Calories 437; Fat 11g; Chol. 37mg; Prot. 26g; Carbo. 59g; Sod. 356mg.

Tastefully Oregon

Spaghetti Pie

8 ounces spaghetti, cooked, drained
2 tablespoons butter
2 large eggs, well beaten
½ cup plus 2 tablespoons grated
   Parmesan cheese, divided

1 cup ricotta cheese
1 cup spaghetti sauce
½ cup grated mozzarella cheese

Heat oven to 350°. In large bowl, toss hot spaghetti with butter. In small bowl, combine eggs and ½ cup Parmesan. Stir into spaghetti. Pour spaghetti mixture into a lightly greased 10-inch pie plate, and form into a crust. Spread ricotta evenly over the crust, but not quite to the edge, and top with spaghetti sauce. Bake uncovered for 25 minutes. Remove from oven; top with mozzarella. Return to oven and bake 5 more minutes until cheese melts. Remove from oven and sprinkle with remaining Parmesan. Cool 10 minutes before cutting into wedges.

Oregon Cook Book

Marinara Salsa

1 clove garlic, minced
¼ cup olive oil
1 (2-pound) can tomatoes, drained

1 teaspoon salt
Oregano and parsley to taste

Sauté garlic in oil. Remove garlic and add tomatoes and spices. Cook slowly for about 45 minutes. Best on spaghetti and light pasta.

Cooking Italian

The diminutive D River in Lincoln City is the world's shortest river at an abbreviated 120 feet, flowing from Devils Lake into the ocean.

Walnut Rice

2 tablespoons butter
½ cup chopped celery
3 large garlic cloves, minced, divided
1 cup long grain white rice
2 cups chicken stock

1 tablespoon walnut oil
½ cup chopped walnuts
Dash cayenne
Salt to taste (omit if using canned stock)

Melt butter in a saucepan and add celery and half the garlic. Sauté 2 minutes, add rice, and cook an additional 3 minutes, stirring constantly. Add stock and bring to a boil. Reduce heat, cover, and simmer 15 minutes.

Meanwhile, heat walnut oil in a skillet and add remaining garlic and walnuts. Sauté, stirring constantly, until walnuts start to brown. Remove from heat.

After rice has cooked for 15 minutes, remove from heat. Add sautéed walnut mixture and cayenne. Taste. Add salt, if necessary. Replace lid and let set to season 5–10 minutes. Serves 4.

Thyme and the River

Frey Workshop Chicken Pilaf

3 (10½-ounce) cans condensed cream of mushroom soup (undiluted)
3¾ cups boiling water
¼ cup dry sherry
1½ envelopes dry onion soup mix
4 cups long grain white rice

6 tablespoons chopped, canned pimiento
15 or so pieces chicken (breasts and thighs)
Butter (optional)
Salt, pepper, and paprika to taste
Broccoli (optional)

In a 4- to 5-quart casserole, combine first 6 ingredients. Brush chicken with butter; season with salt, pepper, and paprika and place on top of rice mixture. Cover. Bake at 375° for 1¼ hours or until chicken and rice are tender. During the last 10–15 minutes, add several handfuls of broccoli, if you like. Serve when the whole business is tender. Feeds about 20 normal people or 15 Rockaway Beach eaters.

Seasoned with Words

Jasmine's Jambalaya

¼ stick margarine
1 cup diced onion
½ cup diced green pepper
1 garlic clove, diced
½ cup uncooked white rice
1 cup water

1 (8-ounce) can tomato sauce
1 tablespoon vinegar
4–5 dashes hot pepper sauce
½ teaspoon salt, or to taste
1 cup cubed cooked ham
1 cup cooked shrimp

Melt butter in a large skillet or saucepan; sauté onion, green pepper, and garlic until tender. Add remaining ingredients except ham and shrimp; cover and simmer until rice is tender. Add ham and shrimp and simmer another 3–4 minutes.

West Coast Seafood Recipes

Beans and Rice

Many overlanders ate beans and rice during the last part of the journey. These dried foods had not spoiled during the months on the Oregon Trail.

1 tablespoon vegetable oil
1 small onion
¾ cup long grain rice, uncooked
1½ cups water
½ teaspoon dried thyme

½ teaspoon salt
¼ teaspoon black pepper
⅛ teaspoon red (cayenne) pepper
1 (16-ounce) can cooked light red
    kidney beans

Heat oil in Dutch oven or large saucepan over medium-high heat. Remove skin from onion. Chop onion; cook in oil until tender, turning occasionally. Stir in rice. Cook 2 minutes, stirring frequently. Add water, thyme, salt, pepper, and red pepper. Red pepper is spicy; if you do not like spicy food, you may wish to add just a pinch.

Reduce heat to low. Cover. Cook 25 minutes or until all liquid is absorbed. Gently stir in beans. Makes 6–8 servings.

Oregon Trail Cooking

The Tillamook Naval Air Museum is housed in the world's largest wooden clear-span building. It is over 15 stories tall (192 feet), 206 feet wide, 1,072 feet long and covers 7 acres (6 football fields).

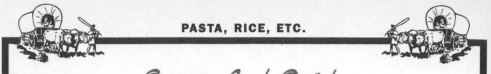

Oregon Crab Quiche

This simple quiche is so elegant; good at any time, but try it for a special luncheon. It's also a splendid way to stretch and share a small amount of expensive crabmeat.

1 cup (4 ounces) shredded natural Swiss cheese
1 (9-inch) pastry shell, unbaked
$\frac{1}{2}$ pound fresh Dungeness crabmeat, flaked, or 1 ($7\frac{1}{2}$-ounce) can crabmeat, drained and flaked
2 fresh green onions (including tops), sliced

3 eggs, beaten
1 cup light cream or half-and-half
$\frac{1}{2}$ teaspoon salt
$\frac{1}{2}$ teaspoon grated lemon peel
$\frac{1}{4}$ teaspoon dry mustard
Dash of mace
$\frac{1}{4}$ cup sliced almonds

Sprinkle cheese evenly over bottom of pastry shell. Spread crabmeat over cheese; sprinkle green onions over crabmeat.

Combine beaten eggs, cream, and seasonings; pour over all. Sprinkle top with sliced almonds. Bake at 325° for about 45 minutes or until set (when knife blade inserted in center comes out clean). Remove from oven and let stand for 10 minutes before cutting and serving.

Begged, Borrowed and Stöllen Recipes

Calico Quiche

1 (9-inch) pie shell, homemade or frozen
$\frac{1}{4}$ cup seeded, deveined, and chopped red bell pepper
$\frac{1}{2}$ cup seeded, deveined, and chopped green bell pepper
1 cup grated Cheddar cheese
1 cup grated Swiss cheese
1 cup cubed, cooked chicken

$\frac{1}{4}$ cup ($\frac{1}{2}$ stick) butter
$\frac{1}{2}$ cup coarsely chopped onion
1 tablespoon all-purpose flour
$\frac{1}{2}$ cup half-and-half
$\frac{1}{2}$ cup sour cream
4 eggs, beaten
$\frac{1}{4}$ teaspoon ground nutmeg
1 tablespoon chopped parsley

Preheat oven to 350°. In pie shell, layer chopped peppers, cheeses, and chicken. In sauté pan, melt butter and sauté onion until soft. Whisk in flour thoroughly. Stir in half-and-half and simmer until thickened, about 3–5 minutes. Let cool.

In large bowl, combine sour cream, eggs, nutmeg, and parsley. Stir into sautéed onion mixture. Pour filling into pie crust. Bake 35–40 minutes or until set. Yields 6–8 servings.

From Portland's Palate

Cabernet Onion Quiche

We make quiche for dinner knowing it will be a great lunch the next day, too! Sautéing the onions in Cabernet gives this quiche a truly satisfying richness. We serve this with a fresh green salad alongside our Chardonnay or Reisling.

1 tablespoon olive oil	1 cup milk
2 cloves garlic, chopped	3 eggs
1 large onion, diced	¼ teaspoon each, salt and pepper
1 teaspoon thyme or oregano	Homemade or prepared pie crust
½ cup Hood River Vineyards Cabernet Sauvignon	1 cup grated Cheddar cheese
	¼ teaspoon paprika

Preheat oven to 375°. Heat oil in a large skillet on medium-high heat. Add garlic and onion and sauté for a minute or so. Add thyme or oregano (or whatever flavored herbs you like) and stir in. Add Cabernet, stirring till it reduces and most of the liquid is gone. Remove from heat and set aside.

In a bowl, whisk milk and eggs together until frothy and smooth. Mix in salt and pepper.

Place pie crust in deep-dish pie pan or quiche pan on baking sheet. Layer grated cheese so the bottom is completely covered. Layer onion mixture evenly over this. Pour milk mixture over everything and sprinkle with paprika.

Bake in oven for 35–45 minutes (checking after 30 minutes—baking time will vary from oven to oven), until knife inserted in center comes out clean. Let cool 10 minutes before serving. Serves 4–6.

Recipe by Hood River Vineyards
The Fruit Loop Cookbook

Cheese Enchiladas Verde

¾ cup shredded Jack cheese
¾ cup shredded Cheddar cheese
2 small zucchini, shredded
¼ cup diced onion
1 tablespoon finely chopped, fresh
  cilantro

8 corn tortillas
1 (14-ounce) can green chili
  enchilada sauce
1 cup green salsa (salsa verde)
1 avocado, diced

Mix cheeses, zucchini, onion, and cilantro in a small bowl. In skillet with small amount of oil on medium heat, place 1 tortilla at a time and cook 10 seconds on each side. Drain on paper towels. Place green enchilada sauce in a separate bowl . Dip 1 tortilla at a time in enchilada sauce and place on waxed paper. Top each with ⅛ of the cheese mixture. Roll up and place in 9x13-inch casserole. Top with remaining enchilada sauce. Cover and bake at 350° for 30 minutes. Top with salsa and avocado and serve. Serves 4.

Recipes for the Weekend Gourmet

Meats

Outstanding public art, dozens of urban parks, a lively downtown, and a world-class transportation system make Portland a marvel of urban planning. These bronze seals by artist Georgia Gerber are just one example of the unique art you'll find throughout area.

Sauerbraten or German Pot Roast

I know the gingersnaps sound weird but that is what makes the great gravy. We love this over mashed potatoes.

MARINADE:

2 cups sliced onions	1½ teaspoons cloves
2 cups white vinegar	1 teaspoon allspice
1½ cups water	2–3 bay leaves

Bring to a boil and boil for 5 minutes; let cool.

1 (3- to 6-pound) chuck roast or any pot roast cut	Salt and pepper
Flour	1 cup grated carrots (optional)
	12 gingersnaps

When Marinade is cool, put in meat. Cover and put into refrigerator for 4 days, turning meat over in Marinade at the end of second day. When 4 days are up, take meat out of Marinade (reserve Marinade) and wipe dry with paper towels. Flour, salt and pepper the meat. Brown in hot fat until golden brown.

Place in Dutch oven or something comparable. Pour ⅔ of Marinade over meat. Place in oven at 325° and cook until tender, about 2½–3 hours. During cooking, if liquid evaporates, just add more Marinade. At this point, you can add grated carrots.

Remove meat to hot platter. Into roaster or Dutch oven that meat has been cooked in, add the remainder of the Marinade. Crumble the gingersnaps into liquid. Heat, stirring and blending to a smooth gravy. Taste for additional salt.

Favorite Recipes from Ruralite Readers

 Tillamook's first white settler, Joe Champion, made his home in a hollowed-out spruce stump. Coincidentally, he was also Tillamook's first resident to use the phrase "going back to my roots."

Round Steak Sauerbraten

1½ pounds round steak	1 tablespoon wine vinegar
1 tablespoon oil	1 teaspoon Worcestershire sauce
1 package brown gravy mix	¼ teaspoon ground ginger
2 cups water	1 bay leaf
1 onion, sliced	½ teaspoon salt
1 tablespoon brown sugar	¼ teaspoon pepper

Cut meat into 1-inch pieces each, about ½ inch thick. Brown in hot oil, then remove from pan. Add gravy mix and water, and bring to a boil, stirring constantly. Add onion, brown sugar, vinegar, Worcestershire sauce, and seasonings. Add meat and mix well. Turn into 1½-quart casserole. Cover and bake 1½ hours at 350°. Remove bay leaf and serve with noodles. Serves 6–8.

Note: Can be made the day before and just heated up.

Manna by the Sea

Mushroom-Stuffed Flank Steak

1 (2- to 2½-pound) beef flank steak, 1 inch thick	2 tablespoons butter or margarine
2 (4-ounce) cans sliced mushrooms	Meat tenderizer
2 tablespoons crumbled blue cheese	Salt and pepper
	1 clove garlic

Have a pocket cut in steak at the market. Combine mushrooms, cheese, and butter or margarine. Spread mushroom mixture inside pocket; close with skewers. Use meat tenderizer on flank steak according to manufacturer's directions. Sprinkle with salt and pepper. Rub surface with garlic. Broil steak about 5 minutes on each side. Remove to platter. Cut diagonally across grain. Makes 6 servings.

Cookin' with Capital Press

Old-Fashioned Pot Roast

Years ago, when most women didn't work outside of the home, this was a very popular menu item because they had more time to devote to their cooking. Although the recipe calls for beef, it is also very good with venison, elk, or moose (for my Canadian friends). I always add potatoes, too, and sometimes cabbage, turnips, or other fresh vegetables that I have on hand.

1 boneless beef chuck roast (about 3 pounds)
6 tablespoons flour, divided
6 tablespoons butter or margarine, divided
3 cups hot water
2 teaspoons beef bouillon granules

2 large onions, quartered (or 8 small whole onions)
1 celery rib, cut into pieces
1 teaspoon salt
$\frac{1}{2}$ teaspoon pepper
4 carrots, cut in quarters

Sprinkle roast with 1 tablespoon flour. In a Dutch oven, brown the roast on all sides in half the butter. Add water, bouillon, onion, celery, salt and pepper and bring to a boil. Reduce heat; cover and simmer for 1 hour. Add carrots (and other vegetables you may choose to use), cover, and simmer 45–60 minutes or until meat is tender. Remove meat and vegetables to a serving platter and keep warm.

Strain cooking juices and set aside. In the Dutch oven, melt remaining butter, stir in remaining flour, and cook and stir until bubbly. Add 2 cups of the cooking juices and blend until smooth. Cook and stir until thickened; add additional cooking juices until the gravy is of desired consistency. Makes 6–8 servings.

Recipes and Remembering

Corned Beef

1 (4- to 5-pound) corned beef brisket	2 small onions, cut in wedges
1 bay leaf	(per serving)
A few whole black peppercorns	1 large potato, cut in wedges
1 tablespoon mustard	(per serving)
1/2 cup brown sugar	1 wedge cabbage (per serving)
2 carrots, cubed (per serving)	

Wash corned beef under running water (try to get most of the spices off). Put in a large kettle and cover with cold water. Add bay leaf and peppercorns. Bring to a boil, then simmer until tender, about 4 hours. Remove meat to a shallow pan, reserving liquid; spread meat with mustard and brown sugar. Bake at 375° for 20 minutes or until nicely browned.

Remove fat from reserved liquid. Cook vegetables in liquid. Cook carrots and onions for 1/2 hour; add potatoes and cook 15 minutes longer; add cabbage and cook another 15 minutes or until all is tender. Put meat on a platter and arrange vegetables around it. Garnish with parsely and serve with horseradish, mustard, and vinegar.

Gems from the Kitchen

Swedish Meat Ring

A good one-dish meal as well as being decorative and very inexpensive.

1 pound ground beef or hamburger	1 egg, beaten
2 tablespoons chopped onion	1/4 cup tomatoes
1 cup grated carrots	1 teaspoon salt
2 tablespoons cooking oil	Biscuit dough

Fry beef, onion, and carrots in hot oil until lightly browned; add egg, tomatoes, and salt. Cool. Roll biscuit dough to a sheet about 1/2 inch thick; spread mixture over dough. Roll up like jellyroll; bring ends together to form a ring. Cut halfway through ring at intervals of 2 inches. Bake at 400° until golden brown. Fill center with creamed peas or any creamed vegetable.

Favorite Recipes from Ruralite Readers

Make-Ahead Barbecued Meatballs

These are so handy to have in the freezer for unexpected company or a quick meal anytime.

MEATBALLS:

3 pounds ground beef
1 cup quick oats
1 cup cracker crumbs
1/2 cup chopped onion
1 (12-ounce) can evaporated milk

2 eggs
2 teaspoons chili powder
1/2 teaspoon garlic powder
2 teaspoons (or less) salt
1/2 teaspoon pepper

Combine all ingredients (mixture will be soft) and shape into walnut-size balls. Arrange in a single layer on wax paper-lined cookie sheets. Freeze until solid and store frozen Meatballs in freezer bags. Makes 80 Meatballs.

BARBECUE SAUCE:

2 cups ketchup
1/2 teaspoon liquid smoke
1/4 cup chopped onion

1 cup brown sugar
1/2 teaspoon garlic powder

Combine all ingredients and stir until sugar dissolves. To serve, place 20–30 Meatballs in a 9x13-inch pan and pour Sauce over Meatballs. Bake at 350° for 1 hour.

Note: These are very versatile and may be added to spaghetti sauce and simmered until done, or cooked with a mushroom soup sauce in the oven and served with mashed potatoes.

Then 'til Now

Bavarian Stuffed Meatloaf

Boiling water
3 medium onions, chopped
2 large eggs
1/4 cup milk
6 slices white bread, torn in pieces
1 1/2 teaspoons salt
1/4 teaspoon black pepper
1/2 teaspoon whole marjoram
2 pounds ground beef

10 slices bacon, cooked crisp and
  drained, divided
12 ounces cream cheese, sliced
6–8 dried prunes, cooked
1/3 cup butter, melted, divided
3 tablespoons red wine
Cooked vegetables for garnish,
  such as small carrots and onions,
  Brussels sprouts, etc.

Preheat oven to 350°. Grease a 1 1/2- to 2-quart oval baking dish or a 5x9-inch loaf pan.

Pour boiling water over onions and let stand 5 minutes. Drain. Beat eggs and milk together. Beat in bread until well blended. Stir in drained onions, salt, pepper, and marjoram. Mix in ground beef with hands. Shape into a loaf and fit in baking dish or pan. Bake, uncovered, about 1 hour, until loaf begins to pull from pan sides. Pour off fat. Chill, covered.

Preheat oven to 325°. Grease an oven-proof serving dish 3–4 inches larger on all sides than loaf.

Halve loaf horizontally. Set bottom half on dish. Layer with half the bacon, all the cheese, and remaining bacon. Fit top layer on and press down lightly. Garnish top with prunes. Combine half the butter with 3 tablespooons wine and drizzle over loaf. Surround with garnish vegetables. Brush with remaining butter. Bake 20–30 minutes until heated through. Serves 8–10.

Fiddlin' in the Kitchen

In Oregon, the cowboy way really hasn't changed very much in the past 100 years. There are something like 1.5 million head of cattle in the state, making it little wonder that beef and its byproducts are the state's second largest industry.

Little Cheddar Meat Loaves

1 egg
3/4 cup milk
1 cup (4 ounces) shredded
  Cheddar cheese
1/2 cup quick cooking oats
1/2 cup chopped onion

1 teaspoon salt
1 pound ground beef
2/3 cup ketchup
1/2 cup packed brown sugar
1 1/2 teaspoons prepared mustard

Beat egg and milk. Stir in cheese, oats, onion, and salt. Add beef and mix well. Shape into 8 loaves. Place in greased 9x13x2-inch baking dish. Combine ketchup, brown sugar, and mustard; spoon over loaves. Bake, uncovered, at 350° for 45 minutes or until meat thermometer reads 160°. Yields 8 servings.

Recipes from the Kitchens of Family & Friends

Sweet-Sour Meat Loaf

1 (15-ounce) can tomato sauce
1/2 cup brown sugar
1/4 cup vinegar
1 teaspoon prepared mustard
2 pounds ground beef
1 pound pork or veal (or all ground
  beef)

2 eggs, slightly beaten
2 small onions, chopped
1/2 cup fine soft bread crumbs
1 tablespoon salt
1/2 teaspoon pepper

Mix the first 4 ingredients until thoroughly blended. Set aside. Combine remaining ingredients in large mixing bowl. Mix 1 cup of sauce into meat mixture. Bake at 350° for 1 hour (maybe a little longer). Baste after 30 minutes with 1/4 cup sauce. Heat remaining sauce and pour over meat loaf at serving time.

A Taste of Tillamook

Twenty Minute Tamale Pie

2 tablespoons butter
1 onion, chopped
1 pound ground beef
1 (16-ounce) can stewed tomatoes
1 (17-ounce) can whole-kernel
   corn, undrained
1 cup sour cream
1 cup cornmeal

1 (4½-ounce) can sliced ripe olives
2 teaspoons salt
1 tablespoon chili powder
½ teaspoon cumin
3 teaspoons monosodium glutamate
   (optional)
2 cups shredded Monterey Jack
   cheese

Heat butter in 10- to 12-inch skillet with cover. Add onion and meat and cook until lightly browned. Add remaining ingredients, except cheese, and stir until thoroughly mixed. Sprinkle with shredded cheese. Cover and simmer for 20 minutes. Serves 6–8.

Gems from the Kitchen

Pancho Pie

1 sweet green pepper, chopped
1 clove garlic, chopped
1 onion, chopped
1 pound hamburger
1 tablespoon butter or oil
1 teaspoon chili powder
2 teaspoons salt

½ cup tomatoes
½ cup cornmeal
1 can cream-style corn
1 cup milk
½ cup sliced olives
½ cup sliced mushrooms

Sauté pepper, garlic, onion, and hamburger in butter or oil. Add seasonings and cook 10 minutes. Add remaining ingredients and pour into baking dish. Bake at 350° for 1 hour.

Sagebrush Surprises Cookbook

Bellfountain Park, between Corvallis and Junction City, boasts the world's longest picnic table at a staggering 82 feet. Chances are you may need a megaphone to ask someone to pass the potato salad!

Beef in Phyllo

A taco in a party wrap.

1 pound ground beef
½ pound bulk pork sausage
1 medium onion, chopped
1 large clove garlic, minced
¼ teaspoon salt
¼ teaspoon pepper
½ teaspoon chili powder
3 cups grated Monterey Jack
  cheese
1 (4-ounce) can diced green chiles,
  drained

1 (4-ounce) can sliced ripe olives
¾ pound phyllo dough
½ cup butter, melted
Paprika
1 cup sour cream (optional)
1 medium ripe avocado, peeled and
  sliced (optional)
Guacamole (optional)
Salsa (optional)

Preheat oven to 350°. Brown beef and sausage, then add onion, garlic, salt, pepper, and chili powder. Cook about 12 minutes and drain fat. Cool. Mix cheese, chiles, and olives with the cooled meat. To keep phyllo from drying out while using, unroll package and place on a large tray. Cover with plastic wrap and then a damp towel. Cover each time you remove sheets of phyllo.

To make beef phyllo packets, place 2 sheets of phyllo together on a tray and brush top sheet with melted butter. Place ⅛ of meat mixture 2 inches from one end, in the center. Fold the 2 inches of phyllo over, then fold both sides evenly toward center. Roll to form a package. Repeat until 8 packages are formed. Place in buttered baking dish and brush top and sides of package with melted butter.

Bake 15–20 minutes until flaky and golden. Sprinkle with paprika. Serve with sour cream, avocado slices or guacamole and salsa. Serves 8.

Albertina's Exceptional Recipes

Oregon's state flag pictures a beaver, the state animal, on its reverse side. It is the only state flag to carry two separate designs. The front includes a shield with an eagle on top, surrounded by thirty-three stars. (It was the thirty-third state admitted into the Union.) The scene on the shield shows a sun setting over the Pacific Ocean, mountains, forests and a covered wagon. The flag is emblazoned with the words "State of Oregon" above the shield, and 1859 below, denoting the date of statehood.

Enchilada Casserole

1½ pounds lean ground beef
1 small onion, chopped
1 garlic clove, minced
1½ cups picante sauce
2 (10-ounce) packages frozen,
    chopped spinach, thawed and
    squeezed dry
1 (8-ounce) can tomato sauce
2 medium tomatoes, chopped

1 large pepper, diced
1 tablespoon lime juice
1½ teaspoons salt
12 corn tortillas
1 cup dairy sour cream
¾ cup shredded Jack cheese (or
    mozzarella)
½ cup sliced ripe olives (optional)
Shredded lettuce (optional)

Brown meat with onion and garlic; drain. Add picante sauce, spinach, tomato sauce, tomatoes, pepper, lime juice, and salt. Simmer, uncovered, 15 minutes, stirring occasionally. Arrange 6 tortillas on bottom and up sides of lightly greased 9x13-inch baking dish, overlapping as necessary. Top with half meat mixture. Arrange remaining tortillas over, overlapping. Spread sour cream over tortillas. Top with remaining meat mixture. Bake at 350° for about 30 minutes or until hot and bubbly. Remove from oven; sprinkle with cheese. Let stand 10 minutes. Cut into squares and serve. Garnish with olives and shredded lettuce, if desired. Serve with additional picante sauce. Makes 8 servings.

Look What's Cooking

Frito Casserole

1 pound hamburger
Chopped onion, garlic powder, salt
    and pepper to taste
1 can Cheddar cheese soup
1 can chili

1 can enchilada sauce
1 small can tomato sauce
½ bag Fritos
1½–2 cups Cheddar cheese

Brown meat and onion with garlic powder, salt and pepper. Drain. Add soup, chili, and sauces. Heat well. Stir in Fritos. Pour into casserole dish; top with cheese. Bake at 350° until cheese melts.

Potluck and Patchwork

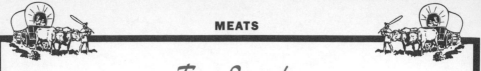

Taco Smacho

You can add green onions to diversify the performance of this dish, which plays like a symphony to the taste buds.

1½ pounds ground beef
1 (3-ounce) package cream cheese, cubed and softened
2 teaspoons salt
2 teaspoons chili powder
18 jumbo pasta shells, cooked, rinsed, and drained

2 tablespoons butter, melted
1 cup taco sauce
2 cups shredded Cheddar cheese
1½ cups crushed tortilla chips
1 cup sour cream
3 green onions, chopped

Heat oven to 350°. In large skillet, brown ground beef; drain fat. Add cream cheese, salt, and chili powder; simmer for 10 minutes. Toss shells with butter; fill with meat mixture (use hands to fill pasta shells). Arrange shells in buttered 9x13-inch baking pan. Pour taco sauce over each shell. Cover with foil; bake for 15 minutes. Uncover, top with Cheddar cheese and tortilla chips. Bake for 15 minutes more or until bubbly. Garnish with sour cream and onions. Makes 6–8 servings.

Serving Up Oregon

Barbecued Beef Cubes

1 pound beef cubes
2½ tablespoons flour
Dash of pepper
¼ cup chopped onion
1½ teaspoons brown sugar
½ teaspoon chili powder
½ teaspoon dry mustard

1 (10-ounce) can tomato soup
½ cup water
1 tablespoon vinegar
½ teaspoon Worcestershire sauce
Dash of Tabasco
3 cups cooked rice

Dredge beef cubes in flour seasoned with pepper. Brown meat in large skillet; add onion. Combine brown sugar, chili powder, dry mustard, tomato soup, water, vinegar, Worcestershire sauce, and Tabasco. Pour over meat mixture. Bring to a boil. Cover. Cook over low heat or in a 350° oven for 1½ hours or until tender. Stir occasionally during cooking time. Serve over cooked rice. Makes 3–4 servings.

Look What's Cooking

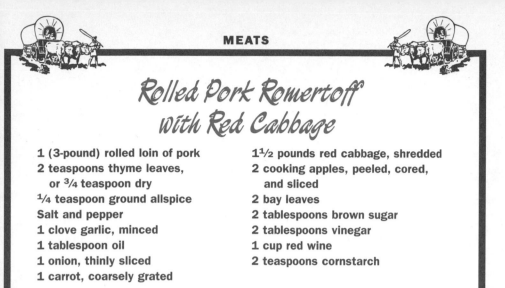

Rolled Pork Romertoff with Red Cabbage

1 (3-pound) rolled loin of pork	1½ pounds red cabbage, shredded
2 teaspoons thyme leaves, or ¾ teaspoon dry	2 cooking apples, peeled, cored, and sliced
¼ teaspoon ground allspice	2 bay leaves
Salt and pepper	2 tablespoons brown sugar
1 clove garlic, minced	2 tablespoons vinegar
1 tablespoon oil	1 cup red wine
1 onion, thinly sliced	2 teaspoons cornstarch
1 carrot, coarsely grated	

Rub the pork all over with thyme, allspice, seasoning, and garlic. Heat oil in a large skillet, then roll the pork in it over high heat to sear outside. Mix onion, carrot, cabbage, and apples together in a soaked clay pot. Tuck bay leaves into the vegetables. Sprinkle with seasoning, if desired; add sugar, vinegar, and wine. Place pork, along with the oil from searing, on top of cabbage mixture. Cover pot and place in a cold oven. Set oven at 425°. Cook for 1½ hours.

Mix cornstarch with a little water; add a little of the cooking liquor before stirring the mixture into the vegetables and their juices around the pork. Cook, covered, for 15 minutes, then uncover pot and cook for a final 15 minutes. Transfer meat to a serving platter and serve cut in thick slices. Turn cabbage into a serving dish. Creamy mashed potatoes are an excellent accompaniment. Serves 6.

What's Cooking??

Pork Roast with Thyme

If you can handle a little 'kick', use a little more spice than what the recipe calls for—but not too much more.

1 (4-pound) pork roast, loin or center cut
3 garlic cloves, slivered
1 teaspoon salt

$^1/_2$ tablespoon ground black pepper
3 bay leaves
$^1/_2$ cup apple cider vinegar
1 teaspoon dried thyme

Heat oven to 325°. Trim excess fat off roast. With small knife, pierce roast on top. Force slivers of garlic into the cuts. Sprinkle with salt and pepper. Place bay leaves in bottom of roasting pan and place roast on top of bay leaves, fat-side-up. Combine vinegar and thyme. Pour over top of roast and bake for 35 minutes per pound or until an internal temperature of 160° is reached. Using a baster or spoon, baste drippings over roast frequently while it is cooking. When done let roast stand for 10 minutes before slicing. Serves 5.

Serving Up Oregon

Whiskey Pork with Mustard Sauce

$^1/_2$ cup soy sauce
$^1/_2$ cup bourbon whiskey
$^1/_4$ cup packed brown sugar

3 ($^3/_4$-pound) pork tenderloins, or
2–3 pork chop steaks

In a shallow dish, blend soy sauce, bourbon, and brown sugar. Add the meat, turning to coat with liquid; marinate in refrigerator for several hours.

MUSTARD SAUCE:

$^1/_2$ cup sour cream
$^1/_2$ cup mayonnaise
1 tablespoon dry mustard

1 tablespoon chopped scallions
$1^1/_2$ tablespoons white wine vinegar

While meat is marinating, prepare sauce in medium bowl. Mix sour cream, mayonnaise, mustard, scallions, and vinegar. Let stand at room temperature at least 4 hours.

Preheat oven to 325°. Bake meat in marinade for 45 minutes, basting frequently. Serve with Mustard Sauce. Serves 4.

Get Cookin' with Sound Construction

Spiced Pork Chops

A make-ahead recipe.

¼ cup flour	2 tablespoons oil
½ teaspoon dry mustard	1½ cups apple juice
¼ teaspoon pepper	2 tablespoons brown sugar
⅛ teaspoon ground allspice	½ teaspoon cinnamon
4 pork chops, cut 1 inch thick	2 apples, peeled and sliced

Combine flour, dry mustard, pepper, and allspice. Dredge pork chops in mixture, reserving remaining flour mixture. In skillet, brown chops in oil; remove and keep warm. To drippings add apple juice, brown sugar, and remaining flour mixture. Cook and stir until bubbly. Return pork chops to skillet, and sprinkle with cinnamon. Pour juice mixture over all. Cover and simmer for about 60 minutes until pork is no longer pink. Add apples during the last 20 minutes of cooking. Cool and place in Ziploc bag to freeze.

Thaw. Arrange in baking dish sprayed with nonstick spray. Bake covered at 350° until fully heated and bubbly. Serves 4.

Note: Ham slices can be a yummy replacement for the pork chops.

Per serving: Calories 421; Fat 22g; Calories from Fat 47%.

What's for Dinner?

Margaret's Sesame Pork Chops

6 pork chops	½ cup water
¼ cup soy sauce	3 tablespoons honey
1 tablespoon ketchup	1 small onion, finely chopped
¼ teaspoon ground ginger	1 tablespoon sesame seeds, toasted
⅛ teaspoon pepper	

Brown chops in a small amount of fat. Place in a 9x13-inch pan. (Do not salt.) Combine soy sauce, ketchup, ginger, pepper, water, honey, and chopped onion. Pour over chops and sprinkle with sesame seeds. Cover and bake 1 hour at 325°.

Christian Bakers Cookbook

Smoked Pork Chops with Pasta and Cheese

4 smoked loin pork chops
6 ounces wagon wheel or bow tie
pasta
1 (10-ounce) package frozen peas
1 tablespoon butter
1 large onion, chopped

1 tablespoon flour
1½ cups milk
1 tablespoon Dijon mustard
¼ teaspoon pepper
1 cup shredded Swiss cheese

Brown pork chops in skillet; remove and set aside, keeping warm. Cook pasta according to package directions. Stir peas into cooked pasta; drain and set aside. In skillet, sauté onion in butter. Stir in flour; remove pan from heat and smoothly stir in milk, mustard, and pepper. Return sauce to heat and stir until boiling. Add cheese and mix until melted. Remove from heat, add pasta, and mix well. Pour pasta onto platter, top with pork chops, and serve. Serves 4.

Recipes for the Weekend Gourmet

Pork Chops à la Rogue

An appropriate main course for an elegant dinner.

8 pork chops
½ teaspoon oil
Salt and pepper
6 fresh pears, peeled, halved and
cored
3 tablespoons orange juice

¼ cup firmly packed brown sugar
¼ teaspoon cinnamon
⅓ cup dry sherry
1½ tablespoons butter or margarine
1 teaspoon cornstarch
1 tablespoon water

Preheat oven to 350°. In a skillet, over medium heat, brown pork chops in oil. Place pork chops in shallow pan; sprinkle with salt and pepper. Place pears rounded-side-down on and around pork chops. Pour orange juice over all; sprinkle with brown sugar and cinnamon. Pour sherry over all. Divide butter and place in hollows of pears. Cover and bake 20 minutes. Continue baking uncovered for an additional 20 minutes.

Remove from oven and place pears and pork chops in a warm serving dish. Dissolve cornstarch in water, add to juices in pan, and cook until mixture thickens. Pour over chops and pears. Yields 6–8 servings.

Rogue River Rendezvous

Gourmet Pork Chops

This is wonderful reheated and served again the next day—one of those two-meal, one-cook meals.

8 center cut pork chops
Butter
1 (2½-ounce) can button
  mushrooms (or use fresh)
1 envelope dry onion soup mix

1 cup white table wine
1 cup chicken broth
2 teaspoons bottled garlic or
  2 cloves, crushed
½ pint sour cream

Brown chops in small amount of butter. Remove from pan. Add mushrooms to pan and brown lightly. Add soup mix, wine, broth, and garlic. Stir until blended. Return chops to pan. Cover and simmer slowly, about 45 minutes or until chops are tender. Let chops and liquid cool down. Then, add sour cream slowly, whisking as you add. Heat gently; do not boil.

Recipes from the Kitchens of Family & Friends

Pork Chops with Corn Dressing

1 egg, beaten
2 cups soft bread crumbs
1 can whole-kernel corn, drained,
  or 1½ cups cooked whole-
  kernel corn
¼ cup water
½ cup chopped green pepper
1 small onion, chopped

1 teaspoon Worcestershire sauce
2 tablespoons cooking oil
6 boneless pork chops (about 1 inch
  thick)
Salt and pepper to taste
1 can condensed cream of
  mushroom soup (undiluted)
½ soup can milk

In a bowl, combine egg, bread crumbs, corn, water, green pepper, onion, and Worcestershire sauce; set aside. In a large oven-proof skillet or Dutch oven, heat oil over medium heat. Lightly brown pork chops on both sides. Season with salt and pepper. Top with corn dressing mixture. Add enough water to cover bottom of pan. Bake, uncovered, at 350° for about 1 hour or until pork is tender. Add additional water to pan, if necessary. Remove pork chops and dressing to serving platter; keep warm. Add soup and milk to pan drippings. Cook and stir over medium heat until hot and bubbly. Serve with pork chops.

A Taste of Tillamook

Hearty Ham Pie

½ cup fresh broccoli
¼ cup chopped green pepper
¼ cup chopped fresh mushrooms
3 tablespoons chopped onion
1 garlic clove, minced
2 teaspoons vegetable oil

2 cups chopped cooked ham, divided
1½ cups (6 ounces) shredded
  Swiss cheese, divided
1 unbaked (9-inch) pastry shell
4 eggs, beaten
1 cup light cream

In a saucepan, sauté the broccoli, green pepper, mushrooms, onion, and garlic in oil until tender. Sprinkle half the ham and cheese in the pie crust and cover with vegetables. Cover with remaining ham and cheese. Combine eggs and cream and pour over ham and cheese. Bake at 350° for 45–50 minutes or until a knife inserted near center comes out clean. Makes 6 servings.

Note: It may be necessary to cover edge of crust with foil the last part of baking to prevent over-browning.

Then 'til Now

Poultry

This sign marks the route of the historic Oregon Trail through La Grande. Wagon trains rested here and prepared for the treacherous climb over the Blue Mountains, considered to be the most difficult portion of the journey—steeper and more rugged than the pass through the Rockies.

Cranberry Chicken

1 (8-ounce) bottle Catalina French
  Dressing
1 package powdered onion soup mix

1 can whole cranberries
6–8 chicken breasts

Mix together the dressing, soup mix, and cranberries. Arrange chicken pieces in a 9x13-inch casserole and pour sauce mix over chicken. Bake for 1 hour at 350°.

Dilley Family Favorites

Asparagus Chicken

8 boneless, skinless chicken breast
  halves
Mrs. Dash Herb Seasoning

24 uncooked asparagus spears
1–2 cups sliced fresh mushrooms

Pound breast pieces thin. Sprinkle with herb seasoning. Place 3 asparagus spears on each and roll. Place seam-side-down in reased 9x13-inch baking dish. Cover with sliced mushrooms. Cover and bake for 30 minutes at 350°.

Cooking with Love

Chicken and Broccoli

2 cans cream of chicken soup
3/4 cup mayonnaise
1 1/2 teaspoons curry powder
1 teaspoon lemon juice

2 packages frozen broccoli, cooked
6 chicken breasts, cooked and
  sliced
1 cup shredded Cheddar cheese

Mix soup, mayonnaise, curry powder, and lemon juice. Layer broccoli, chicken, sauce, and then cheese. Bake at 350° for 30 minutes.

Manna by the Sea

Oneanta Chicken with Rosemary Sauce

6 ounces sliced mushrooms	1 ounce dry white wine
1 red bell pepper, finely diced	4 (6- to 7-ounce) whole boneless,
1 button garlic, minced	skinless chicken breasts
1/4 teaspoon dry thyme	Pinch of salt
4 ounces cream cheese, softened	Pinch of white pepper

Sauté mushrooms, bell pepper, garlic, and thyme. Blend in cream cheese and wine; chill. Pound each chicken breast flat and season with salt and pepper. Pile 1/4 of filling in center of each breast and fold in both sides, then roll to cylinder shape—be sure to completely wrap chicken around all filling. Bake at 400° for 20–23 minutes. Serve with Rosemary Sauce. Serves 4.

ROSEMARY SAUCE:

1/2 cup white wine	3 tablespoons chopped fresh
1 bay leaf	rosemary, divided
2 teaspoons chopped shallots	1/2 cup heavy cream

Combine all ingredients except cream and 1 tablespoon rosemary in a small heavy saucepan. Cook until liquid volume is reduced by half. Strain; add cream and remaining rosemary. Reduce slowly until slightly thickened. Serve over chicken breasts. Great with asparagus or artichokes.

Multnomah Falls Lodge Cook Book

Alsace Chicken

The flavor, the moistness, the aroma, the crust—words can't describe this delicious dish.

½ cup butter	¼ teaspoon paprika
1 clove garlic, minced	⅓ cup dried parsley flakes
5 teaspoons Dijon mustard	(optional)
1½ cups Panko crumbs or coarse	8 (4-ounce) chicken breast halves,
bread crumbs	boned and skinned
⅓ cup grated Parmesan cheese	

Make marinade by melting butter in saucepan. Add garlic and sauté on medium-low heat for 5 minutes. Blend in Dijon mustard, stirring well. Cool enough to touch but not to solidify. Whip vigorously until mixture thickens. Marinate chicken at least an hour.

Mix bread crumbs with Parmesan cheese, paprika, and parsley to make a breading mixture. Roll marinated chicken in breading mixture; place in greased 9x13-inch pan. Can be refrigerated up to several hours at this point.

Preheat oven to 350°. Bake chicken for 30 minutes or until done. Serve with parsleyed rice. Spoon Dijon Sauce over the top. Serves 8.

DIJON SAUCE:

2 tablespoons Dijon mustard	¼ cup mayonnaise

Blend mustard and mayonnaise.

Albertina's Exceptional Recipes

Crater Lake is the nation's clearest, deepest lake at 1,932 feet. Its "crystal-blueness" is phenomenal on sunny days and extraordinary in winter when the rim is covered with snow. It is so blue that supposedly, when the very first color photos were sent to the lab, the processor thought the lake looked so unbelievably blue that he thought the photographer used a blue lens! He later wrote him an apology and sent him a free roll of film.

Zesty Chicken Italiano

2 tablespoons butter or margarine	1 (14½-ounce) can tomatoes,
1 pound boneless chicken breast,	undrained and quartered
cut into 1-inch pieces	½ teaspoon dried oregano
1 clove garlic, minced	½ teaspoon lemon pepper
1½ cups thinly sliced zucchini	Salt and pepper to taste
1½ cups sliced fresh mushrooms	8 ounces vermicelli (or other pasta)
1 (15-ounce) can tomato sauce	Grated Parmesan cheese

In a large skillet, melt butter and sauté chicken pieces until lightly browned. Add garlic, zucchini, and mushrooms, and sauté 2 minutes. Stir in remaining ingredients except pasta and Parmesan cheese. Simmer, uncovered, 10 minutes to blend flavor and thicken sauce. Meanwhile, cook pasta according to directions on package; drain. Serve sauce over hot cooked pasta and sprinkle with Parmesan cheese.

What's Cooking in Sisters

Stove Top Barbecue Chicken

A make-ahead recipe.

2 teaspoons vegetable oil	1 tablespoon Worcestershire sauce
½ cup chopped onion	1 teaspoon chili powder
⅔ cup ketchup	½ teaspoon celery seed
⅔ cup water	1½ pounds chicken breasts
¼ cup white vinegar	without skin
¼ cup brown sugar	

Heat oil in skillet, and sauté onion until tender. Stir in remaining ingredients except chicken. Cool and place in freezer bag with chicken and freeze.

Thaw in refrigerator several hours to marinate. Place in large nonstick skillet. Bring to a boil and reduce heat. Cover and simmer for 30 minutes. Turn chicken pieces and simmer covered for about 20 minutes more or until chicken is cooked through. Serve over rice or noodles. Serves 6.

What's for Dinner?

Chicken with Black Beans

4 boneless, skinless chicken breasts	2 tablespoons lime juice
Oil	1/2 teaspoon salt
1 cup cubed mangos, or 1 (8-ounce) can peaches	1 clove garlic, minced
1 tablespoon grated ginger root	2 green onions, chopped
1 teaspoon grated lime peel	2 (15-ounce) cans black beans, undrained

Brown chicken in large skillet in oil, cooking approximately 10 minutes. Add other ingredients directly into skillet; simmer another 10–20 minutes. Serves 4.

Caveman Classic Cuisine

Chicken Picadillo

Serve this in a tortilla or with French bread. It is also good served with rice.

1 pound boneless, skinless chicken breasts	1/2 teaspoon chopped garlic
1 teaspoon cumin	1 onion, sliced
3/4 cup salsa (thick and chunky)	1 green pepper, sliced

Cut chicken into 1-inch strips. Sprinkle with cumin. Spray skillet with nonstick coating and stir-fry chicken until tender and no longer pink. Add salsa, garlic, onion, and green pepper. Cover and simmer for 10 minutes or until vegetables are tender. Yields 4 servings.

Serving size: 1/4 recipe; Calories 190; Carbo. 10g; Prot. 30g; Fat 4g; Exchanges 4 very lean meat, 1 vegetable.

Quick & Healthy Recipes and Ideas (ScaleDown)

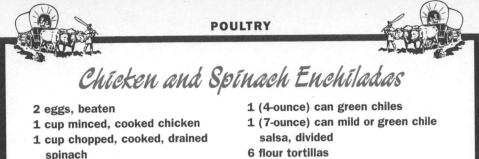

Chicken and Spinach Enchiladas

2 eggs, beaten
1 cup minced, cooked chicken
1 cup chopped, cooked, drained
  spinach
¼ cup heavy cream
1 clove garlic, minced
2 tablespoons hot salsa
1 cup grated Monterey Jack cheese
⅓ cup freshly grated Parmesan
  cheese

1 (4-ounce) can green chiles
1 (7-ounce) can mild or green chile
  salsa, divided
6 flour tortillas
1 tomato, diced
1 cup grated Cheddar cheese
Garnish: chopped green onion,
  picante sauce, sour cream

Preheat broiler. Combine first 9 ingredients in a bowl and mix well. Add 2 tablespoons green chile salsa and transfer the mixture to a saucepan. Warm over medium heat until cheeses are melted and well blended. Fill each tortilla with ⅙ of the chicken-salsa mixture. Divide the tomato evenly between the tortillas and fold tortillas to close. Place side-by-side in a buttered baking dish. Sprinkle the top with Cheddar cheese and pour remaining salsa on top. Place the enchiladas on lowest level of broiler and broil for 5–10 minutes, or until cheese on top is melted and bubbly. Don't allow tortillas to become crisp. Serve immediately; garnish with green onion, picante sauce, and sour cream.

Heavenly Temptations

Sour Cream Chicken Enchiladas

2 whole chicken breasts
2 (10½-ounce) cans cream of
 chicken soup
1 pint sour cream
1 (4-ounce) can chopped green
 chiles (save some for garnish)

Vegetable oil
1 dozen corn tortillas
¾ cup chopped onion
3 cups grated Cheddar or Monterey
 Jack cheese, or combination
Ripe olives

Boil chicken breasts 20–25 minutes. Remove meat from bone and chop. Mix chicken meat, soup, sour cream, and chiles together. Heat oil in small fry pan; dip each tortilla into the hot oil until softened, and drain on paper towels. Spread a thin layer of creamed mixture down the middle of each tortilla (reserve some creamed mixture for top) and sprinkle with chopped onion and cheese (reserve some cheese for top). Roll up tortilla and place seam-side-down in prepared pan. Pour remaining mixture over the top of rolled tortillas and sprinkle with remaining cheese. Bake 25–30 minutes at 350°. Garnish with black olives and additional chiles. Serves 6–8.

Note: Can be prepared ahead of time and refrigerated before baking.

A Taste of Oregon

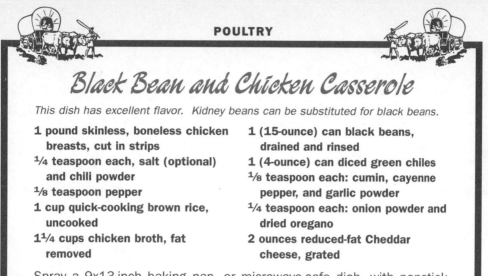

Black Bean and Chicken Casserole

This dish has excellent flavor. Kidney beans can be substituted for black beans.

1 pound skinless, boneless chicken breasts, cut in strips	**1 (15-ounce) can black beans, drained and rinsed**
¼ teaspoon each, salt (optional) and chili powder	**1 (4-ounce) can diced green chiles**
⅛ teaspoon pepper	**⅛ teaspoon each: cumin, cayenne pepper, and garlic powder**
1 cup quick-cooking brown rice, uncooked	**¼ teaspoon each: onion powder and dried oregano**
1¼ cups chicken broth, fat removed	**2 ounces reduced-fat Cheddar cheese, grated**

Spray a 9x13-inch baking pan, or microwave-safe dish, with nonstick cooking spray. Arrange chicken in pan and top with salt, if desired, chili powder, and pepper. Follow directions below for conventional oven or microwave.

Conventional Oven: Preheat oven to 350°. Bake for 20 minutes or until chicken is done.

Microwave Oven: Cover with plastic wrap. Cook on HIGH for 6–8 minutes, depending on thickness of chicken. Rotate dish halfway through cooking time.

Meanwhile, cook rice according to package directions, substituting chicken broth for water and omitting salt and butter. When rice is done, mix in black beans, chiles, and remaining seasonings. Pour drippings from cooked chicken into rice mixture and mix well. Spread over chicken. Top with grated cheese. Return to conventional oven for 5 minutes (microwave oven for 30 seconds) or until cheese is melted. Yields about 6 cups.

Serving size: 1¼ cups; Calories 272; Carbo. 26g; Prot. 31g; Fat 5g; Exchanges 2 starch, 3½ very lean meat.

Quick & Healthy Volume II (ScaleDown)

Hood River, previously known for growing luscious apples, pears, cherries, peaches and other fruits, and for the view of the majestic snowcapped peak of Mt. Hood, has become the destination of choice for wind surfers from around the world. The winds from the Columbia River Gorge, best during the middle of the day, create ideal conditions for riding the waves. "Wind surfing capital of the world" is Hood River's newest distinction.

Brushy Bar Chicken Casserole

The fresh taste and crisp texture of this casserole make it a natural alternative to those with rich and creamy sauces and it comes together in a snap!

2 cups cooked chicken breasts,
  chopped into $\frac{1}{2}$-inch pieces
2 cups chopped celery
$\frac{1}{2}$ cup minced onion
1 cup mayonnaise

2 tablespoons lemon juice
$\frac{1}{2}$ cup toasted slivered almonds
$\frac{1}{2}$ cup sliced stuffed green olives
$\frac{1}{2}$ cup grated sharp Cheddar cheese
1 cup crushed potato chips

Preheat oven to 375°. Combine chicken, celery, onion, mayonnaise, and lemon juice in large bowl. Add almonds, green olives, and cheese; fold gently to mix. Spread in 9x13-inch casserole and top with potato chips. Bake for 20–30 minutes, until heated through and cheese melts. Yields 6–8 servings.

Rogue River Rendezvous

Chicken Broccoli Casserole

1 (16-ounce) package frozen
  broccoli or 2 large fresh bunches
4 cups cooked chicken or turkey,
  cubed
2 cans cream of chicken soup

1 tablespoon lemon juice
$\frac{1}{2}$ cup mayonnaise
1 cup grated cheese
1 cup soft buttered bread cubes

Preheat oven to 350°. Cook broccoli until just tender. Place in bottom of 9x13-inch baking dish. Mix together chicken, soup, lemon juice, and mayonnaise. Pour over broccoli. Sprinkle cheese over chicken. Sprinkle bread over top and bake for 30 minutes.

Favorite Recipes, Second Edition

Oregon is the 10th largest state in size, but only 28th in population. Nearly half of its 3.3 million people live in the Portland area.

Chicken Pie

1 medium fryer	1½–2 cups water
½ large white onion	3–4 carrots, sliced
⅓ bay leaf	1½–2 cups frozen peas (uncooked)
1 teaspoon salt	Salt and pepper to taste

Cook fryer with onion, bay leaf, salt, and water until tender. Chill; remove skin and bones. Chill broth until fat has risen to top, then skim. Partially cook carrots, saving cooking water to add to chicken broth. In 2 (10-inch) pie pans, layer chicken, peas, and carrots. Make sauce with chicken broth and carrot water; thicken with a ratio of 2 tablespoons flour and 1 tablespoon butter. Season to taste with salt and pepper. Pour while hot over pie filling. Liquid should be close to top of pie plate. Cover ingredients with crust; cut slits to allow steam to escape. Design a center hole to check doneness of vegetables. Seal edges. Bake at 425° for 20–25 minutes.

Our Favorite Recipes

Chicken Quick Meal

This is a good recipe to use when you are too tired to cook or need to have a good meal to cook for a person living alone, a family, or for company. This recipe is low calorie, low cholesterol, low salt, and low sugar, yet, it's delicious.

PER PERSON:

2 pieces skinless chicken	Salt and pepper
1 medium potato, peeled	1 medium onion, sliced
2 carrots, cut in chunks	

Place chicken, potato, and carrots in ungreased casserole dish; add salt and pepper. Arrange onion slices over top. Add no water. Cover. Put in oven at 375°; set the timer for 1 hour; forget it. In 1 hour it's ready to eat!

Note: Chicken can be used still frozen from the refrigerator or fresh; makes no difference as to time or taste. Stick with these recommended vegetables. No other combination seems to work.

Coastal Flavors

Chicken Squares

A make-ahead recipe.

2 cups cooked and cut-up chicken thighs, without skin	**1 tablespoon parsley**
6 ounces low-fat cream cheese, softened	**Salt and pepper, to taste**
	2 packages crescent rolls
2 tablespoons milk	**3 tablespoons margarine, melted**
	$1/4$ cup bread crumbs, seasoned

Prepare filling ahead by mixing together well the first 5 ingredients. Freeze in a Ziploc bag.

Thaw filling. Open crescent rolls and separate each can into 4 rectangles by pressing together triangles at the seams. (Each rectangle is made from 2 triangles.) Press seams together well so that the filling will not leak out during cooking. Divide filling onto all 8 rectangles. Pull up corners and pinch side seams together, sealing well. Dip top of each "square" first into melted butter, then bread crumbs. Place onto a baking sheet sprayed with nonstick spray. Bake at 350° for 25 minutes until golden brown. Serve with turkey or chicken gravy, if desired. Serves 6.

Note: This recipe can also be made with cooked and cut-up turkey, and is an excellent way to use holiday leftovers.

Per serving: Calories 287; Fat 20g; Calories from Fat 62%.

What's for Dinner?

No Peek Chicken

2 cups regular rice	**$1/3$ cup water**
1 can cream of onion soup	**1 chicken, cut in serving pieces**
1 can cream of celery soup	**Salt and pepper to taste**

Mix rice, soups, and water. Place mixture in well-greased 9x13-inch pan. Put chicken pieces on top of mixture. Sprinkle with salt and pepper. Cover tightly with foil. Bake at 350° for $2^1/2$ hours. Do not lift foil while baking.

Pig Out

Rock Cornish Hens on Dressing

Great for a party. Everything can be done in the morning except the final half hour of baking.

9 tablespoons butter or margarine, divided
4 cups coarsely chopped celery
4 cups coarsely chopped mushrooms
2 teaspoons salt
½ teaspoon rosemary
½ teaspoon thyme
Pepper
⅔–1 cup coarsely chopped water chestnuts
8 (1½-pound) rock cornish hens, thawed
Salt and pepper

In large skillet melt 1 tablespoon butter. Add celery, mushrooms, salt, rosemary, thyme, and pepper. Simmer until celery is tender. Add water chestnuts. Mix well. Clean hens; tie feet together and wings to body. Place hens on a tray (or cookie sheet with edges) back-side-up, brush with 4 tablespoons melted butter or margarine and sprinkle with salt and pepper. Broil 12–15 minutes until nicely browned. Remove birds from tray and put the dressing into the tray; place hens breast-side-up on the dressing; brush with remaining melted butter. Salt and pepper to taste. Broil lightly or bake in slow oven, 325° about 30 minutes or more; baste occasionally.

Heavenly Temptations

Peppered Duck Breast with Marionberry Catsup

With Pepper Mix for the duck and the Marionberry Catsup prepared in advance, this can be finished in less than 15 minutes.

PEPPER MIX:

1 tablespoon salt
2 teaspoons black peppercorns
6 juniper berries
$\frac{1}{2}$ teaspoon thyme
$\frac{1}{4}$ teaspoon sugar

Blend all ingredients in a small blender jar until finely ground.

MARIONBERRY CATSUP:

4 cups marionberries (or blackberries)
$\frac{1}{4}$ cup butter
$\frac{1}{2}$ cup minced shallots
8–10 tablespoons brown sugar, divided
2 tablespoons balsamic vinegar
Pinch ground cloves

Purée and strain berries. You should end up with $2\frac{1}{2}$–$2\frac{3}{4}$ cups purée. (If you want a thicker purée, strain berries with a wire mesh strainer instead of a food mill.) Set aside.

Melt butter in a nonreactive sauté pan. Add shallots. Sauté, stirring constantly, until softened. Add berry purée and 6 tablespoons brown sugar, mixing well. Cook over low heat 8–10 minutes, stirring occasionally. Add vinegar and ground cloves. Taste and add remaining 2–4 tablespoons of brown sugar to taste (depends on berry sweetness). Let cook an additional 5 minutes. The catsup will have thickened slightly. Remove from heat and keep warm if using immediately. Otherwise, set aside to cool. When cool, refrigerate in an air-tight container. This can be made well in advance, as it stores quite well. Reheat carefully before serving with the duck. Makes $2\frac{1}{2}$ cups catsup.

DUCK BREAST:

2 tablespoons flour
$1\frac{1}{2}$ teaspoons Pepper Mix
3 whole duck breasts, skinned, boned, and cut in half
12 tablespoons Marionberry Catsup
$1\frac{1}{2}$ teaspoons butter
1 tablespoon olive oil

Combine flour and Pepper Mix. Lightly coat both sides of each duck breast half. Gently heat Marionberry Catsup and keep warm. Heat butter and olive oil in a skillet, and sauté breasts for 3 minutes per side. They should be light pink and moist inside. Do not overcook. Transfer to dinner plates and nap each with 2 tablespoons Marionberry Catsup. Serve immediately. Serves 4–6.

Thyme & the River, Too

Gobbler Cobbler

PASTRY:

1½ cups flour
⅛ teaspoon salt
½ cup shortening

¼ cup milk
⅓ cup shredded Cheddar cheese

Combine flour and salt; cut in shortening. Add milk; blend in cheese and mix lightly. Roll out on floured board, place Pastry in 9-inch pie pan and prick with a fork. Bake at 425° for 12–15 minutes or until lightly browned.

FILLING:

2 cups chopped cooked turkey
1 cup pineapple chunks, drained
1 cup chopped walnuts
¼ cup chopped celery
¼ cup chopped onion

1 (8-ounce) carton sour cream
⅔ cup mayonnaise
3 tablespoons shredded Cheddar
  cheese
Sliced black olives

Combine turkey, pineapple, nuts, celery, and onion and mix well. In a separate bowl mix sour cream and mayonnaise. Add just enough sour cream mixture to the turkey mixture to moisten it. Pour turkey mixture into the pie shell, top with remaining sour cream mixture. Garnish with cheese and olives and bake 20 minutes at 350°. Makes 6 large servings.

Recipes and Remembering

Hood River Turkey

4 apples	1 cup water
4 onions	1 cup soy sauce
1 fresh (10-pound) turkey	1 cup white wine

Cut up apples and onions. Stuff turkey with apples and onions. Secure legs and wings. Put turkey in large pan. Mix water, soy sauce, and wine. Cook on LOW setting of gas grill with lid closed. Baste the turkey with the soy mixture every 20–30 minutes. If the turkey becomes too brown, cover it with aluminum foil. The entire cooking time will be $1\frac{1}{2}$–2 hours depending upon the exact size of the turkey. Serves 4–6.

Savor the Flavor of Oregon

Cranberry Relish

1 (8-ounce) package cherry Jell-O	1 cup raw cranberries
1 cup boiling water	1 orange (including rind)
1 cup sugar	3 large apples, peeled
1 tablespoon lemon juice	1 cup drained crushed pinapple
1 cup pineapple juice	

Dissolve Jell-O in boiling water. Add sugar and juices. Put in refrigerator until nearly set. Grind cranberries, orange, and apples. Add to Jell-O mixture. Stir in pineapple. Jar and chill.

Treasured Recipes

Seafood

Seafood is abundant in Oregon—from the sea and the many lakes and streams. Fresh tuna, salmon, trout, bass, bluegill, catfish, halibut, lingcod, snapper, Dungeness crabs and shellfish can sometimes be bought directly from fishermen.

Grilled Wild Salmon with Fresh Tarragon Butter

This simple method for grilling salmon is the salmon recipe most requested at our house. The grilled fish is paired with the subtle flavor of fresh tarragon and Walla Walla sweet onions that have been slowly cooked in lemon butter. We like the flavor of the fish when it is cooked directly on the grill, but it can also be cooked on a sheet of heavy-duty foil. If you use the latter method, grill the fish, skin-side-down, on the foil and do not turn the fish over while it is cooking. When the fish is served, the skin will stick to the foil, making it easy to serve pieces of the fillet.

½ cup chopped Walla Walla
  sweet onion
2 tablespoons chopped parsley
8 tablespoons (½ cup) butter or
  corn oil margarine
2 tablespoons lemon juice
1 teaspoon minced fresh tarragon,
  or ½ teaspoon crushed dried
  tarragon

1 (3-pound) Chinook, silver, or
  sockeye salmon or steelhead
  fillet
Salt and pepper
2 lemon slices
2 sprigs fresh parsley

In a saucepan, cook the onion, parsley, butter, lemon juice, and tarragon over medium-low heat until the onion is tender, about 20 minutes. Brush fish with a small amount of the melted butter mixture to keep it from sticking to the grill, and sprinkle with salt and pepper. Put the fillet, skin-side-up, on a moderately hot grill and cook for 15 minutes. Turn the fillet over and carefully stack onion from the tarragon butter over the fish. Cook for another 10 minutes, basting with butter often. (The fish needs to be turned only once while cooking.) Serve grilled fish on a warm platter garnished with slices of lemon and sprigs of fresh parsley. Serves 4–6.

Dungeness Crabs and Blackberry Cobblers

Grilled Citrus Salmon

1½ tablespoons freshly-squeezed
   lemon juice
2 tablespoons olive oil
1 tablespoon butter
1 tablespoon Dijon mustard
4 garlic cloves, minced

2 dashes cayenne pepper
2 dashes salt
1 teaspoon dried basil
1 teaspoon dried dill
2 teaspoons capers
3 pounds fresh salmon fillets

In a small sauté pan over medium heat, combine lemon juice, olive oil, butter, mustard, garlic, pepper, salt, basil, dill, and capers. While stirring, bring to a boil. Reduce heat and simmer for 5 minutes.

While sauce is still hot, brush on fish. Place salmon fillets skin-side-down on a piece of heavy-duty foil with edges folded up, to make a pan. Pour remaining sauce evenly over fish. Place fish on grill and cover with a lid. Barbecue over medium-hot coals for 10–12 minutes, depending on thickness of fillets. Fish will be flaky and light pink in color when cooked. Yields 6 servings.

Note: May wrap fish in foil and bake in 350° oven for 15–20 minutes.

From Portland's Palate

Grilled Salmon Fillets

Over the years we have presented salmon to our guests in many forms. We now feel marinating and barbecuing salmon is the best way to retain its fresh flavor. The marinade and barbecuing technique we have developed is a "never-fail" method. The fish remains moist, and the fresh salmon flavor is unencumbered by rich sauce.

1 (4- to 5-pound) whole, fresh
   salmon, filleted (with head and
   tail on, 1 pound per person)
¼ cup vegetable oil

2 tablespoons lemon juice
3 tablespoons soy sauce
1 large garlic clove, minced
½ teaspoon dried thyme

Place salmon fillets in a glass or other non-corrosive baking pan. Combine oil, lemon juice, soy sauce, garlic, and thyme. Pour over salmon fillets. Marinate 1 hour, turning the fish occasionally.

Prepare the barbecue. Cover barbecue grate with aluminum foil. Remove the fillets from the baking pan, reserving marinade, and place skin-side-down on the foil. Basting with reserved marinade, grill fish over medium heat 20–25 minutes, until fish flakes easily with a fork. Do not turn fish.

When fillets are cooked, you should be able to transfer them to a serving platter, leaving the skin behind on the foil! Serves 4–5.

Thyme and the River

Salmon Squares à la Janet

3 tablespoons butter or margarine
2 pounds salmon fillets, cut into
  1-inch squares
1 teaspoon salt

½ teaspoon pepper
2 eggs, slightly beaten
Soda crackers, crushed

Heat butter or margarine in frying pan. Season salmon squares to taste. Dip salmon squares in beaten egg and then in cracker crumbs until all sides are coated. Brown in butter until cooked. Serve with lemon wedges and a sauce of your choice. Serves 6.

"Pacific"ally Salmon

Sweet and Sour Salmon

4 salmon steaks, cut about
  ¼ inch thick
Salt and pepper
Flour

2–3 tablespoons butter or margarine
1 large onion, chopped
½ cup red wine vinegar
2 tablespoons sugar

Sprinkle salmon on both sides with salt and pepper, then coat lightly with flour. Brown in heated butter in a large heavy frying pan until golden brown on each side. Remove salmon and keep warm. In the same pan, cook onion until lightly browned, adding more butter, if needed. Stir in vinegar and sugar and bring to a boil. Return salmon to pan; reduce heat and simmer for 3 minutes. Remove from heat and let stand, covered, for 10 minutes. To serve, spoon sauce over salmon.

Fresh-Water Fish Cookbook

 As surely as the salmon return to the Rogue River each spring, the osprey or fish hawk returns to build its high-rise nest in the top of a tree snag along the river. When it comes to fish-catching style, this bird has no equal.

Baked Salmon Fillets

2 pounds salmon fillets	1/4 cup chopped onion
Salt and pepper to taste	1 teaspoon dill weed
1 tablespoon lemon juice	Bread crumbs
1/2 cup sour cream	1 tablespoon butter

Place fillets, skin-side-down, in baking pan. Season with salt and pepper. Squeeze fresh lemon juice over salmon. Spread sour cream over fillets and sprinkle chopped onion and dill weed over the cream. Brown bread crumbs in butter, then scatter on dilled salmon. Cover and bake at 325° for 45 minutes or until fish flakes.

Our Favorite Recipes

Herb's Salmon Steak

1/4 stick margarine, melted	2 tablespoons onion flakes
2 tablespoons lemon juice	Salt and pepper to taste
1/2 teaspoon marjoram	1/2 pound salmon steaks or fillets
1/2 teaspoon lemon pepper	Paprika as desired

Combine margarine with lemon juice, marjoram, lemon pepper, and onion flakes; pour over seasoned salmon and marinate for an hour or so. Lay in a greased oven pan, sprinkle with paprika, if desired, and bake 20–25 minutes at 350°.

West Coast Seafood Recipes

Roast Salmon with Sweet and Sour Onion Confit

This Venetian-inspired dish is traditionally done with sole that has been marinated overnight, then fried, but we like the sweet and sour flavors with the rich taste of the salmon. It is a perfect foil for Pinot Gris. The spinach and polenta round out this dish for an elegant meal. Make the polenta the night before and this dish is put together in less than an hour.

POLENTA CROUTONS:

4 cups cold water	¼ cup unsalted butter
1 cup polenta or coarse cornmeal	½ cup freshly grated Parmesan
Salt to taste	cheese

In a heavy-bottomed saucepan, stir cold water and polenta together. Cook over medium-low heat, stirring every few minutes to prevent sticking, until it is thick, smooth and no longer tastes raw or grainy. This will take 25–30 minutes. Stir in butter and Parmesan and taste for seasoning. Spoon hot mixture into a well-buttered loaf pan and chill in refrigerator overnight. To make croutons, unmold polenta, cut into 1-inch slices, then cut each slice into squares.

4 (6-ounce) salmon fillets	Salt and freshly ground black pepper
Olive oil for coating salmon and	Polenta Croutons
sautéing polenta and spinach	1 pound cleaned spinach leaves

Preheat oven to 450°. Lightly oil, salt and pepper salmon and roast until done, approximately 7–10 minutes. Meanwhile fry Polenta Croutons in olive oil until golden brown and crispy. Drain on paper towels. Sauté spinach in olive oil with a little salt and pepper until just wilted. Set aside, covered, until ready to use. When salmon is done, remove from oven.

SWEET AND SOUR ONION CONFIT:

2 large yellow onions, chopped	1 tablespoon sugar
1 tablespoon butter	3 bay leaves
2 tablespoons olive oil	12 or so black peppercorns
1½ cups dry white wine	Salt and pepper to taste
½ cup white wine vinegar	¼ cup toasted pine nuts for
¼ cup raisins	garnish

Sauté onions in butter and oil over medium heat until wilted, soft and slightly golden, about 15 minutes. Add remaining ingredients except pine nuts and simmer for 15 minutes. Turn off heat and keep warm. Taste again for salt and pepper.

(continued)

(Roast Salmon with Sweet and Sour Onion Confit continued)

To assemble, divide spinach among 4 dinner plates, placing it in the center. Put a salmon filet on top of the spinach and spoon some Sweet and Sour Onion Confit over the fish. Place 3 Polenta Croutons on each plate and garnish the dish with a sprinkling of roasted pine nuts on top of the onion mixture. Serves 4.

Recipe by Christopher Israel of Zefiro, Portland, Oregon
King Estate New American Cuisine Pinot Gris Cookbook

Ginger Salmon with Kiwi Salsa

GINGER SALMON:

4 salmon fillets

2 tablespoons thinly sliced fresh
  gingerroot

2 tablespoons chopped green onions
Soy sauce
4 teaspoons vegetable oil (optional)

Rinse salmon fillets and pat dry. Arrange on a microwave-safe plate. Sprinkle with sliced gingerroot and green onions. Top each with a splash of soy sauce. Cover plate with plastic wrap, venting 1 edge. Microwave on HIGH for 7 minutes or until fish flakes easily. Heat oil in a small microwave-safe dish on HIGH for 30 seconds or until hot. Drizzle hot oil over salmon.

KIWI SALSA:

6 ripe kiwifruit, peeled, diced

2 tablespoons minced red onion

1/2 teaspoon finely chopped
  jalapeño chile

2 tablespoons finely chopped fresh
  cilantro

2 teaspoons grated lime zest
2 tablespoons (or more) fresh lime
  juice
1/2 teaspoon (or more) salt

Mix kiwifruit, red onion, jalapeño, cilantro, lime zest, lime juice, and salt in a bowl. Add more lime juice or salt, if desired. Serve with Ginger Salmon. Yields 4 servings.

Note: You may substitute pineapple in place of kiwifruit if kiwifruit is not in season. May also serve the salsa with chicken or tortilla chips.

Cooking from the Coast to the Cascades

Salmon à la King

¼ stick margarine
¼ cup diced green pepper
½ cup diced celery
1 (4-ounce) can mushroom pieces,
  with liquid

2 tablespoons flour
Milk as needed
1 (8-ounce) can salmon
Salt and pepper to taste

In a skillet, sauté green pepper and celery in margarine until tender. Add mushrooms and flour, slowly stirring in milk until thickened. Add salmon and seasonings, stirring until hot.

West Coast Seafood Recipes

Savory Salmon Loaf

½ cup bread crumbs
½ cup milk
1 teaspoon lemon juice
½ teaspoon salt
½ teaspoon sage
1 tablespoon chopped parsley

2 eggs, slightly beaten
1 pound flaked salmon (fresh or
  canned)
Dash of pepper
2 tablespoons chopped onion
1 tablespoon melted butter

Mix all ingredients except butter together in order given. Pack firmly into a buttered loaf pan. Bake at 350° for 30–40 minutes. Serves 6.

Fresh-Water Fish Cookbook

Honey Mustard Salmon

2 tablespoons honey
1 teaspoon Dijon mustard

Approximately 2 pounds salmon

Mix honey and mustard well. Place foil on barbeque grill. Poke holes in foil approximately 3 inches apart. Place salmon on foil. Baste salmon several times with honey and mustard mixture. Turn salmon over and baste several times. Cook fish until done (when it flakes).

Fresh-Water Fish Cookbook

Baked Snapper
with Spicy Tomato Sauce

1 tablespoon oil	½ teaspoon chili powder
¼ cup chopped onion	½ lemon, finely sliced
1 celery stem, chopped	1 bay leaf
1 tablespoon chopped green pepper	1 clove garlic, minced
1 (16-ounce) can unsalted	Few grains cayenne pepper
tomatoes, drained	2 pounds red snapper or other white
¾ teaspoon Worcestershire sauce	fish fillets
1½ teaspoons low-sodium ketchup	1 tablespoon flour

Heat oil and sauté onion, celery, and green pepper. Add tomatoes, Worcestersauce sauce, ketchup, chili powder, lemon, bay leaf, garlic, and cayenne. Simmer until celery is tender and mixture is thick.

Preheat oven to 350°. Coat fish with flour and place in baking dish. Spread sauce over fish. Cover and bake 20–30 minutes or until fish flakes easily with a fork. Makes 4 servings.

Favorite Recipes Cookbook

Halibut Steak with Sauce

1–1½ pounds halibut steak	½ cup sour cream
Salt and pepper	Juice of ½ lemon
1 small onion, sliced and separated	½ cup grated Cheddar cheese
into rings	Parsley flakes
⅓ stick butter, melted	Garlic salt

Place halibut steaks in a baking dish and sprinkle with salt and pepper. Place rings of onion on top of steaks. Combine melted butter, sour cream, and lemon juice. Mix by hand and pour over steaks. Place cheese over fish/sauce. Garnish with parsley flakes and garlic salt. Bake at 350°, uncovered, for 30 minutes.

Grade A Recipes

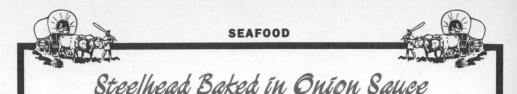

Steelhead Baked in Onion Sauce

⅓ cup butter or margarine
3 cups sliced onions
4 tablespoons flour
1 teaspoon salt

2 cups milk
1 pound fish fillets
½ cup dry buttered bread crumbs

Melt butter in frying pan; add onions. Stir frequently over low heat until onions are yellow; add flour and salt. Stir until flour is moistened. Add milk; bring to a boil. Place fillets in a greased 6x10-inch baking dish; cover with sauce. Top with crumbs. Bake for 30 minutes at 375°. Serve from baking dish. Yields 5 servings.

Fresh-Water Fish Cookbook

Fillet of Steelhead

1 large (2-pound) fillet
Onion salt
Mayonnaise
Italian seasoning
Dill

1 cup crushed saltine crackers
½ cup margarine, melted
Lemon pepper
Seafood seasoning

Put fillet in baking dish. Sprinkle fillet with onion salt. Spread mayonnaise over fillet. Sprinkle Italian seasoning and dill to taste. Sprinkle cracker crumbs over fillet. Pour melted margarine over fish and top with lemon pepper and seafood seasoning. Bake in a 350° oven for 20 minutes or until done.

Fresh-Water Fish Cookbook

 Oregon is the nation's leading producer of Christmas trees, growing more than 8 million firs for holiday decorating around the world. Some reach up to 130 feet high.

Stuffed Fillet of Sole

¼ cup chopped onion
¼ cup butter or margarine
1 small can mushrooms, drained
  (reserve liquid)
1 small can crabmeat, drained
½ cup cracker crumbs
2 tablespoons parsley
½ teaspoon salt
¼ teaspoon pepper

2 pounds sole fillets
3 tablespoons butter
3 tablespoons flour
¼ teaspoon salt
Milk
⅓ cup dry white wine
1 cup shredded Swiss cheese
½ teaspoon paprika

Sauté onion in butter until lightly browned; add mushrooms, crabmeat, cracker crumbs, parsley, salt and pepper. Spread mixture over fillets. Roll and place seam-side-down in oblong baking pan.

In saucepan, melt butter; blend in flour and salt. Add enough milk to mushroom liquid to make 1½ cups. Add with wine to saucepan. Cook until thickened. Pour over the fillets. Bake in a 400° oven for 25 minutes. Sprinkle with cheese and paprika; bake an additional 5 minutes or until cheese is melted.

Scallops and Sole Food

Chilean Sea Bass with Ginger Sesame Sauce

It is nice to serve this fish with steamed rice so every drop of the delicious sauce can be enjoyed. To shorten the cooking time, simply sprinkle the marinade ingredients on the fish and bake, microwave, or grill it.

1 pound Chilean sea bass, red snapper, or halibut, cut into 4 pieces

Rinse fish under cold water and pat dry. Place fish in shallow baking dish.

MARINADE:

1 teaspoon lower-sodium soy sauce   **1/2 teaspoon grated fresh gingerroot**
1/4 teaspoon sesame oil

Combine soy sauce, sesame oil, and ginger; drizzle over fish and let stand, uncovered, for 30–60 minutes.

GINGER SESAME SAUCE:

1 teaspoon sesame seeds
1 teaspoon vegetable oil
1/2 teaspoon grated fresh gingerroot
1 teaspoon minced garlic
2 teaspoons lower-sodium soy sauce

2 teaspoons freshly squeezed lemon juice
1/2 teaspoon cornstarch
1/4 cup water
2 tablespoons finely chopped green onions

Preheat oven to 400°. Bake fish, uncovered, 8–15 minutes (time depends on thickness of the fish). While fish is baking, prepare Ginger Sesame Sauce. Toast sesame seeds in nonstick skillet over medium heat, stirring constantly, until golden brown. Set aside. Heat oil in nonstick skillet; add ginger and garlic and cook 1 minute. Combine soy sauce, lemon juice, cornstarch, and water; stir into ginger-garlic mixture and cook until slightly thickened and mixture is clear.

Remove fish from oven and place on warm serving platter. Stir sesame seeds and juices from baking dish into sauce and bring to a boil. Spoon sauce over fish and sprinkle with green onions. Serve immediately. Makes 4 servings.

Per Serving: Calories 128; Sod. 245mg; Fiber Trace; Total Fat 3g; Sat. Fat 1g; Chol. 60mg; Chol-saturated Fat Index 4.

The New American Diet Cookbook

Baked Fish with Bread Crumbs and Tomatoes

(Psari ala Spetsiota)

Named for the island of Spetsai, this dish is very easy to prepare and very tasty. The elements are simple: impecably fresh fish, flavorful vine-ripened tomatoes and good quality bread crumbs. You may serve hot or cold.

2 pounds firm white fish fillets or steaks
6 tablespoons olive oil, divided
1 tablespoon fresh lemon juice
Salt and freshly ground pepper to taste
2 cups peeled, seeded and chopped tomatoes, or 1 (14½-ounce) can stewed tomatoes, drained

4 garlic cloves, finely minced
½ cup dry white wine
1 tablespoon sugar or honey
4 tablespoons chopped fresh flat-leaf (Italian) parsley
1 teaspoon dried oregano or ground cinnamon (optional)
1 cup fine dried bread crumbs

In a large enough baking dish, arrange fish in a single layer. In a small bowl, whisk together 2 tablespoons oil, lemon juice, salt and pepper and pour over the fish. Let stand for about 30 minutes at room temperature.

In a saucepan over medium heat, combine tomatoes, garlic, wine, sugar or honey, parsley, and oregano or cinnamon. Bring to a simmer and cook for about 10 minutes. Season to taste with salt and pepper. Pour tomato sauce evenly over fish. Scatter bread crumbs evenly over top. Drizzle with remaining 4 tablespoons oil. Bake in a preheated 400° oven about 15 minutes until fish is cooked through and bread crumbs are golden brown. Serve immediately. Serves 4–6.

Flavor it Greek!

Hells Canyon National Recreational Area is 700,000 acres of some of the most rugged, spectacular wildlands on earth, and at its heart is the wildest whitewater stretch of the Snake River.

Fish Salad Bunwiches

4 pounds rockfish, poached and chilled	$\frac{1}{4}$ cup finely chopped onion
2$\frac{1}{2}$ cups finely chopped celery	$\frac{1}{4}$ cup lemon juice
2$\frac{2}{3}$ cups mayonnaise	1 teaspoon salt
$\frac{1}{2}$ cup sweet pickle relish	25 hamburger buns, toasted
	Lettuce leaves

Flake fish; add celery. Combine and mix mayonnaise, pickle relish, onion, lemon juice, and salt. Add to fish and celery; mix carefully. Cover bottom half of each bun with a lettuce leaf and top with about $\frac{1}{3}$ cup salad mixture. Cover with bun tops. Serves 25.

Clam Dishes and Rock Fishes

Craburgers

1$\frac{1}{2}$ cups Dungeness crabmeat	$\frac{1}{3}$ cup mayonnaise
2 hard-cooked eggs, chopped	$\frac{1}{3}$ cup chili sauce
3 tablespoons chopped ripe olives	4 hamburger buns
Juice of $\frac{1}{2}$ lemon	Cheddar cheese slices

Combine crabmeat with remaining ingredients except hamburger buns and Cheddar cheese. Mix. Spread on split hamburger buns; place on broiler pan. Broil 5 inches from heat 6–7 minutes. Cover with cheese slices and return to oven until cheese is melted.

Huckleberries and Crabmeat

Crab Newberg

¼ stick margarine
2 tablespoons flour
¼ teaspoon salt, or to taste
¼ teaspoon nutmeg
3–4 drops hot pepper sauce

1 cup milk, half-and-half or
   non-dairy liquid creamer
2 egg yolks, beaten
1 (6-ounce) can crabmeat
¼ cup dry white wine

Melt margarine in a saucepan or double boiler; add flour, salt, nutmeg, and pepper sauce, then stir in milk until thickened.

Beat egg yolks and stir into sauce. Add flaked crab and wine, continuing to stir until heated. Serve over hot rice. (Don't discard egg whites; use with another recipe.)

West Coast Seafood Recipes

Jake's Dungeness Crab Tortellini

1 tablespoon butter
6 mushrooms, sliced
1 tablespoon garlic
4 ounces heavy cream

Salt and pepper
8 ounces tortellini, cooked
4 ounces crabmeat
2 tablespoons Gorgonzola cheese

Heat butter in skillet until it starts to bubble. Sauté mushrooms in butter until they start to brown, approximately 2 minutes. Add garlic and stir; before garlic starts to brown, add cream and salt and pepper. Allow cream to start to reduce so that it begins to thicken. Add tortellini and toss together. Add crab and cheese and heat. Makes 1 serving.

Serving Up Oregon

Dungeness crab is the world's standard for super-premium crab. It is unmatched for quality, texture and taste. Dungeness is unique to the West coast of the United States. The crab season on the Oregon coast begins on December 1, and continues through August 15. Peak harvest occurs during the first eight weeks, with up to 75% of the annual production landed during this period. Oregon fishermen land, on average, 10 million pounds of Dungeness crab annually.

Dungeness Crab Cakes with Red Pepper Sauce

We like these Crab Cakes with the Red Pepper Sauce, although they taste great by themselves.

RED PEPPER SAUCE:
2 cloves garlic
3/4 cup roasted and peeled red
   peppers

2 teaspoons freshly squeezed lemon
   juice
1/4 cup nonfat mayonnaise

Purée garlic, red peppers, lemon juice, and mayonnaise in food processor or blender until smooth. Place in covered container and chill in refrigerator.

CRAB CAKES:
3 teaspoons olive oil, divided
1/4 cup minced green onions
3 tablespoons minced red bell
   pepper
1 tablespoon rice vinegar or other
   vinegar
3/4 pound (2 cups) fresh crabmeat,
   or 1 (14³/₄-ounce) can salmon
   (2 cups), or 1 (12-ounce) can
   tuna

3 tablespoons freshly squeezed
   lemon juice
1/2 cup dried bread crumbs, divided
2 egg whites, lightly beaten, or 1/4
   cup egg substitute, lightly beaten
1 teaspoon Dijon-style mustard
1/4 cup chopped fresh parsley
1/8 teaspoon Tabasco sauce
1/4 teaspoon paprika
1/8 teaspoon pepper

Heat 1 teaspoon olive oil in a small nonstick skillet. Add green onions and bell pepper and sauté, stirring often, until green onions are wilted. Add vinegar and boil rapidly until it has evaporated. Set aside to cool.

Place crabmeat in a bowl and sprinkle with lemon juice. If using canned salmon, discard skin; mash bones well. If using tuna, mash well. Blend in cooled green onion-pepper mixture. Stir in 1/4 cup bread crumbs, egg whites or egg substitute, mustard, parsley, Tabasco sauce, paprika, and pepper. Cover and chill at least 2 hours.

When ready to cook, mold mixture into 8 cakes. Coat lightly on both sides with remaining 1/4 cup bread crumbs. Do not coat salmon or tuna cakes. Heat remaining 2 teaspoons oil in a nonstick skillet. Add cakes, cover, and cook over medium heat 4 minutes or until nicely browned. Turn carefully and cook, uncovered, 4 minutes or until browned. Makes 8 Crab Cakes and 1 cup sauce.

Per Cake and 2 tablespoons Sauce: Calories 109; Sod. 411mg; Fiber 1g; Total Fat 3g; Sat Fat Trace; Cho.l 43mg; Chol-saturated Fat Index 3.

The New American Diet Cookbook

Cracked Dungeness Crab with Herb Mayonnaise

Fresh crabs are most commonly sold precooked in the Pacific Northwest, but when I have time I like to buy them live and steam them myself. When they are eaten as soon as they are cooked, their meat is always succulently sweet and mild.

2 live Dungeness crabs	Herb Mayonnaise or Homemade
4 lemon wedges	Herb Mayonnaise

Use tongs to put live crabs in a pan of ice to numb them before cooking. Steam the crabs over boiling water for 20 minutes. When crabs are cool enough to handle, remove backs. Discard viscera and gills and rinse under cold water. Separate legs from body. Lay each leg on its edge and crack shell by gently hitting it with a mallet. Place crab on a platter and garnish with lemon wedges. Serve with Herb Mayonnaise or Homemade Herb Mayonnaise. Serves 4.

HERB MAYONNAISE:

1 cup commercial mayonnaise	2 teaspoons chopped fresh dill
1/2 teaspoon drained capers	2 scallions or green onions,
2 teaspoons chopped fresh basil	trimmed and chopped

Blend all ingredients together and place in a small bowl to accompany the cracked crab.

HOMEMADE HERB MAYONNAISE:

1 egg	2 tablespoons fresh dill
1 teaspoon fresh lemon juice or	1 1/2 cups corn oil or 3/4 cup mild
wine vinegar	olive oil and 3/4 cup corn oil
1/2 teaspoon salt	1 tablespoon drained capers
2 tablespoons fresh basil leaves	

Put egg, lemon juice, salt, basil, and dill in the bowl of a food processor and process for 30 seconds. Gradually add oil until the mixture thickens. Stir in the capers. Makes about 2 cups.

Dungeness Crabs and Blackberry Cobblers

Crab Wavecrest

1½ cups packed cooked crabmeat
  (a 2-pound Pacific crab)
1–1½ tablespoons drained
  pimentos
1–1½ tablespoons chopped
  green olives
½ cup mayonnaise
1 tablespoon bottled chili sauce

½ teaspoon Worcestershire sauce
3–4 drops Tabasco sauce
Salt to taste
1 whole green olive per serving
Paprika
2–3 tablespoons coarsely chopped
  fresh parsley

Preheat oven to 350°. Butter 2 (6-ounce) or 3 (4-ounce) crab shells, small casseroles or custard cups.

Mix all ingredients except whole olives, paprika, and parsley. Divide among bakers. Decorate each with an olive. Sprinkle with paprika. Bake 20 minutes. Sprinkle with parsley. Serve with garlic bread and a tossed salad.

Fiddlin' in the Kitchen

Baked Crab-Filled Avocados

2 tablespoons butter
2 tablespoons flour
1 cup milk
¼ teaspoon salt
Dash of lemon pepper

¼ teaspoon Worcestershire sauce
2 tablespoons chopped black olives
1 pound Dungeness crabmeat
3 large ripe avocados, halved
¼ cup grated cheese

Melt butter and blend in flour. Add milk gradually and cook until thick and smooth, stirring constantly. Add seasonings, olives and crabmeat. Fill centers of avocado halves with crab mixture. Sprinkle cheese over top of each avocado. Place in greased baking pan. Bake at 350° for 20 minutes.

Huckleberries and Crabmeat

In 1880, a sea cave was discovered near what is now known as Florence. Sea Lion Caves is known to be the largest sea cave in the world.

Crab or Shrimp Stuffed Mushrooms

16 extra large mushrooms	1/2 cup mayonnaise
1/2 cube of butter	2 shallots, minced and sautéed
1 pound crab or small salad shrimp	1 teaspoon prepared mustard

Remove stem from mushrooms and sauté the caps, top-side-down, in butter for 1 minute. Place in ovenproof dish and set aside.

Mix crab or shrimp with mayonnaise, shallots, and mustard. Fill mushrooms with equal amounts of this mixture. Place in oven for 20 minutes at 300°. Remove from oven and cover lightly with Mornay Sauce. Garnish with fresh, chopped parsley.

MORNAY SAUCE:

3 tablespoons flour	1 teaspoon salt
2 tablespoons butter, melted	1/2 teaspoon white pepper
1 1/2 cups hot milk	
1 1/2 cups shredded cheese (Cheddar, Swiss, Jack)	

Add flour to melted butter in saucepan; cook a few minutes (do not brown). Add milk, stirring constantly until smooth and creamy. Add cheese; continue stirring. Mix in salt and pepper. Remove from heat and serve.

Multnomah Falls Lodge Cook Book

Cantonese Shrimp with Rice

2 cups sliced celery (sliced diagonally)	1 (16-ounce) can mixed Chinese vegetables
2 cups sliced onions	1/4 teaspoon lemon pepper
2 tablespoons vegetable oil	1/4 cup soy sauce
1 quart fresh spinach leaves	1 1/4 cups chicken broth
3 cans shrimp, drained	2 tablespoons cornstarch

Sauté celery and onions in vegetable oil about 2 minutes, stirring often. Add spinach, shrimp, and vegetables, which have been rinsed and drained. Cover and cook 1 minute. Blend pepper, soy sauce, chicken broth, and cornstarch. Stir into shrimp-vegetable mixture. Cook, stirring until sauce is clear and thickened, about 2 minutes. Serve over hot fluffy rice. Serves 6.

"Cate"ring to Shrimp

Steve Perry's Hungry Barbarian Shrimp Stir-Fry

The trick to doing good stir-fry is the timing. Once you start, it all goes very fast and you won't be able to step far away from the stove. All the ingredients should be ready before you crank the fire up; so the ginger should be grated or finely sliced— about a tablespoon is usually enough—the shrimp peeled, the vegetables peeled and sliced—and angle cuts are better. (It is not necessary to peel the eggplant, which looks kinda like a purple cucumber, but do take the ends off before you slice it with angle cuts.)

3–4 tablespoons hot pepper oil	Soy sauce
1 small ginger root	1 cup sugar or snow peas, ends
½ cup cashews	trimmed
1 pound medium-sized shrimp	½ cup Mung bean sprouts
2 medium carrots	1 package Chinese noodles (fresh
2 medium Chinese eggplants	are better, but you can use dried)
1 cup raw cabbage, green or red	Black pepper

You should have your pot, with about 1–2 quarts of water, heating. Stir-fry noodles cook very fast, so you want to wait until you are nearly finished with the vegetables before starting the noodles. Bring the water to a boil slowly.

Over a hot fire, in a large skillet or wok—you'll need a lid, later—heat oil until it starts to smoke. Add grated ginger, stir, then add cashews. When the ginger starts to crisp, add shrimp. Stir and turn frequently. A pair of bamboo or wooden spatulas works best; do it like tossing a green salad. Don't overcook, no more than 2 minutes or until the shrimp have turned completely pink. Remove from heat; put shrimp into a bowl or colander. Add another dab of oil to skillet, return to stove, then add carrots. Stir, cook for 1–2 minutes, then add eggplant and cabbage. Continue to stir for another 1–2 minutes.

Put shrimp back into skillet; add 3–4 tablespoons soy sauce—it'll hiss some—add sugar peas (or snow peas) and bean sprouts. Stir and cover with lid. Add more soy sauce to keep a bit of liquid in skillet; from here on out, you're steaming instead of frying. Put noodles into water; stir. The water will probably stop boiling. Allow it to come back to a boil; add 1 cup cold water to pot. When it starts to boil again, noodles will be about done. Don't overcook them. Drain noodles in colander, then add them to skillet. Sprinkle noodles liberally with soy sauce (you don't need salt—this stuff is loaded with sodium) and pepper to

(continued)

(Steve Perry's Hungry Barbarian Shrimp Stir-Fry continued)

taste. Stir for about 45 seconds. Remove from heat. Serves 3–4 polite people; 2 barbarians.

Note: You can use mushrooms or other vegetables if you like, potatoes, even sliced apples, just about anything; just remember to cook the harder ones like carrots first, then add softer ones later. If you are a vegetarian, use a bit more oil and try hard tofu with the water pressed out in place of shrimp.

Seasoned with Words

Succulent Shrimp Cakes

1 pound small raw prawns, peeled, deveined, and cut into 2 or 3 pieces
1 large stalk celery, chopped in small pieces
1/2 onion, chopped in small pieces (can use green onions)
1/4 cup chopped green pepper (optional)

1/2 teaspoon salt
1/4 teaspoon pepper
1/2 teaspoon Lawry's Seasoned Salt
1 tablespoon lemon juice
1 teaspoon Worcestershire sauce
2 tablespoons cocktail sauce
3 eggs, slightly beaten
3/4 cup cracker meal/crumbs

Mix all ingredients in a mixing bowl. Heat skillet over medium heat and spray or coat bottom of pan with olive oil. Drop spoonfuls of mixture into skillet and shape into 4-inch patties. Cook approximately 5 minutes on each side or until brown and center is done. Serve with Shrimp Dipping Sauce or with hot Knorr's Newberg Sauce. Serves 4 people.

SHRIMP DIPPING SAUCE:

1/2 cup mayonnaise or salad dressing
1/4 cup ketchup

1 teaspoon lemon juice
1 teaspoon Worcestershire sauce

Combine ingredients. Serve cold or room temperature with seafood.

A Taste of Tillamook

Shrimp Curried Eggs

8 eggs, hard-cooked
1/3 cup mayonnaise
1/2 teaspoon salt
1/2 teaspoon paprika
1/2 teaspoon curry powder
1/4 teaspoon dry mustard
3 tablespoons butter, divided

2 tablespoons flour
1 (10½-ounce) can frozen cream
  of shrimp soup, thawed
1 soup can milk
1/2 cup Cheddar cheese, shredded
1/2 cup Pacific shrimp, drained
1 cup bread crumbs

Remove yolks from eggs; mash. Mix with mayonnaise, salt, paprika, curry powder, and mustard. Refill egg whites; place in a baking dish. Melt 2 tablespoons butter; blend in flour. Add soup and milk. Cook, stirring until thickened. Add cheese and shrimp. Cover eggs with sauce. Mix crumbs and 1 tablespoon melted butter; sprinkle over casserole. Bake at 350° for 15 minutes.

"Cate"ring to Shrimp

Gardes Me Feta

1/2 cup minced onion
1½ tablespoons butter
1½ tablespoons olive oil
1/2 cup dry white wine
4 ripe tomatoes, peeled, seeded and
  chopped, or 1 (28-ounce) can
  tomatoes, drained and chopped

1 clove garlic, minced
1 teaspoon salt
1/2 teaspoon pepper
1/2 teaspoon oregano
4 ounces feta cheese
1 pound raw shrimp, peeled and
  deveined

Sauté onion in butter and oil until tender. Add wine, tomatoes, garlic, salt, pepper, oregano, and feta cheese. Bring to a boil; simmer until thickened. Add shrimp and cook 3–5 minutes or just until shrimp turn pink.

Sauce can simmer on low for up to 2 hours, so you can entertain your guests and then add the shrimp just before serving. Serve with crusty French bread for soaking up the sauce. Serves 4, but can easily be doubled.

Collection Extraordinaire

Alta's Clam Fritters

1 pint frozen ground clams
  (or 2 cans ground)
1 beaten egg
1/2 cup dry bread crumbs

Salt to taste
1/4 cup pancake flour
1/4 cup canned milk
1 tablespoon oil

Mix all except oil. Drop by spoonfuls to form small patties in skillet with small amount of heated oil. Fry quickly until golden brown on both sides. Serve hot with tartar sauce, lemon juice or maple syrup. Serves 2 or 3.

Begged, Borrowed and Stöllen Recipes

Northwest Clam Bake

6 dozen clams (steamers)
12 small onions
6 medium potatoes
6 ears of corn in the husks

3 Dungeness crabs, cleaned
Lemon wedges
Melted butter or margarine

Wash clam shells thoroughly. Peel onions; parboil for 15 minutes along with the potatoes. Drain. Remove corn silk and replace husks. Cut 12 pieces of cheesecloth and 12 pieces of heavy-duty aluminum foil, 18x36 inches each. Place 2 pieces of cheesecloth on top of 2 pieces of foil. Place 2 onions, a potato, an ear of corn, 1 dozen clams and 1/2 Dungeness crab on cheesecloth. Tie opposite corners of the cheesecloth together. Pour 1 cup of water over the package. Bring foil up over the food and close all edges with tight double fold. Make 6 packages. Place packages on grill, about 4 inches from hot coals. Cover with hood or aluminum foil. Cook for 45–60 minutes, or until onions and potatoes are cooked. Serve with lemon wedges and butter.

Clam Dishes and Rock Fishes

There are nine lighthouses along Oregon's coastline. Five are still being used; the others are designated historic monuments.

Creamy Oyster Bake

12 crackers crushed
1 (10-ounce) jar oysters, drained
1/2 cup milk

1/2 teaspoon salt, or to taste
1/4 teaspoon onion salt
1/4 stick margarine

Spread half the cracker crumbs over bottom of a small greased casserole dish. Lay oysters on cracker crumbs; add seasonings and milk; cover with remaining cracker crumbs, dot with margarine, and bake 30 minutes at 350°.

West Coast Seafood Recipes

Oysters Florentine

6 tablespoons butter, divided
4 bunches fresh spinach, cleaned
  and stems trimmed
3 cloves garlic, finely chopped
1/4 teaspoon salt
1/4 teaspoon ground white pepper
4 tablespoons flour
20 medium-sized oysters, shucked,
  rinsed, and dried

Egg wash (2 eggs whisked with 1
  tablespoon water)
2 tablespoons Worcestershire sauce
2 tablespoons lemon juice
1 tablespoon chopped shallots
1 teaspoon chopped fresh parsley

Melt 2 tablespoons butter into sauté pan; add spinach, chopped garlic, salt, and pepper to taste. Cook until wilted. Flour oysters lightly and dip in egg wash. Fry over medium heat in separate pan in 2 tablespoons melted butter until golden brown.

Divide spinach onto 4 dinner plates; place 5 oysters on top of spinach. Return saucepan to medium heat and add remaining butter, Worcestershire sauce, lemon juice, shallots, and parsley. Deglaze and pour mixture over oysters. Serve.

Serving Up Oregon

Scalloped Oysters

½ cup thinly sliced onion
½ cup minced celery heart
1 button garlic, minced
¼ cup butter, divided
1 pint extra small oysters

3 eggs
½ cup heavy cream
½ teaspoon white pepper
1 teaspoon celery salt
½ cup bread crumbs

Sauté onion, celery, and garlic in half the butter until tender. Remove from the pan and set aside. Using the same pan, add remaining butter and oysters. Sauté until firm. Place in shallow baking dish and add sautéed vegetables. Mix eggs, cream, and seasonings; beat well. Pour over oysters and cover with bread crumbs. Bake for 30 minutes at 325°.

Multnomah Falls Lodge Cook Book

Baked Scallops

This recipe is deceptively simple to make and the results are wonderful.

1 pound scallops, raw
½ cup cream or half-and-half
Salt and pepper to taste

Dash of nutmeg
1 cup cracker crumbs, divided
1½ tablespoons butter, melted

Mix scallops with the cream. Add salt, pepper, nutmeg and most of the cracker crumbs. Place in baking dish and cover with remaining cracker crumbs and sprinkle with melted butter. Bake in preheated 375° oven for 25 minutes.

What's Cooking in Sisters

Scallops Wrapped in Smoked Salmon with Caviar and Beurre Blanc

12 large sea scallops, muscles
   removed
12 (3- to 4-inch) strips of cold-
   smoked salmon, approximately
   1-inch wide (lox can be
   substituted)

Beurre Blanc
1 tablespoon unsalted butter
1 teaspoon finely chopped
   lemon zest
1 tablespoon finely chopped chives
1/2 teaspoon red lumpfish caviar

Wrap each scallop with a strip of smoked salmon and secure with a wooden toothpick. Refrigerate, covered, until ready to assemble. This can be done up to 2 hours ahead. Meanwhile, make Beurre Blanc.

BEURRE BLANC:

1 1/2 tablespoons white wine vinegar
1 1/2 tablespoons lemon juice
2 teaspoons finely minced shallots
1/4 teaspoon salt

Freshly ground white pepper
1 tablespoon butter for the
   reduction, plus 4 ounces chilled
   unsalted butter, cut into 8 pieces

Combine vinegar, lemon juice, shallots, salt, pepper, and 1 tablespoon butter in a small, heavy, non-reactive saucepan and boil over medium-high heat until reduced to about 1 tablespoon.

Remove saucepan from heat and whisk in a few pieces of chilled butter until they melt creamily into the reduction. Return saucepan to burner, and over very low heat, add remaining pieces of butter, one piece at a time, whisking constantly. The sauce should be creamy and pale. Season with salt, pepper, and lemon juice as needed. Hold the sauce in a warm spot.

To assemble, sauté the scallops in butter for about 2 minutes on each side. Remove from heat and cover for a minute so that scallops are warmed through. On 4 warmed plates, ladle a tablespoon of Beurre Blanc, swirling to coat the surface. Remove toothpicks from scallops and place 3 scallops in the center of each plate. Scatter the lemon zest, chopped chives, and caviar around the scallops and serve immediately. Serves 4 as a first course.

Recipe by Stephanie Pearl Kimmel, King Estate Winery, Eugene, Oregon
King Estate New American Cuisine Pinot Gris Cookbook

Oregon Seafood Stir-fry

¾ pound sole
¼ pound scallops
⅓ pound shrimp
2 teaspoons cornstarch
¼ cup white wine
1½ tablespoons soy sauce
¾ cup orange juice
2 tablespoons vegetable oil

2 teaspoons grated ginger root
1 tablespoon minced garlic
2 ounces pea pods
1 medium red pepper, thinly sliced
½ cup sliced green onions
½ teaspoon sesame oil
½ pound Oriental noodles

Rinse fish and shellfish briefly with cold water; pat dry with paper towels. Cut sole into large chunks. Combine cornstarch, wine, soy sauce, and orange juice. Add fish chunks and marinate in refrigerator 30 minutes. Drain fish, reserving marinade.

Heat oil in skillet; add ginger and garlic. Sauté 5–10 seconds. Add fish chunks and stir-fry for 4 minutes, or until medium-rare. Add scallops, vegetables, and sesame oil; stir-fry 2 minutes. Add shrimp and continue cooking just until sauce thickens. Serve immediately over Oriental noodles.

Scallops and Sole Food

Oriental Seafood

I make this dish with jumbo shrimp that is shelled and deveined. It is easily found in the freezer section. Scallops and halibut are also very good in this recipe.

2 cups chicken broth, fat removed
1 tablespoon soy sauce
1/2 teaspoon ground ginger
1/4 teaspoon garlic powder
3-ounce coil vermicelli (fine
   noodles), dry
1 onion, cut in wedges
1 red bell pepper, sliced
1 (8-ounce) can sliced water
   chestnuts, drained

1/2 cup sliced carrots
1 cup broccoli pieces
1 tablespoon cornstarch
1/4 cup water
1 pound seafood, such as a firm fish
   (cod, halibut), cut in bite-size
   pieces, scallops, and/or shelled
   and deveined shrimp

Add all but the cornstarch, water, and seafood in a large skillet. Bring to a boil. Reduce heat to low, cover, and simmer for 8–10 minutes or until vegetables are almost done. Mix cornstarch with water. Add to skillet and bring to a slow boil, stirring until thickened. Reduce heat, add seafood, and simmer just until seafood is cooked. Yields 7 cups.

Serving size: 1³/₄ cups; Calories 260; Carbo. 30g; Prot. 30g; Fat 2g; Exchanges 1 starch, 3 lean meat, 3 vegetable.

Quick & Healthy Volume II (ScaleDown)

Cakes

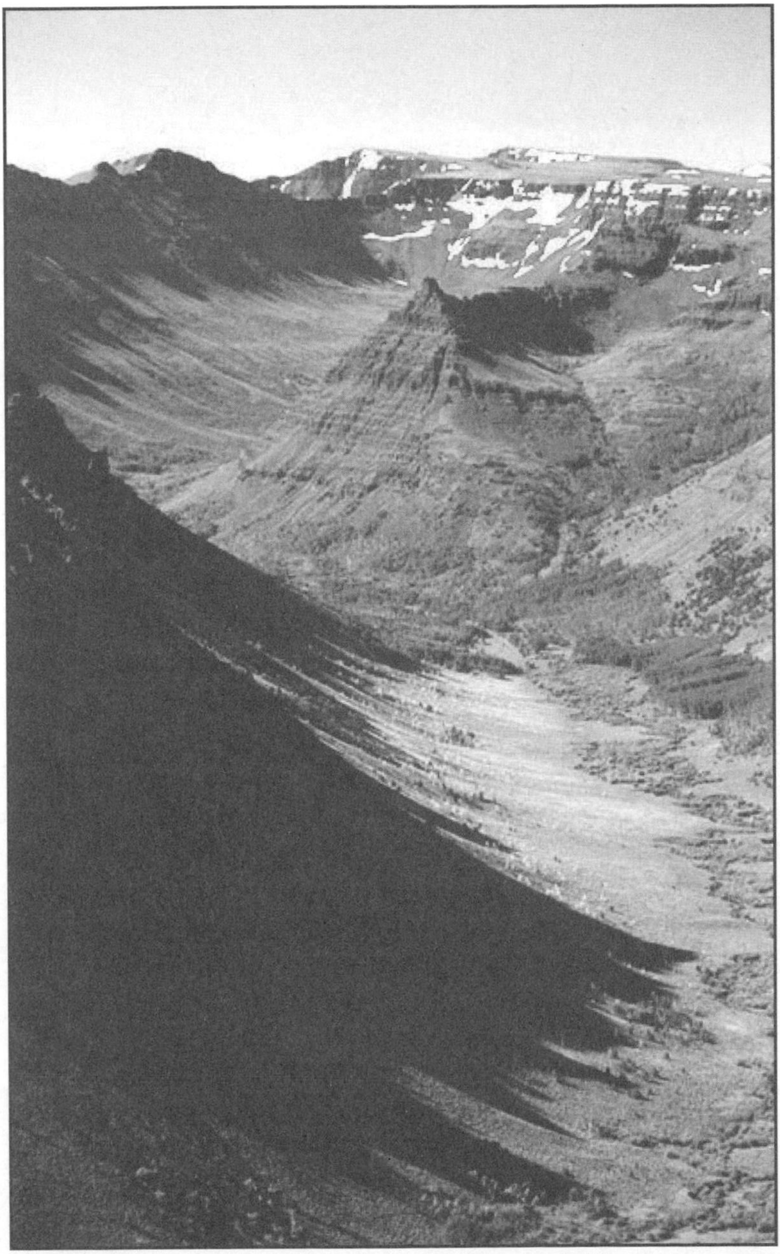

Because of its unique geology, Steens Mountain is the only Cooperative Management and Protection Area in the United States. One feature is the glaciated Kiger Gorge, shown above.

PHOTO BY JOHN CRAIG, COURTESY OF USDI BLM.

Caramel Apple Cake

1 cup cooking oil	2 cups flour
2 cups sugar	1 teaspoon salt
3 eggs	1 teaspoon baking soda
1½ teaspoons vanilla	3 cups diced apples

Mix all ingredients together and pour into a greased and floured 9x13-inch pan. Bake in preheated 350° oven for 1 hour. Remove cake from oven and poke holes across the entire surface using a fork or toothpick.

TOPPING:

½ cup butter	¼ cup milk
1 cup brown sugar	

Mix together in a saucepan. Boil for 3 minutes. Pour over cake.

What's Cooking in Sisters

Apple Pie Cake

½ cup butter	2½ cups chopped apples
1 cup sugar	1 teaspoon baking soda
1 egg	1 cup flour
¼ teaspoon salt	½ cup nuts
1 teaspoon cinnamon	2 tablespoons hot water
1 teaspoon nutmeg	1 teaspoon vanilla

Mix ingredients in order listed. Put in greased 10-inch pie plate. Bake at 350° for 35 minutes. Check for doneness. Cake will be a dark brown.

Our Favorite Recipes

The small village of Bickelton, know as the "Bluebird Capital of the World" is filled with bluebird houses which are perched on many fence posts.

Crockpot Apple Cake

2 cups sugar	1 teaspoon soda
1 cup oil	1 teaspoon nutmeg
2 eggs	2 cups finely chopped, unpeeled
2 teaspoons vanilla	Delicious apples
2 cups flour	1 cup chopped walnuts
1 teaspoon salt or less	

Beat sugar, oil, and eggs together well; add vanilla. Sift flour, salt, soda, and nutmeg together. Add apples to sugar mixture; mix well. Stir in flour mixture and nuts; mix well. Pour batter into greased and floured 2-pound can. Fill can no more than ²/₃ full. Place in crockpot; cover top of can with 4–6 paper towels. Cover and cook on HIGH about 3½ hours. Crockpot lid should not be tightly closed—slightly raise lid to allow release of excess moisture. Add no water and do not peek until last hour.

Oregon: The Other Side

Rhubarb Crunch Cake

2 cups brown sugar, divided	¼ teaspoon salt
½ cup shortening	1½ cups chopped rhubarb
1 cup sour milk or buttermilk	1 teaspoon vanilla
2 eggs	1 teaspoon butter
2 cups flour	½ teaspoon cinnamon
1 teaspoon soda	½ cup chopped nuts

Combine ½ cup brown sugar, shortening, milk, and eggs. Beat until smooth. Add flour, soda, salt, and rhubarb. Add vanilla and mix well. Pour into greased 9x15-inch loaf pan. Mix remaining sugar, butter, cinnamon, and nuts. Sprinkle over cake and bake at 350° for 35 minutes.

Look What's Cooking

Hummingbird Cake

3 cups flour
2 cups sugar
1 teaspoon salt
1 teaspoon soda
1 teaspoon cinnamon
3 eggs, beaten

1½ cups salad oil
1½ teaspoons vanilla
1 (8-ounce) can crushed pineapple, undrained
2 cups chopped nuts, divided
2 cups chopped bananas

Combine dry ingredients in a large mixing bowl. Add eggs and salad oil; stir until dry ingredients are moistened. Do not beat. Stir in vanilla, pineapple, 1 cup nuts, and bananas. Spoon batter into 3 well-greased and floured 9-inch cake pans. Bake at 350° for 25–30 minutes, or until cake tests done. Cool in pans 10 minutes. Remove from pans and cool completely. Spread Frosting between layers and on top and sides of cake. Sprinkle top with 1 cup chopped nuts. Also makes a great Bundt cake.

FROSTING:

1 (3-ounce) package cream cheese, softened
½ cup margarine, softened

2 pounds powdered sugar
3 teaspoons vanilla
4 teaspoons grated orange peel

Combine cream cheese and butter; cream until smooth. Add remaining ingredients and beat until light and fluffy.

Favorite Recipes, Second Edition

Refrigerator Cake

1 (2-layer) yellow cake mix	1 (12-ounce) container whipped
1 (14-ounce) can sweetened	topping
condensed milk	1½ cups (or less) flaked coconut
1 (20-ounce) can crushed	
pineapple, drained	

Bake cake in 9x13x2-inch pan according to directions. Remove directly from oven and pierce all over top with toothpick. Pour milk all over the top of the hot cake. Spread pineapple over cake. Let cake cool in pan. When cool, spread with whipped topping and sprinkle top with coconut. Refrigerate until serving time.

Christian Bakers Cookbook

Mother's Rich Orange Cake

No worries about this cake drying out when cut; it doesn't last that long.

Juice of 1 orange	1 cup chopped walnuts
1⅔ cups sugar, divided	1¾ cups flour
½ cup shortening	½ teaspoon soda
2 eggs, unbeaten	1 teaspoon baking powder
1 cup ground raisins	¾ teaspoon salt
Grated peel of 1 orange	⅔ cup milk

Mix orange juice and ⅔ cups sugar; set aside. Mix 1 cup sugar, shortening, and eggs; add raisins, orange peel, and walnuts. Blend dry ingredients and mix with milk; add to sugar mixture. Beat well; pour into greased, floured tube or Bundt pan. Bake 50–60 minutes at 350°. Remove from oven. Turn hot cake out of pan onto deep plate and immediately pour and spread the orange juice mixture over it. Set cake plate on rack to cool. Serve warm or cold.

Begged, Borrowed and Stöllen Recipes

Pumpkin Cake

½ cup shortening
1¼ cups sugar
2 eggs, beaten
1¼ cups sifted cake flour
1 tablespoon baking powder
½ teaspoon salt
½ teaspoon cinnamon

½ teaspoon ginger
½ teaspoon nutmeg
1 cup cooked and cooled pumpkin
¾ cup milk
½ teaspoon baking soda
½ cup chopped nuts

Preheat oven to 350°. Grease and flour an 8-inch-square glass baking dish.

Cream shortening. Gradually add sugar, creaming until light and fluffy. Beat in eggs. Sift flour, baking powder, salt, and spices together 3 times. Combine pumpkin and milk. Stir in soda. Add flour and pumpkin mixtures alternately to creamed mixture, beating well after each addition. Fold in nuts. Turn into baking dish. Bake 50–55 minutes. Cool in pan on wire rack 10 minutes. Turn out onto rack and cool completely. Frost top and sides with Raisin-Brown Sugar Icing.

RAISIN-BROWN SUGAR ICING:
1 large egg white
1 cup light brown sugar

3 tablespoons water
½ cup halved raisins

Beat egg white, brown sugar, and water together, just enough to blend, in top of a double boiler. Place over rapidly boiling water and beat with a rotary egg beater or electric mixer until mixture is light and fluffy and holds a firm shape (5–7 minutes). Off-heat, carefully fold in raisins (raisins will thin icing slightly).

Fiddlin' in the Kitchen

Pumpkin Pie Cake

1 large can (3½ cups) pumpkin
3 eggs
1 cup sugar
½ teaspoon salt
2½ teaspoons cinnamon
½ teaspoon nutmeg

½ teaspoon ginger
1 large can evaporated milk
1 box yellow cake mix
1½ sticks (¾ cup) butter
1 cup chopped nuts

Mix pumpkin, eggs, sugar, salt, cinnamon, nutmeg, ginger, and milk together and pour into slightly oiled 9x13-inch pan. Spread the cake mix over mixed ingredients. Melt butter and drizzle over cake mix. Sprinkle chopped nuts over all. Bake at 350° for 60 minutes. Cool. Serve with Cool Whip or whipped cream. Easy and delicious.

Favorite Recipes Cookbook

Quick Gingerbread

½ cup margarine
½ cup sugar
1 egg
¾ cup dark molasses
2¼ cups flour
1 teaspoon ginger

1 teaspoon cinnamon
¼ teaspoon cloves
1 teaspoon soda
½ teaspoon salt
1 cup sour milk or buttermilk

Cream margarine, sugar, and egg. Beat in molasses for 1 minute. Blend in dry ingredients and milk alternately for 2 minutes or only until batter is smooth. Bake in greased 9x9x2-inch pan at 350° for 35–40 minutes.

The Miller Cookbook

The Oregon Trail is the longest of the overland routes used in the westward expansion of the United States. Used between 1840 and 1860, it was about 2,000 miles long, starting in Missouri and ending in Oregon.

Buckeroo Carrot Cake

This cake has been popular during our Barn Sale for many years.

3 eggs
¾ cup cooking oil
¾ cup buttermilk
2 teaspoons vanilla
2 cups sugar
2 cups all-purpose flour
2 teaspoons baking soda

2 teaspoons cinnamon
½ teaspoon salt
2 cups finely grated carrots
1 cup chopped walnuts
1 cup flaked coconut
½ cup drained crushed pineapple

In a large mixing bowl, combine eggs, oil, buttermilk, and vanilla. Add sugar; beat to mix well. Sift together flour, baking soda, cinnamon, and salt. Add to sugar mixture. Beat at medium speed for 1 minute. Add carrots, walnuts, coconut, and pineapple; mix well. Pour mixture into 2 greased and floured 9-inch-round cake pans. Bake in 350° oven for 30–35 minutes, or until cake tests done. Also can be baked in a Bundt or 9x13-inch baking pan. Frost with cream cheese frosting.

Favorite Recipes, Second Edition

Blue Ribbon Carrot Cake

An extremely moist, rich cake.

BUTTERMILK GLAZE:

1 cup granulated sugar
1/2 teaspoon baking soda
1/2 cup buttermilk

1/4 cup (1/2 stick) butter
1 tablespoon light corn syrup
1 teaspoon vanilla extract

In small saucepan over high heat, combine sugar, baking soda, buttermilk, butter, and corn syrup. Bring to a boil. Cook 5 minutes, stirring occasionally. Remove from heat and stir in vanilla. Set aside until cake is baked.

CAKE:

2 cups all-purpose flour
2 teaspoons baking soda
2 teaspoons cinnamon
1/2 teaspoon salt
3 eggs
3/4 cup vegetable oil
3/4 cup buttermilk
2 cups granulated sugar

2 teaspoons vanilla extract
1 (8-ounce) can crushed pineapple, drained
2 cups grated carrots
3 1/2 ounces shredded coconut
1 cup seedless raisins
1 cup coarsely chopped walnuts

Generously grease a 9x13-inch baking pan or 2 (9-inch) cake pans. Sift flour, baking soda, cinnamon, and salt together; set aside. In a large bowl, beat eggs. Add oil, buttermilk, sugar, and vanilla and mix well. Add flour mixture, pineapple, carrots, coconut, raisins, and walnuts and stir well. Pour into prepared pan. Bake 45–55 minutes or until a toothpick inserted in the center comes out clean.

Remove cake from oven and slowly pour Buttermilk Glaze over the hot cake. Cool cake in pan until Glaze is totally absorbed, about 15 minutes.

FROSTING:

1/4 cup (1/2 stick) butter, room temperature
1 (8-ounce) package cream cheese, room temperature
1 teaspoon vanilla extract

2 cups powdered sugar
1 teaspoon freshly squeezed orange juice
1 teaspoon grated orange peel

In a large bowl, cream butter and cream cheese until fluffy. Add vanilla, powdered sugar, orange juice, and orange peel. Mix until smooth. Frost cake and refrigerate until Frosting is set. Serve cake chilled. Yields 20–24 servings.

From Portland's Palate

Special Oatmeal Cake

CAKE:

1¼ cups boiling water
1 cup dry oatmeal
½ cup margarine
1 cup granulated sugar
1 cup brown sugar
½ cup egg substitute, or 3 egg
   whites

1 teaspoon vanilla
1½ cups flour
½ teaspoon Lite Salt
½ teaspoon baking soda
1 teaspoon cinnamon

Pour boiling water over oatmeal. Let stand 10 minutes. Preheat oven to 350°. Spray a 9x13-inch baking pan with nonstick cooking spray. Cream margarine and sugars. Add egg substitute or whites and vanilla; blend well. Add oatmeal. Blend in flour, Lite Salt, baking soda, and cinnamon. Pour in prepared pan. Bake 30–40 minutes, or until wooden pick inserted in center comes out clean.

TOPPING:

3 tablespoons margarine, melted
½ cup brown sugar
¼ cup evaporated skim milk

1 teaspoon vanilla
½ cup dry oatmeal

Near the end of baking time, combine melted margarine and brown sugar. Add evaporated milk, vanilla, and oatmeal. Spread evenly on top of warm cake. Brown under broiler 3–5 minutes, watching carefully. Serves 15.

Nutritional analysis per serving: Serving size 2½x3-inch piece; Calories 267; Fat 9g; Chol. trace mg; Prot. 4g; Carbo. 43g; Sod. 204mg.

Tastefully Oregon

Blueberry-Raspberry Upside-Down Cake

I bake this wonderfully moist cake in my 9-inch cast-iron frying pan—the heavy pan keeps the butter from burning and the handle makes it easy to flip the cake upside down when it is done. It can be served warm from the oven for dessert or as a coffee cake for a brunch, but once it has cooled, the cake needs to be tightly wrapped in plastic wrap—it will get more moist the longer it sits.

7 tablespoons butter, divided
1 cup brown sugar
2 eggs
1 cup sugar
1/2 cup milk
1/4 teaspoon salt
1 cup all-purpose flour

1 teaspoon baking powder
1 pint fresh raspberries
1 pint fresh blueberries
1 pint (2 cups) heavy cream
1/4 cup powdered sugar
1 teaspoon vanilla

Preheat oven to 375°. Melt 5 tablespoons butter in a heavy skillet and stir in brown sugar. Cook over medium heat until sugar dissolves. Keep warm over low heat. Beat eggs and sugar together until light, about 4 minutes. Melt remaining 2 tablespoons butter in milk over low heat or in microwave, on HIGH, for 1 minute. Sift together salt, flour, and baking powder. Add dry ingredients and warm milk to beaten eggs and sugar. Stir brown sugar and butter mixture in a cast-iron skillet and sprinkle raspberries and blueberries over it. Pour batter over berries and bake cake for 45 minutes, or until a toothpick inserted in center of cake comes out clean.

As soon as it is done, carefully turn cake upside down onto a large platter with a lip, to catch the juices. Whip cream with powdered sugar and vanilla. Serve cake warm with a dollop of whipped cream. Makes 8 servings.

Dungeness Crabs and Blackberry Cobblers

Oregon leads the nation in many products, including peppermint, grass seed, raspberries, blackberries, hazelnuts, and even Christmas trees. And their cranberry harvest is second only to New England.

Jenny's "Evil" Cake

1 package devil's food cake mix
1 can fat-free condensed milk
½ jar caramel topping

1 carton low-fat Cool Whip
3–4 Heath candy bars, crumbled

Bake cake per recipe on box in a 9x13-inch pan, but underbake about 5 minutes. Make holes in top of cake with end of wooden spoon and slowly pour condensed milk over top of cake. Pour caramel topping over top of cake and let set about 1 hour.

Spread top with Cool Whip and grate or crumble Heath candy bars on top of Cool Whip.

Recipes from the Kitchens of Family & Friends

Earthquake Cake

1 cup coarsely chopped pecans
  or walnuts (optional)
1 cup coconut
1 German chocolate cake mix
1 (8-ounce) package cream cheese,
  softened

½ cup margarine
1 pound powdered sugar
1 teaspoon vanilla

Grease bottom of a 9x13-inch pan. Mix nuts and coconut; spread in bottom of pan. Prepare cake mix per instructions. Pour over nut and coconut mixture. Mix cream cheese, margarine, sugar, and vanilla. Immediately spoon cream cheese mixture in large mounds on top of cake batter. Bake in 350° oven for 45–50 minutes.

Cookin' with Capital Press

Most people have heard of Nike CEO Phil Knight, a middle-distance runner who turned selling shoes out of his car into a footwear-and-apparel colossus. But few know of Nike cofounder Bill Bowerman, Knight's coach, or of Steve Prefontaine, the now-deceased runner who was also coached by Bowerman and whose crusade for better equipment inspired Bowerman and Knight to build the Nike empire.

The famous Nike "swoosh" logo was designed by University of Oregon student Carolyn Davidson in 1964, four years after the company was founded. She was paid $35 for her design.

Nike's corporate headquarters are located in Beaverton, Oregon.

Harvey Wallbanger Cake

A powerful cake, but delicious.

1 (2-layer-size) package orange cake mix	½ cup oil
1 small package instant vanilla pudding mix	½ cup orange juice
	½ cup Galliano liqueur
4 eggs	2 tablespoons vodka

Combine cake and pudding mixes. Add eggs, oil, orange juice, Galliano, and vodka. Beat at low speed 5 minutes. Do not underbeat. Pour into fluted greased and floured tube pan. Bake at 350° for 40 minutes. Cool in pan 10 minutes. Remove to rack.

GLAZE:

1 cup sifted powdered sugar	1 tablespoon Galliano
1 tablespoon orange juice	1 teaspoon vodka

Combine and mix until smooth. Glaze cooled cake.

Treasured Recipes

Fresh Tomato Cake

1 cup dark brown sugar	1 teaspoon salt
½ cup shortening	3 cups peeled, seeded, chopped
2 eggs	fresh ripe tomatoes
3 cups flour	½ cup chopped nuts
2 teaspoons baking powder	½ cup chopped dates
1 teaspoon baking soda	½ cup raisins
1 teaspoon nutmeg	

Cream sugar and shortening. Add eggs. Mix dry ingredients together and add to egg mixture, mixing well. Stir in tomatoes, nuts, dates, and raisins. Put into a greased and floured 9x13-inch baking pan. Bake at 350° for 35 minutes. Cool. Frost with Cream Cheese Frosting.

CREAM CHEESE FROSTING:

½ cup butter or margarine	2 teaspoons vanilla
1 (8-ounce) package cream cheese	1 pound powdered sugar

Beat margarine, cream cheese, and vanilla until well blended. Gradually beat in powdered sugar. Spread on cooled cake.

Recipes and Remembering

Gum Drop Cake

For those who don't like fruit cake because of the candied fruit peel, this alternative is made with gum drops!

4 cups sifted flour
1 teaspoon soda
1/4 teaspoon each salt, cloves, nutmeg
1 teaspoon cinnamon
1 cup butter or margarine, softened
2 cups sugar
2 eggs

1 1/2 cups applesauce
1 teaspoon vanilla
1 pound raisins
1 pound small gum drops (take out the black ones)
1/2 cup shredded coconut
1 cup chopped walnuts (optional)

Sift flour and measure, then sift with soda, salt, and spices. Cream butter and sugar until light and fluffy. Add eggs and beat well. Add flour mixture, applesauce, and vanilla to creamed mixture. Add raisins and gum drops that have been sprinkled with a little flour. Add coconut and walnuts, if desired. Grease 3 small loaf pans; put wax paper in bottoms. Bake in 300° oven for about 2 hours or until cake springs back when lightly touched with finger.

Favorite Recipes from Ruralite Readers

French Almond Cake

Fantastic!

1 cup (8 ounces) almond paste, room temperature
3 eggs
2/3 cup sugar
1/2 cup butter, softened
1/4 cup cake flour
1/2 teaspoon baking powder

1/4 teaspoon salt
Sliced almonds (optional)
Powdered sugar (optional)
Fresh berries or berry sauce (optional)
Whipped cream (optional)

Preheat oven to 350°. Grease and flour a 9-inch springform pan. Beat almond paste until soft and pliable. Add eggs, one at a time. Beat in the sugar. Add butter and beat until the batter is well creamed.

Sift together dry ingredients. Stir into creamed mixture. Pour into the prepared pan. (Sliced almonds may be sprinkled on top.) Bake for 40–45 minutes. Cool.

Serve sprinkled with powdered sugar and fresh berries on the side, or with berry sauce and whipped cream.

Albertina's Exceptional Recipes

Whacky Cake

3 cups flour
2 teaspoons soda
1 teaspoon salt
2 cups sugar
4 tablespoons cocoa

$\frac{1}{2}$ cup oil
1 teaspoon vanilla
2 tablespoons vinegar
2 cups cold water

Mix dry ingredients in pan. Make 3 holes in dry ingredients. Add oil, vanilla, and vinegar. Add cold water and mix well. Bake 30 minutes at 350°.

Pig Out

Milky Way Cake

4 Milky Way bars
1 stick butter
2 cups sugar
$\frac{3}{4}$ cup oil
4 eggs
1 cup buttermilk

$1\frac{1}{2}$ cups flour
1 teaspoon salt
$\frac{1}{2}$ teaspoon baking soda
2 teaspoons vanilla
1 cup chopped pecans

Melt candy and butter for 4 minutes in microwave. Add sugar, oil, eggs, and milk. Sift flour, salt, and soda, and add to wet mixture. Beat 2 minutes until smooth and creamy. Add vanilla and nuts; stir. Coat a tube or Bundt pan with cooking spray and pour in mix. Bake at 350° for 1 hour and 15 minutes.

Dilley Family Favorites

Vanilla Cream Cheesecake

CHEESECAKE:

1 pound cake
2½ pounds cream cheese, softened
1¾ cups sugar
2 tablespoons flour
3 eggs

1 tablespoon vanilla
1 tablespoon finely grated lemon zest
1 tablespoon finely grated orange zest

Cut ½-inch lengthwise slices of pound cake; fit slices into bottom of greased 10-inch springform pan, cutting pieces so bottom is completely covered. With an electric mixer, beat softened cream cheese until smooth. Gradually add sugar, scraping often. Add flour, 1 tablespoon at a time. Add eggs, 1 at a time. Add vanilla and zests. Pour cream cheese mixture into pan. Bring heavy-duty foil up and around bottom and side of pan.

Place springform pan in a larger pan with enough water to reach 1 inch up sides. Bake 10 minutes at 350°, then 1 hour and 15 minutes at 275°. Cake is done when it jiggles like a custard. Do not overcook. Cool to room temperature, then top with Glaze. Refrigerate at least 4 hours. Add Blueberry Topping and serve.

GLAZE:

1½ cups cultured sour cream
2 tablespoons sugar

½ teaspoon vanilla
⅛ teaspoon salt

Heat oven to 425°. Mix well and pour over room temperature cheesecake. Bake at 425° for 5 minutes or until Glaze smooths and sets. Refrigerate at least 4 hours before adding Blueberry Topping.

BLUEBERRY TOPPING:

⅛ cup water
1½ tablespoons cornstarch
½ cup sugar
½ teaspoon lemon zest

½ teaspoon orange zest
2 cups blueberries, picked and cleaned, divided
½ tablespoon butter

In a heavy bottom saucepan, add enough water to dissolve cornstarch, then add sugar, zests, and 1 cup of the blueberries. Cook, stirring, over medium heat till sauce begins to simmer and thicken. Remove from heat; add butter. Cool until lukewarm, then fold in remaining blueberries; spread carefully over chilled cheesecake. Chill 30 minutes or until set.

Coastal Flavors

Double Lemon Cheesecake

12 ounces cream cheese, at room
   temperature
¾ cup plus 2 tablespoons sugar,
   divided
2 eggs
¼ cup fresh lemon juice

1 teaspoon grated lemon peel
1 teaspoon vanilla
1 (9-inch) graham cracker crust
1 cup sour cream
1 teaspoon vanilla

Preheat oven to 350°. Blend cream cheese, ¾ cup sugar, eggs, lemon juice, lemon peel, and vanilla until smooth. Pour mixture into crust. Bake until filling is just set, about 35 minutes. Cool cheesecake slightly. Combine sour cream, 2 tablespoons sugar, and vanilla in small bowl. Spread mixture evenly over cheesecake. Bake 10 minutes. Cool. Refrigerate overnight. Cut into wedges and serve. Serves 8.

Christian Bakers Cookbook

Miniature Cheese Cakes

1 package of vanilla wafers
2 (8-ounce) packages cream
   cheese, softened (not reduced-fat)
1 cup sugar

2 eggs
1 teaspoon vanilla
1 can pie filling (cherry or blueberry)

Line 24 muffin pan cups with fancy paper muffin cup liners; put a vanilla wafer in the bottom. Blend cream cheese, sugar, eggs, and vanilla on medium speed of mixer until light and fluffy. Fill the cups ⅔ full. Bake at 325° for 20 minutes. Do not brown. Cool and fill rest of way up with pie filling. I like to add a dollop of whipped cream on top just before serving.

Seasoned with Words

The northern and central regions of Oregon are known for wheat production; Portland ranks among the nation's top wheat ports.

Apple Bake Cheesecakes

An easy and elegant dessert.

FILLING:

1 (8-ounce) package cream cheese, room temperature

1 large egg

$\frac{1}{2}$ cup sugar

1 teaspoon vanilla

1 teaspoon finely grated lemon zest

Preheat oven to 350°. Combine all ingredients in a food processor and process until smooth. Transfer into a bowl. Cover and refrigerate.

APPLES:

8 medium-sized dessert apples (Criterion, Rome, Golden Delicious or Honeycrisp)

$\frac{2}{3}$ cup honey

8 cookies (vanilla wafers, ginger snaps, biscotti, etc.)

Core apples, being careful not to cut through all the way to the bottom. Spoon out core in sections and scoop out most, but not all of the flesh. Put apples in a baking dish and spoon $1\frac{1}{2}$–2 tablespoons of the Filling into each cavity. Pour enough warm water or cider into the dish to reach a level of $\frac{1}{2}$ inch–$\frac{3}{4}$ inch. Cover with foil and place the pan in the lower third of the oven and bake 30–40 minutes or until the apples are fork-tender. Remove from oven (the filling will be soft). Serve warm, or for a traditional cheesecake consistency, refrigerate for at least 2 hours. If chilled, remove from refrigerator 1 hour before serving. Drizzle honey over apples and crumble cookies over top. Serves 8.

Recipe by Mt. Hood Organic Farms
The Fruit Loop Cookbook

Chocolate Amaretto Cheesecake

CRUST:

1 pound vanilla wafers, ground   ¼ cup butter, melted

Combine and press into springform pan.

FILLING:

10 ounces good semisweet   16 ounces cream cheese, softened
   chocolate   4 eggs
1 cup sugar   1 egg yolk
3 tablespoons flour   ¼ cup amaretto

Melt chocolate in double boiler and set aside. Mix sugar and flour together. Blend cream cheese and sugar mixture until smooth. Add eggs and yolk 1 at a time; blend until smooth. Add melted chocolate, then amaretto. Pour into crust and bake at 250° until set, about 1½–1¾ hours.

TOPPING:

1½ cups sour cream   3 tablespoons amaretto
¼ cup honey   Melted chocolate

Mix first 3 ingredients well and top warm cheesecake. Chill well then drizzle top with a little melted chocolate.

Multnomah Falls Lodge Cook Book

Boysenberry Swirl Cheesecake with a Hazelnut Crust

Many pioneers of Irish and British descent settled in the Pacific Northwest, and cheesecake recipes were part of their heritage. It was natural for them to make use of indigenous nuts and berries; this recipe reflects that kind of adaptation. In this recipe I use the intensely flavorful boysenberry—the commercial blackberry I consider number one for flavor. It's a cross between a wild blackberry, a raspberry, and a loganberry and features the best of each berry.

CRUST:

8 tablespoons (½ cup) butter, softened

1 cup all-purpose flour

½ cup finely ground, roasted hazelnuts

½ cup sugar

Put all ingredients in a bowl and blend with a fork or pulse 8–10 times in a food processor. Put mixture in an 11-inch springform pan and pat crust into bottom and sides of pan. Chill crust in refrigerator while preparing filling.

FILLING:

3 (8-ounce) packages cream cheese, softened

2 cups sugar

3 eggs

1½ cups fresh or frozen boysenberries (or any variety of blackberry or raspberry), thawed and drained

Preheat oven to 375°. Using a mixer, blend cream cheese, sugar, and eggs together until smooth. Run berries through a food mill or purée them in a blender or food processor and push them through a sieve to remove seeds.

Layer half the cheese mixture over crust, then spread on all the puréed berries. Carefully add remaining cheese filling over berries and cut through batter with a knife, using a circular motion, to create swirls. Bake for 45–50 minutes. Remove from oven and let cool to room temperature. Chill in refrigerator for 3–4 hours before serving. Serves 8–10.

Dungeness Crabs and Blackberry Cobblers

Cookies and Candies

Plummeting 620 feet from its origins on Larch Mountain, the magnificent Multnomah Falls is the second highest year-round waterfall in the nation. Benson Bridge, where you can feel the falls' cool mists, crosses between the upper and lower cataracts.

Snow-Cap Cookies

In some circles, these rich, chewy cookies are known as chocolate crinkles because each cookie acquires a crinkled white topping during the baking process. In this recipe, dark chocolate and espresso make the contrast even greater, giving the cookies a snow-capped appearance and a superb flavor. If you're a real chocolate lover, try adding semisweet chocolate chips to the dough before chilling. You won't be sorry.

4 tablespoons unsalted butter	1 cup granulated sugar
2 ounces unsweetened chocolate	1 cup all-purpose flour
2 eggs, room temperature	1 teaspoon baking powder
1 teaspoon vanilla extract	1/4 teaspoon salt
1 tablespoon instant espresso powder	1/2 cup sifted powdered sugar

In small saucepan, melt butter and chocolate over low heat. Stir to blend and set aside to cool slightly.

In medium bowl combine eggs, vanilla, espresso powder, and granulated sugar. Using an electric mixer on medium speed, beat until light and fluffy, about 3 minutes. In another bowl, whisk together flour, baking powder, and salt. Alternately blend dry ingredients and chocolate mixture into egg mixture in 3 increments. Cover and refrigerate until firm, at least 3 hours.

Preheat oven to 350°. Shape chilled dough into 1-inch balls and roll in powdered sugar to form a thick coat. Place about 2 inches apart on an ungreased baking sheet. Bake until set, about 15 minutes. Transfer to wire rack and let cool completely. Makes about 2 1/2 dozen cookies.

The New Complete Coffee Book

Snow White Bunnies or Chocolate Brown Bears

4 bunny cookie cutters,
  each 7 inches tall
3 tablespoons unsalted butter
4 cups miniature marshmallows
  or 40 large marshmallows
5 cups puffed rice cereal
1 cup flaked sweetened coconut
½ cup white chocolate chips

Flaked sweetened coconut for tail
  (optional)
Red Hots (cinnamon candies)
  or round miniature M&Ms for eyes
  (optional)
Ribbon in any color, ⅛ inch wide
Clear cellophane gift bags

In a large saucepan, melt butter over low heat. Add marshmallows and stir until completely melted, about 5 minutes. Remove from heat, add rice cereal, and stir until coated. Add coconut and white chocolate chips and stir until blended. The mixture will be sticky. Using a spatula coated with nonstick cooking spray, press rice cereal mixture into a 9x13x2-inch baking pan coated with nonstick cooking spray. (The recipe can be made ahead to this point, covered with plastic wrap, and kept at room temperature for several hours or overnight.)

To make each bunny, press a cutter into cereal mixture. Press your fingertips around the perimeter of cutter to make sure cutter touches bottom of pan. Wriggle filled cutter free and set aside on waxed paper. Repeat with remaining cutters. Round out or fill in each cutter with any leftover cereal to make each bunny plump. If desired, press coconut on top of cereal to make a fuzzy bunny tail and press in Red Hots to create eyes.

To make a Christmas collar, use the ribbon to tie a bow around each bunny's neck. Place each bunny in a gift bag and tie bag closed with additional ribbon. Makes 4 large bunnies. The cookies taste best if eaten within 5 days.

To make Chocolate Brown Bears, proceed as directed, but use 12 (3½–4-inch) bear cookie cutters instead of bunny cookie cutters, 6 cups instead of 5 cups puffed rice cereal and substitute ½ cup Nutella hazelnut chocolate spread or other chocolate spread and ½ cup semisweet chocolate chips for the coconut and white chocolate chips. Makes 12 bears.

To give a gift platter of ready-to-nibble snow bunnies or brown bears, use 1 cookie cutter and slip the cookie out of the cutter after it's formed. Other animal or holiday shapes may also be used.

Christmastime Treats

Peanut Butter Cookies

1 cup shortening	1 teaspoon vanilla
1 cup brown sugar	2¹/₂ cups flour
1 cup white sugar	¹/₂ teaspoon salt
1 cup peanut butter	2 teaspoons baking soda
2 eggs	

Cream shortening, sugars, and peanut butter. Add eggs and vanilla and beat very well. Add sifted flour, salt, and baking soda, and mix well. Roll into small balls and place on ungreased cookie sheet. Press down with tines of fork. Bake at 375° 8–10 minutes. Makes 4 dozen.

Dilley Family Favorites

Date Pinwheel Cookies

1 cup finely cut dates	1 tablespoon lemon juice
1¹/₂ cups packed brown sugar, divided	1³/₄ cups flour
¹/₃ cup plus ¹/₄ cup evaporated milk, divided	³/₄ teaspoon baking soda
¹/₂ cup chopped nuts	¹/₂ cup shortening
	³/₄ teaspoon salt
	¹/₄ teaspoon grated lemon rind

In a mixing bowl, combine dates, ¹/₂ cup brown sugar, and ¹/₃ cup milk. Cook over medium heat in a saucepan until very thick. Remove from heat then add nuts and lemon juice. Set aside to cool.

In a separate bowl, sift together flour and soda. Set aside. In another bowl, combine shortening, salt, lemon rind, 1 cup brown sugar and ¹/₄ cup milk. Stir in flour mixture and mix until well blended. Divide dough into 2 or 3 balls. With a floured rolling pin, flatten each ball into a 12-inch square (use wax paper if too soft). Spread with cooled date mixture over the squares. Roll each into a log and chill until firm. Cut into ¹/₂-inch slices. Bake on greased cookie sheet at 375° for 10 minutes or until done.

Note: Prepared dough logs can be frozen until ready to slice and bake.

Grandma Jean's Rainy Day Recipes

Raw Apple Cookies

2 cups sugar
1/2 cup shortening
1 teaspoon vanilla
2 eggs
1 teaspoon soda
3 1/2 cups flour
1/4 teaspoon salt

1 teaspoon cloves
1 teaspoon nutmeg
1 teaspoon cinnamon
1/2 cup sour milk
1 cup raisins
1/2 cup nuts
2 cups chopped raw apples

Cream sugar, shortening, and vanilla. Add eggs. Mix in dry ingredients. Add milk; mix in raisins, nuts, and chopped apples. Drop by spoonfuls on greased baking sheet. Bake 10 minutes at 350°.

Pig Out

Ranger Cookies

1 cup butter or margarine
1 cup sugar
1 cup brown sugar
2 eggs
2 cups flour
1 teaspoon baking powder

1/2 teaspoon baking soda
1/2 teaspoon salt
1 teaspoon vanilla
2 cups quick-cooking oats
2 cups cornflakes, unbroken
1 cup shredded coconut

Cream butter; add sugars gradually. Blend in eggs and beat well. Sift flour, baking powder, soda, and salt; add to creamed mixture, then add vanilla, oatmeal, cereal, and coconut. Drop by teaspoonfuls on a greased baking sheet. Do not beat the cornflakes or coconut—just stir! Bake 12–15 minutes at 375°. Makes 5 dozen.

Manna by the Sea

For 40 years, Millican, 24 miles southeast of Bend, was literally a one-man town. Its lone resident, a bachelor by the name of William Rahn, ran the town's post office, gas pump, and general store. Rumor has it that he once took a two-month vacation, and nobody noticed.

Ginger Bread Boy Cookies

Ginger cookies may be decorated before baking with colored sugar and Red Hots for Christmas and Valentine's Day. Grandchildren love to roll, cut and decorate these cookies.

¾ cup molasses	2 teaspoons ginger
¾ cup butter	1 teaspoon cinnamon
¾ cup packed brown sugar	¼ teaspoon cloves
2 eggs	1 teaspoon soda
¼ teaspoon vanilla	½ teaspoon baking powder
3½ cups flour	

In microwave, heat molasses to a slight simmering point. Add butter and stir to melting. Add brown sugar and stir. Cool slightly. In a separate bowl, beat eggs and add vanilla. In another bowl, mix flour, spices, baking soda, and baking powder. When molasses mixture is cooled, add egg mixture to it. Now pour this wet mixture into the dry mixture; stir as in kneading bread. Chill for several hours. Using ¼ of the dough at a time, roll to ⅝ inch on a floured pastry cloth with a flour-covered rolling pin. Cut out cookies (decorate if you like). Bake in preheated 375° oven for 11–14 minutes.

What's Cooking in Sisters

Lemon Frosted Pecan Cookies

1 cup unsalted butter	¾ cup cornstarch
¾ cup powdered sugar	2 tablespoons milk
1½ cups flour	¾ cup chopped pecans

Mix butter, sugar, flour, cornstarch, and milk until well blended. Chill. Place small spoonful of chopped pecans 2 inches apart on ungreased cookie sheet. Place small balls of dough on pecans and flatten. Bake at 350° for 12–15 minutes. Cool.

FROSTING:

2½ cups powdered sugar	3 tablespoons fresh lemon juice
1 tablespoon soft butter	

Mix Frosting ingredients, and frost cookies.

Rainy Day Treats and Sunny Temptations

Lemon Cookies

1 box lemon cake mix	1 egg
2 cups (8 ounces) Cool Whip	Powdered sugar

Mix together and form into small balls. Drop in powdered sugar and bake on ungreased cookie sheet at 350° for 12–15 minutes.

Savor the Flavor

Pecan Pie Cookies

PECAN FILLING:

1/2 cup powdered sugar	3 tablespoons dark corn syrup
1/4 cup butter or margarine	1/2 cup chopped pecans

Combine sugar, butter or margarine, and corn syrup in saucepan; stir to blend. Cook over medium heat, stirring occasionally, until mixture reaches a full boil. Remove from heat; stir in pecans. Cool. Roll 1/2 teaspoon balls and put in freezer.

COOKIE:

1 cup butter or margarine	2 eggs, separated
1/2 cup sugar	2 1/2 cups unsifted all-purpose flour
1/2 cup dark corn syrup	

Cream butter or margarine and sugar on low speed in large bowl of electric mixer. Add corn syrup and egg yolks; beat until thoroughly blended. Stir in flour gradually. Chill several hours. Beat egg whites slightly. Using one tablespoonful of dough for each cookie, roll into balls. Brush very lightly with egg white. Place on greased cookie sheet, leaving a 2-inch space between each cookie. Bake at 375° for 5 minutes. Remove from oven.

Press a frozen Pecan Filling ball into the center of each cookie. Return to oven; bake 5 minutes longer or until lightly browned. Cool 5 minutes on cookie sheet. Remove; cool completely on rack. Makes about 4 dozen.

Recipes, Recipes, Recipes!

Pumpkin Chocolate Chip Cookies

1 (29-ounce) can pumpkin
3½ cups packed brown sugar
1½ cups vegetable oil
2½ teaspoons vanilla
5½ cups flour

1 tablespoon baking powder
1 tablespoon baking soda
1½ teaspoons salt
2 teaspoons pumpkin pie spice
1–2 cups mini-chocolate chips

Mix pumpkin, brown sugar, oil, and vanilla in a large bowl. Mix flour, baking powder, baking soda, salt, and pumpkin pie spice in a separate bowl. Add dry ingredients to pumpkin mixture and stir until well combined. Stir in chocolate chips.

Drop by tablespoonsful 2 inches apart onto a greased cookie sheet. Bake at 350° for 15 minutes. Remove cookies to a wire rack to cool. Yields 4 dozen.

Cooking from the Coast to the Cascades

Chocolate Bourbon Pecan Pie Bars

A variation of this sumptuous cookie might include substituting walnuts or Oregon hazelnuts for the pecans. Recipe may be successfully halved or doubled.

3 cups all-purpose flour
2 cups sugar, divided
1 cup butter, softened
½ teaspoon salt
1¼ cups light corn syrup

6 ounces semisweet chocolate
¼ cup bourbon
4 eggs, beaten
1½ teaspoons vanilla
3 cups pecans, chopped

Preheat oven to 350°. Grease bottom and sides of a 9x13-inch baking pan. In a large mixing bowl, beat flour, ½ cup sugar, butter, and salt at medium speed until mixture resembles coarse crumbs. Press firmly and evenly into pan. Bake for 20 minutes.

Meanwhile in a 3-quart saucepan, stir corn syrup and chocolate over low heat until chocolate melts. Remove from heat. Stir in bourbon, remaining sugar, eggs, and vanilla until blended. Stir in pecans. Pour over crust and spread evenly. Bake for 30 minutes or until filling is firm around edges. Cool before cutting. Yields 24 bars.

Rogue River Rendezvous

Pumpkin Bars

1 cup oil
2 cups sugar
4 eggs, beaten until creamy
2 cups pumpkin
½ teaspoon salt

1 teaspoon baking soda
2 teaspoons baking powder
2 cups flour
1 cup chopped nuts

Mix all ingredients and pour into a 13x15-inch jellyroll pan or 2 (9x13-inch) pans. Bake at 350° for 25 minutes.

TOPPING:
1 (3-ounce) package cream cheese, softened
6 tablespoons butter or margarine, softened

1 teaspoon milk
1 teaspoon vanilla
2 cups powdered sugar
Dash of salt

Mix thoroughly and smooth over baked cake. Cut into bars.

Potluck and Patchwork

Fudge Brownies

4 squares unsweetened chocolate or equivalent powdered cocoa
½ cup butter, softened
4 eggs

2 cups sugar
1 teaspoon vanilla
1 cup sifted flour
1 cup coarsely-chopped walnuts

Melt chocolate and butter. Let cool slightly. Beat in eggs, 1 at a time, until fluffy and well mixed. Add sugar, vanilla, flour, and nuts. Mix well; spread into a greased 9x13-inch pan. Bake at 325° for 35–40 minutes.

FROSTING:
6 tablespoons butter
6 tablespoons milk

1½ cups granulated sugar
1½ cups chocolate chips

Melt butter; add milk and sugar. Boil only 30 seconds. Remove from heat and add chocolate chips. Beat with electric mixer. Pour over brownies right out of oven. Cool before cutting. Delicious!

Variation: When out of oven, spread raspberry jam over top, then frost.

What's Cooking??

Mint Brownies

BROWNIES:

4 squares chocolate	4 eggs
1 cup margarine	1 cup flour
2 cups sugar	½ cup nuts

Melt chocolate and margarine. Beat sugar and eggs and combine with chocolate mixture. Combine flour and nuts and add to creamed mixture. Pour in greased 9x13-inch baking pan. Bake at 350° for 20–25 minutes. Cool.

MINT TOPPING:

6 tablespoons margarine, softened	3 cups powdered sugar
4 tablespoons milk	¾ teaspoon peppermint flavoring
Green food coloring	

Mix margarine, milk, food coloring, powdered sugar, and flavoring thoroughly. Cover cooled brownies.

CHOCOLATE TOPPING:

5 ounces semisweet chocolate	2 teaspoons vanilla
4 tablespoons margarine	

Melt chocolate and margarine. Add vanilla. Cool slightly. Spread on top of Mint Topping. Refrigerate before serving.

The Miller Cookbook

Raspberry Shortbread

¾ cup butter (no substitute)	1 teaspoon vanilla
½ cup sugar	2 cups flour

Cream butter and sugar. Add vanilla, then flour. Press in greased 9-inch-square pan. Bake at 325° for 40 minutes. Remove.

TOPPING:

1 cup raspberry jam	½ cup chopped almonds
1 teaspoon almond extract	

Mix jam with almond extract and smooth over shortbread; sprinkle with almonds. Bake another 15 minutes. Cool and cut.

Rainy Day Treats and Sunny Temptations

Toffee-Coffee Crunch Brittle

Chocolate-coated espresso beans and toasted hazelnuts meet here in an irresistible coffee-flavored candy. Broken into shards, this brittle makes a scrumptious after-dinner tidbit with coffee or espresso. And, if you want to make ice cream sundaes and frosted cakes and cookies sparkle, seal several pieces of the candy in a plastic sandwich or storage bag, crush them with a rolling pin or mallet, and dust them over your dessert.

1 cup sugar
1/2 cup light corn syrup
1/4 cup water
2 teaspoons instant coffee powder
1/2 cup (1 stick) unsalted
   butter at room temperature
Pinch of salt

3 tablespoons (about 22) crushed
   chocolate-covered espresso beans
1 1/2 teaspoons finely ground
   espresso beans
1/4 cup toasted, skinned, and
   chopped hazelnuts
1/2 teaspoon baking soda

Generously butter a rimmed baking sheet and set aside. (Preheat the pan in a warm oven for a few minutes because the candy spreads more easily in a warm pan.)

In a 2-quart heavy saucepan, combine sugar, corn syrup, water, instant coffee powder, butter, and salt. Cook over medium-high heat, stirring occasionally, until butter has melted. Continue to cook to 250° on a candy thermometer (hard-ball stage), about 15 minutes. Add crushed chocolate-covered espresso beans and ground espresso beans, and continue to cook to 280° (soft-crack stage), 7–8 minutes.

Remove mixture at once from heat, and quickly stir in nuts, then stir in baking soda until blended. The syrup will foam and expand. Immediately pour syrup onto prepared pan. With a metal spatula, spread hot candy evenly over pan. When cool, break slab into pieces. Store in an airtight container–unless you eat it all first! Makes about 1 pound.

The New Complete Coffee Book

Easy Elegant Truffles

These are limited in flavors only by your imagination. When dipping, decorate truffle tops differently to indicate the center flavor. Have fun! These make wonderful, elegant gifts.

2 (12-ounce) bags real chocolate chips (semisweet, milk, flavored or vanilla or combination)

1 (8-ounce) package cream cheese, room temperature

⅛ teaspoon salt

1 cup powdered sugar

1 tablespoon vanilla

Semisweet or milk chocolate for dipping or almond bark in chocolate or white

Melt chocolate chips in top of large double boiler over barely simmering water until melted. Add cream chese and stir until it is melted in. Remove from heat; add salt, powdered sugar, and vanilla, and beat by hand or with mixer to blend and smooth. Cover and cool to about room temperature. Form into truffle-size balls; chill until firm. Dip into melted chocolate or almond bark coating to cover. Chill until firm.

Variations:

Mocha: Dissolve 3 tablespoons instant coffee in the vanilla before adding.

Orange: Add grated rind of large orange.

Black Forest: Add ½ teaspoon almond extract in place of vanilla and stir in 3 tablespoons very finely chopped, well drained maraschino cherries.

Coconut: Use vanilla chips. Use 1 teaspoon coconut flavoring with vanilla; stir in 4 tablespoons very finely chopped coconut.

Toasted Almond: Vanilla chips, ½ teaspoon almond extract, 2 tablespoons very finely chopped toasted sliced almonds.

German Chocolate: Use milk chocolate chips, add 2 tablespoons very finely chopped coconut and 2 tablespoons very finely chopped toasted pecans.

Mint: Use mint flavored chocolate chips or add 1 teaspoon mint extract.

Raspberry: Use raspberry chocolate chips and stir in 2 tablespoons seedless raspberry jam.

*** Great Recipes from Redeemer's Fellowship***

Lemon Fudge

1 (4-ounce) package lemon pudding
  (not instant)
$\frac{1}{2}$ cup margarine

$\frac{1}{2}$ cup milk
1 teaspoon vanilla
1 (1-pound) box powdered sugar

In a saucepan, mix lemon pudding, margarine, milk, and vanilla. Bring to a boil, stirring constantly. Remove from heat and add sugar. Pour into a buttered dish. Let cool. Cut into squares.

Grade A Recipes

Peanut Butter Fudgies

This tastes quite a bit like fudge.

3 cups quick oats
1 (12-ounce) package mini or
  regular chocolate chips
$\frac{1}{4}$ cup coconut (optional)
$\frac{1}{4}$ cup nuts (optional)

$\frac{1}{2}$–1 cup (or so) peanut butter to
  taste (optional)
2 cups sugar
$1\frac{1}{2}$ sticks margarine or butter
$\frac{1}{2}$ cup canned milk

Mix in large bowl the quick oats, chocolate chips, coconut, nuts, and peanut butter. Blend thoroughly in saucepan the sugar, margarine or butter, and canned milk. Bring ingredients in saucepan to a rolling boil and boil about 2 minutes. Pour over dry mixture. Mix thoroughly until chocolate is melted and all ingredients are mixed. Spread in a cookie sheet and cut into squares.

Coastal Flavors

Microwave Almond Roca

2 cups chopped almonds, divided **1 cup sugar**
1 cup butter, plus some for pan **1 package real chocolate chips**

Spread 1¼ cups almonds in buttered 9x13-inch pan. Cook 1 cup butter and sugar in microwave on HIGH for 1 minute. Stir. Cook an additional 6–8 minutes on HIGH, stirring every 2 minutes. Mixture will be caramelized in color. Pour immediately over almonds. (Don't be surprised if the butter/sugar mixture partially separates.) Pour chocolate chips on hot caramel mixture. When melted, spread evenly. Sprinkle with remaining nuts. Chill or freeze. Break in pieces to serve.

Favorite Recipes Cookbook

Cream Caramels

1¾ cups Karo syrup **½ cup butter**
1 cup white sugar **½ cup margarine**
1 cup brown sugar **1 teaspoon vanilla**
2 cups half-and-half **1½ cups nuts**

Cook syrup, white sugar, brown sugar, half-and-half, butter, and margarine together to firm ball stage (246°). Remove from heat. Stir often until almost like a cake batter. Takes about an hour. Add vanilla and nuts. Pour into well-greased 10x10-inch or 9x13-inch pan. Cut while warm and wrap individually. Makes 100 pieces.

Look What's Cooking

Pies and Other Desserts

Oregon is a dramatic land of many changes. From it's rugged seacoast, high mountain passes, lush greenery and waterfalls, to the desert expanse of Catlow Valley, shown here, Oregon's natural beauty has been preserved for all to enjoy.

Pear Pie

2 (9-inch) pie crusts, unbaked
3 or 4 pears, quartered, or 1 large can
¾ cup sugar for fresh pears, less for canned
1 egg
2 level tablespoons cornstarch
½ cup cream
Dash of crushed cloves

Line pie tin with one pie crust. Fill the unbaked pie crust with quartered fresh pears or with quarters of canned pears. Combine sugar, egg, cornstarch, cream, and dash of cloves, and pour over pears. Top with second pie crust. Bake at 425° for 15 minutes and then reduce heat to 350° for 30 minutes.

Variation: This batter is excellent with rhubard in the spring, or apples with cinnamon instead of cloves. Also try half brown sugar with half white.

Favorite Recipes from Ruralite Readers

Sour Cream Pear Pie

This is our most popular pear dessert at the Pear Party in September. Our daughter-in-law Linda, makes lots so everyone can sample.

PIE:

1 cup sour cream
1 egg
¾ cup sugar
1 teaspoon vanilla
¼ teaspoon salt
2 tablespoons flour
4 cups peeled and diced ripe pears
1 (9-inch) pie shell, unbaked

Preheat oven to 375°. Blend sour cream, egg, sugar, vanilla, salt, and flour until smooth. Fold in prepared pears. Pour into pie shell. Bake for 40 minutes. Sprinkle with Pecan Streusel Topping and bake another 10 minutes. Cool slightly and serve.

PECAN STREUSEL TOPPING:

¼ cup butter, cut in small pieces
¼ cup flour
¼ cup brown sugar
1 teaspoon cinnamon
¼ cup finely chopped pecans

Cut butter into combined flour, sugar, and cinnamon. Add pecans. Serves 6–8.

Recipe by Rasmussen Farms (Hood River)
The Fruit Loop Cookbook

Fresh Strawberry Pie

6 cups fresh strawberries (about
  1½ quarts), divided
3 tablespoons cornstarch
1 cup sugar (may reduce by half
  when strawberries are at their
  sweetest)

½ cup water
1 (9-inch) pie shell, baked
Whipped topping (optional)

Mash enough berries to equal 1 cup. Combine the cornstarch and sugar, then add water. Gradually stir in the crushed berries. Cook mixture over medium heat, stirring constantly, until mixture thickens and boils. Boil and stir 1 minute. Cool. Fill shell with remaining berries. Pour cooked berry mixture over top. Chill at least 3 hours or until set. Serve with whipped topping, if desired.

Cooking with Love

Oregon Strawberry Pie

1 cup whipping cream
1 (8-ounce) package cream
  cheese, softened
1½ cups sugar, divided
1 teaspoon vanilla extract
1 (10-inch) pie shell, baked,
  room temperature

3 tablespoons cornstarch
½ cup water
1 cup mashed fresh
  strawberries
4 cups whole strawberries

In a small mixing bowl, whip cream; set aside. In a medium bowl, beat cream cheese, ½ cup sugar, and vanilla. Fold in whipped cream and beat lightly by hand. Spoon into baked pie shell.

In medium saucepan, combine remaining 1 cup sugar and cornstarch. Add water and mashed berries. Over high heat, bring to a boil, stirring constantly until mixture begins to thicken (about 1 minute). Let cool. Arrange whole berries on top of cheese mixture, then spoon on berry topping. Refrigerate 3–4 hours. Garnish with additional strawberries. Serves 8.

Rainy Day Treats and Sunny Temptations

Apple Blackberry Pie

½ cup sugar
3 tablespoons quick-cooking
  tapioca
1 teaspoon grated lemon zest
½ teaspoon cinnamon
4 cups thinly sliced, cored, and
  peeled Granny Smith apples

3 cups blackberries
1 (9-inch) pie shell, unbaked
⅓ cup marshmallow creme
2 tablespoons butter or margarine,
  melted
¼ cup packed brown sugar
½ cup rolled oats

Mix sugar, tapioca, lemon zest, cinnamon, apples, and blackberries in a large bowl. Let stand for 15 minutes. Spoon into the pie shell. Mix marshmallow creme, melted butter, brown sugar, and rolled oats in a bowl until crumbly. Sprinkle over the fruit to within 1 inch of the edge. Bake at 375° for 60–70 minutes or until bubbly. Cover with foil after 45 minutes if the topping is getting too brown. Yields 8 servings.

Cooking from the Coast to the Cascades

Blueberry Sour Cream Pie

1 cup sour cream
¾ cup sugar
¼ teaspoon salt
5 tablespoons all-purpose flour,
  divided
1 teaspoon vanilla extract

1 egg, beaten
2½ cups fresh blueberries
1 (9-inch) pie crust, unbaked
2 tablespoons butter, softened
3 tablespoons chopped pecans

Preheat oven to 400°. Combine sour cream, sugar, salt, 2 tablespoons flour, vanilla, and egg. Beat 5 minutes at medium speed or until smooth. Fold in blueberries. Pour filling into pastry shell. Bake for 25 minutes. Combine 3 tablespoons flour, butter and pecans, stirring well. Sprinkle over top of pie. Bake 10 additional minutes. Chill before serving. Serves 8.

Recipe by Nelson's Blueberry Farm (Parkdale)
The Fruit Loop Cookbook

Huckleberry-Cherry Pie

3 tablespoons quick-cooking
  tapioca
1 cup sugar
2 cups huckleberries
1 cup canned cherries

1/2 cup cherry juice
1 tablespoon lemon juice
2 (9-inch) pie shells
1 tablespoon butter

Combine tapioca, sugar, huckleberries, cherries, cherry juice, and lemon juice. Pour mixture into prepared 9-inch pie shell. Dot with butter and add top crust. Bake at 400° for 55 minutes.

Huckleberries and Crabmeat

Huckleberry Quickie

2 cups huckleberries
1½ cups sugar, divided
¾ cup flour, divided
¼ teaspoon salt, divided
2 tablespoons butter

1 tablespoon lemon juice
1 cup water
1¼ teaspoons baking powder
1 egg

Combine berries, 1 cup sugar, ¼ cup flour, ⅛ teaspoon salt, butter, lemon juice, and water in a saucepan. Bring to a boil and simmer 5 minutes. Pour into a greased 9-inch-square baking pan. Now mix ½ cup flour, ½ cup sugar, ⅛ teaspoon salt, and baking powder. Add egg; stir quickly and spoon over berry mixture. Bake at 350° for 25 minutes.

Huckleberries and Crabmeat

Huckleberries are a shrub native to the Northwest. Related to blueberries, the fruit is slightly smaller and makes delicious pies, jams, jellies or syrups.

Virginia's Fruit Pie and Foolproof Crust

8 cups fruit
3 cups sugar
⅓ cup tapioca

3 tablespoons lemon juice
2 teaspoons salt

A good mix of fruit is: 4 cups huckleberries; 2 cups blueberries; 2 cups plums. Mix all ingredients; let set 30 minutes. Heat in microwave on HIGH until warm. Pour in 9x13-inch deep dish casserole.

CRUST:
4 cups flour
1¾ cups shortening
1 tablespoon sugar
2 teaspoons salt

1 tablespoon vinegar
1 egg
½ cup water

With a fork, mix first 4 ingredients. In a separate dish, beat remaining ingredients. Combine the 2 mixtures, stirring with a fork until all ingredients are moistened. Then mold dough into a ball. Chill at least 15 minutes before rolling out. Roll out ½ of dough extra thick and place on top of fruit filling. Bake in a 350° oven until bubbly and done, 45–60 minutes.

Note: Dough can be left in refrigerator up to 3 days (it will remain soft and ready to roll) or it can be frozen until ready to use.

Sagebrush Surprises Cookbook

Fresh Peach Pie

1 cup sugar
2 tablespoons cornstarch
1 cup water
1 (3-ounce) package peach-
  flavored gelatin

3 cups sliced peaches
1 pastry shell, baked
Whipping cream, whipped

In saucepan, combine sugar, cornstarch, and water until smooth. Cook and stir over medium heat until bubbly and thickened. Remove from heat; stir in gelatin until dissolved. Cool. Arrange peaches in crust; pour filling over peaches. Chill about 2 hours. Serve with whipped cream.

Our Favorite Recipes

My Own Lemon Meringue Pie

CRUST:

1 cup flour
¼ teaspoon salt
½ teaspoon sugar

¼ cup shortening
2–4 tablespoons water

Mix flour, salt, sugar, and shortening until it is crumbly. Add water and stir until it makes a ball. Roll out on lightly floured board and press into 9-inch pie plate. Flute edges and prick bottom several times with fork. Bake in preheated 400° oven about 10 minutes or until lightly browned.

FILLING:

1½ cups sugar
7¼ tablespoons cornstarch
Dash salt
1¾ cups water
4 egg yolks, reserve whites

2 tablespoons plus 1 teaspoon
  lemon rind
7 tablespoons lemon juice
Few drops yellow color
4 tablespoons butter

Combine sugar, cornstarch, and salt. Boil water in top of double boiler; add combined ingredients and cook until very thick. Beat egg yolks; add 1 heaping tablespoon of thickened cornstarch mixture and beat quickly. Do this 3 more times; return to top of double boiler and cook until done, 7–8 minutes. Remove and add rind, juice, coloring and butter. Let cool and pour into baked Crust.

MERINGUE:

8 tablespoons sugar
1¼ tablespoons cornstarch
8 tablespoons water

⅛ teaspoon salt
4 egg whites

Cook sugar, cornstarch, and water; add salt. Cook until thick and clear. Cool. Beat egg whites until stiff; add cornstarch mixture in 2 separate additions and beat well after each. When cooled mix has been added, beat 5 minutes. Spread on pie and bake at 350° for 15 minutes.

Favorite Recipes from the Kitchen of Alma Irey

Lemonade Pie

1 (6-ounce) can frozen lemonade
1 (10-ounce) container Cool Whip

4 drops green food coloring
1 graham cracker crust

Mix lemonade, Cool Whip, and food coloring. Do not use electric mixer! Fill pie crust. Refrigerate until served. Tastes best when made the day before. Can be garnished with mint leaves, thinly sliced lemon, or berries. Can be frozen.

Recipes, Recipes, Recipes!

Sour Cream Lemon Pie

¼ cup cornstarch
1¼ cups plus 3 tablespoons
  water, divided
1 cup sugar
2 tablespoons butter
9 tablespoons lemon juice

3 egg yolks
2 tablespoons milk
1 (8-inch) pie shell, baked
1 cup sour cream
1 pint whipping cream, whipped

Dissolve cornstarch in 3 tablespoons cold water. In a 2-quart saucepan, mix sugar, remaining water, and butter. Cook over low heat until sugar dissolves. Add cornstarch mixture and cook until clear (about 8 minutes), stirring occasionally. Add lemon juice and cook 2 minutes. Mix egg yolks with milk and add to saucepan. Cook over low heat until mixture boils, stirring occasionally. Cool. Pour ½ of this mixture into pie shell and refrigerate. Add sour cream to the other ½ of the mixture; mix well. When the refrigerated half is set, spread sour cream mixture over top. Refrigerate. Top with whipped cream before serving. Serves 8.

Savor the Flavor of Oregon

Fort Clatsop National Memorial, near Astoria, contains a replica of Lewis and Clark's 1805-1806 winter outpost. The expedition's 33-member party spent the winter here learning from the local Clatsop Indians, making moccasins and buckskin clothing, storing food and reworking their maps and journals in preparation for their long journey back to St. Louis.

Pineapple Philly Pie

1/3 cup plus 1/2 cup sugar, divided
1 teaspoon cornstarch
1 cup crushed pineapple with juice
1 (8-ounce) package cream cheese,
  softened
1/2 teaspoon salt

3 eggs
3/4 cup milk
1/2 teaspoon vanilla
1 (9-inch) pie shell, unbaked
1/4 cup chopped pecans

Blend together 1/3 cup sugar and cornstarch. Add undrained pineapple. Place in saucepan and cook until mixture thickens. Set aside to cool. In a medium bowl, combine cream cheese, 1/2 cup sugar, and salt, stirring until smooth and blended. Add eggs, 1 at a time, stirring well after each egg. Add milk and vanilla. Spread cooled pineapple mixture over bottom of unbaked pie shell. Pour cream cheese mixture over pineapple and sprinkle with chopped pecans. Bake at 400° for 10 minutes then reduce heat to 325° and bake for 50 minutes.

Grandma Jean's Rainy Day Recipes

Farmer's Market Caramel Apple Pie

A Market Fruit original and one of our most popular pies!

PIE:
6–8 Granny Smith apples, peeled
  and sliced
3/4–1 cup sugar
1/4 teaspoon cinnamon

1 (9-inch) pie shell, unbaked
2 tablespoons margarine, cut into
  small pieces

Preheat oven to 400°. Mix sliced apples with sugar and cinnamon. Pour apple mixture into pie shell. Dot with margarine.

TOPPING:
2 cups oats
1/4 cup margarine

1/4 cup brown sugar

Mix ingredients for Topping with a fork until crumbly. Spread evenly on top of apple mixture. Bake for 45–50 minutes, covering with foil the last 10–15 minutes. Serves 6–8.

The Fruit Loop Cookbook

Chocolate Caramel Pecan Pie

CARAMEL SAUCE:

1 teaspoon butter
1 teaspoon flour
$1/8$ teaspoon salt

$1/3$ cup whipping cream
$1/4$ cup sugar
$1/4$ cup firmly packed brown sugar

In a glass bowl, melt butter. Stir in flour and salt. Stir in whipping cream. Add sugar and brown sugar. Mix well. Microwave on HIGH until mixture boils; microwave at a boil for 2 minutes longer. Set aside.

FILLING:

$2/3$ cup sugar
$1/2$ teaspoon salt
$1/3$ cup butter, melted
1 cup light corn syrup
3 eggs

1 cup pecan halves
2 ounces unsweetened chocolate, melted
1 (9-inch) pie crust, unbaked

In a large bowl, combine sugar, salt, melted butter, corn syrup, and eggs. Beat well. Stir $1/2$ cup of Filling mixture into Caramel Sauce; blend well. Set aside. Stir pecans and chocolate into remaining Filling mixture; blend well. Pour into crust-lined pan. Pour Caramel Sauce evenly over Filling. Bake at 375° for 45 minutes or until outer edge of Filling is set and center is partially set. Cool on wire rack. Serve with whipped cream.

Great Recipes from Redeemer's Fellowship

Banana Caramel Pie

1 cup dark brown sugar
$1/4$ cup flour
$1/4$ teaspoon salt
$1 1/4$ cups cold water
2 egg yolks
1 tablespoon butter

$1/2$ teaspoon vanilla
$1/4$ cup evaporated milk
1 (8-inch) pie shell, baked
2–3 bananas
Cool Whip

In saucepan mix sugar, flour, and salt. Add water, egg yolks, butter, vanilla, and milk. Cook and stir until thickened. Cool 5 minutes. Spread in baked pie shell. Cover with plastic wrap. Refrigerate until serving time. At serving time, remove plastic wrap and slice bananas over filling. Spread Cool Whip over bananas. Refrigerate leftovers.

Heavenly Temptations

Peanut Buttercup Pie

½ cup sugar
1 tablespoon flour
2 tablespoons cocoa
¼ cup milk
1 egg, beaten
1½ tablespoons butter, softened
1 teaspoon vanilla, divided

1 (8-inch) pie shell, unbaked
4 ounces cream cheese, softened
4 ounces whipped topping
⅙ cup peanut butter
½ cup powdered sugar
Miniature chocolate chips or grated
   chocolate for garnish

Combine sugar, flour, cocoa, milk, egg, butter, and ½ teaspoon vanilla. Pour into unbaked pie shell. Bake at 350° for about 20 minutes or until set. Cool and chill.

Combine cream cheese, whipped topping, peanut butter, powdered sugar, and ½ teaspoon vanilla and pour over baked chocolate pie. Sprinkle with miniature chocolate chips or grated chocolate. Chill.

The Miller Cookbook

Peanut Butter Pie

1 (8-ounce) package cream cheese
1 cup powdered sugar
½ teaspoon vanilla
½ pint whipping cream

½ cup peanut butter
1 (9-inch) pie shell, baked or crumb
Peanuts for garnish

Mix in bowl the cream cheese, sugar, and vanilla. Whip the cream and fold into above mixture. Add peanut butter and pour into baked or crumb crust. Sprinkle chopped peanuts on top. May serve with whipped cream, if desired. Yummy!

Manna by the Sea

Coffee Toffee Pie

CRUST:

1½ cups chocolate wafer crumbs   ¼ cup butter or margarine, softened
¼ cup brown sugar   Few nuts, finely chopped

Mix wafer crumbs, brown sugar, butter, and nuts together. Press mixture into a 9-inch pie pan. Bake at 350° for 10 minutes. Cool.

FIRST LAYER:

½ cup butter, softened   2 teaspoons instant coffee
¾ cup granulated sugar   2 eggs
1 (1-ounce) square unsweetened
   chocolate, melted

In a small bowl, beat butter at medium speed until creamy. Gradually add sugar. Beat until light. Mix melted chocolate and instant coffee. When chocolate is cooled, blend into butter mixture. Add 1 egg and beat 5 minutes. Add another egg and beat 5 minutes more. Pour into pie shell and refrigerate overnight.

SECOND LAYER:

2 cups cream   ½ cup powdered sugar
2 tablespoons instant coffee   Chocolate curls

The next day combine cream, instant coffee, and powdered sugar. Refrigerate covered for 1 hour. Then whip until stiff. Spread on pie and garnish with chocolate curls. Refrigerate several hours before serving. Remove from refrigerator 5 or 10 minutes before cutting. Yields 8 servings.

A Taste of Oregon

All American Apple Cobbler

6 apples, thinly sliced
½ cup sugar
1 teaspoon cinnamon
3 tablespoons water

1 cup plus 1 tablespoon all-purpose
   flour, divided
½ cup brown sugar
½ cup butter or margarine, melted

Combine apples, sugar, cinnamon, water, and 1 tablespoon flour in medium bowl; mix well. Place in a greased casserole. Combine remaining ingredients in a medium bowl; mix well. Place topping evenly over apples. Bake in preheated 350° oven for 45 minutes or until topping is slightly browned. Serves 8.

Pig Out

Three Berry Cobbler

We were sorry when this recipe was finished, since that meant we would no longer have it at our tasting sessions. Served warm and topped with frozen vanilla yogurt, it is an all-time favorite of our staff members. Frozen berries are available all year long, so you do not have to wait for summer to enjoy this great treat.

1 tablespoon margarine
½ cup whole wheat flour
½ cup white flour
½ cup sugar
1½ teaspoons baking powder

¾ cup skim milk
3 cups fresh berries (blueberries,
   blackberries, and red raspberries)
   or 2 (12-ounce) bags frozen mixed
   berries, thawed about 1½ hours

Preheat oven to 350°. Put margarine in an 8-inch-square baking pan and heat in oven to melt, about 2 minutes. Combine flours, sugar, baking powder, and milk. Pour batter over margarine, but do not mix. Put berries on top of batter (if using frozen berries, do not include juice). Bake 35 minutes (frozen berries will take 45–50 minutes) or until a wooden pick inserted in the center comes out clean. Makes 9 servings.

Per Serving: Calories 134; Sod. 110mg; Fiber 3g; Total Fat 2g: Sat. Fat Trace; Chol. Trace; Chol-saturated Fat Index Trace.

The New American Diet Cookbook

Nut Tart with Apricot Cream

A superb nutty tart.

CRUST:

2 cups flour

¼ cup sugar

¾ cup butter

2 egg yolks, slightly beaten

Combine flour and sugar; cut in butter with pastry blender or food processor. Work in egg yolks with fork or continue in food processor just until dough holds together. Press evenly over ungreased bottom and sides of 11 or 12-inch tart pan with fluted sides and removable bottom. Bake at 325° for 10 minutes; color will be pale. Use hot or cold.

FILLING:

1½ cups whipping cream

1½ cups sugar

1 teaspoon grated orange rind

¼ teaspoon salt

2 cups coarsely chopped walnuts

¼ teaspoon vanilla

¼ teaspoon orange extract

Combine cream, sugar, rind, and salt in large saucepan. Bring to a boil, stirring constantly. Reduce heat to medium; continue cooking for 5 minutes, stirring often. Remove from heat; stir in nuts and extracts. Pour into pastry shell and bake at 375° until lightly browned, about 35 minutes for a 12-inch tart and 40 minutes for an 11-inch tart. Cool in pan on wire rack until just warm to touch. Remove sides, not bottom, and cool to room temperature. May be made a day ahead. Serve in slender wedges topped with Apricot Cream or whipped cream. May also be served unadorned.

APRICOT CREAM:

¼ pound dried apricots

1 cup orange juice

2 tablespoons sugar

2 tablespoons Grand Marnier

1 cup whipping cream

Snip apricots into quarters. Simmer apricots in orange juice until very soft, about 30 minutes. Remove from heat; add sugar, and stir until dissolved. Cool to lukewarm; purée in blender or food processor adding Grand Marnier. Chill. Whip cream, then gently fold in apricot purée. Chill until ready to serve. Leftover Apricot Cream is delicious frozen.

Favorite Recipes Cookbook

Chocolate Mousse Tart

A velvety-smooth filling encased in a nutty crust—oh, so satisfying!

CHOCOLATE NUT CRUST:

4 ounces semisweet chocolate, finely ground
⅓ cup finely ground walnuts
2 cups finely ground vanilla wafers
6 tablespoons butter, melted

Combine chocolate, nuts, and ground wafers. Stir in melted butter until well combined. Press onto sides and bottom of a lightly buttered 10-inch tart pan. Chill 10 minutes. Bake in preheated 375° oven about 10 minutes. Remove and set on a rack to cool.

1 tablespoon cold coffee
1 teaspoon instant coffee powder
1 teaspoon vanilla extract
1 teaspoon brandy, rum, or any nut liqueur
3 egg yolks, room temperature (reserve whites)
3 ounces unsweetened chocolate
3 ounces semisweet chocolate
12 tablespoons sugar, divided
6 tablespoons water
3 egg whites, room temperature
Pinch of cream of tartar
⅓ cup whipping cream

Combine coffee, instant coffee powder, vanilla, brandy, and egg yolks. Set aside.

Chunk up chocolate and place in bowl of food processor. Process until finely ground. Combine 6 tablespoons sugar and water in a small saucepan and heat on high, without stirring, until sugar has dissolved and mixture just starts to boil. Turn on food processor and very carefully pour hot sugar syrup through the feed tube. Process until combined. Scrape down sides of work bowl and let set 2 minutes to cool a bit. Then add coffee-egg yolk mixture and process until smooth. Transfer to a mixing bowl.

Beat egg whites and cream of tartar until foamy. Gradually add remaining 6 tablespoons sugar and continue to beat until stiff, shiny peaks form. Stir ¼ of the whites into chocolate-egg yolk mixture to lighten it. Gently fold in remaining whites.

Whip cream until soft peaks form, and gently fold into chocolate. Pour into prepared crust and chill 4–5 hours or overnight. Serves 10.

Thyme and the River

Sue's Apple Pie in a Jar

3 cups sugar
1 teaspoon salt
$1/2$ teaspoon nutmeg
2 teaspoons cinnamon
1 cup cornstarch

$10^1/2$ cups water
3 tablespoons lemon juice (optional)
7 quart jars filled with peeled and
   sliced apples

Mix all ingredients except lemon juice and apples. Put in large saucepan on medium heat and cook until bubbling. Remove; add lemon juice, if desired. Stir well. Pour over jars of apples. Process in hot water bath for 25 minutes or 10 minutes in pressure canner at 10 pounds pressure. Store on shelves with other fruit. When unexpected guests arrive for a visit, place in pie shell and bake at 400° for 40–50 minutes.

Cookin' with Capital Press

Blackberry Dumplings

We are so blessed here in Oregon to have plentiful blackberries, and this is a good way to use them.

$3/4$ cup sugar
$1/2$ cup water
$1^1/2$ teaspoons lemon juice

$1/8$ teaspoon salt
$1^1/2$ quarts blackberries
1 teaspoon vanilla

Use a saucepan of at least $4^1/2$-quart capacity with a tight-fitting lid. Mix sugar, water, lemon juice, and salt, and heat over low heat 3 minutes. Add the blackberries; cover and simmer 10 minutes. Add vanilla.

DUMPLINGS:

$2^1/4$ cups flour
3 teaspoons baking powder
$1^1/2$ teaspoons sugar
$1/3$ teaspoon salt

$2^1/2$ tablespoons butter or
   margarine, softened
1 cup milk

Mix flour, baking powder, sugar, salt, butter, and milk and beat until smooth. Spoon the batter on the berries and simmer 25 minutes longer, keeping a tight cover in place. Serve the berries ladled over the dumplings while still warm.

Recipes and Remembering

Dried Apple Dumplings

APPLE LAYER:

1 (8-ounce) package dried apples
 or dried mixed fruit
7 cups water
3/4 cup firmly packed brown sugar

1 teaspoon cinnamon
1/2 teaspoon ginger
1 tablespoon lemon juice

Chop apples into small pieces. In saucepan, combine apples, water, brown sugar, cinnamon, and ginger. Bring the mixture to a boil. Reduce heat to medium and simmer for 25 minutes. (Prepare Dumplings while mixture simmers.) Add lemon juice. Cook 5 minutes. Remove cover from apple mixture. Gently drop spoonfuls of Dumplings mixture onto simmering apple mixture. Make sure the Dumplings sit on the top of the apple layer and do not sink. Cover tightly. Cook over medium-low heat for 15 minutes. Do not remove cover during cooking. Makes 6 servings.

DUMPLINGS:

1 cup all-purpose flour
1/4 cup cornmeal
1/4 cup sugar
2 teaspoons baking powder

1 egg
1/2 teaspoon salt
1/4 cup water

In medium bowl, combine flour, cornmeal, sugar, baking powder, and salt. In small bowl, beat together egg and water with hand mixer. Add egg mixture to flour mixture. Mix with spoon just until all ingredients are moistened. Do not overstir or Dumplings will be tough.

To serve, spoon apple mixture into bowls; spoon Dumplings on top.

Oregon Trail Cooking

Oregon has an official state insect—the swallowtail butterfly. The state seashell of Oregon, the Oregon Hairy Triton, is the only shell that shares the name of a state, and one of only three in the world named after a location.

Blackberry Roll

We in Oregon are blessed with abundant blackberries and I am always looking for ways to utilize them. This is a great recipe.

2 cups flour
4 teaspoons baking powder
$\frac{1}{2}$ teaspoon salt
$\frac{1}{4}$ cup cold butter or margarine
1 cup grated sharp Cheddar
   cheese

$\frac{3}{4}$ cup milk
$2\frac{1}{2}$ cups fresh blackberries
$\frac{1}{2}$ cup plus 2 tablespoons sugar,
   divided
$\frac{1}{4}$ cup brown sugar
$\frac{1}{2}$ teaspoon grated nutmeg

Preheat oven to 350°. In a mixing bowl, combine flour, baking powder, salt, and butter. Work until butter is fine crumbs. Blend in cheese and milk; do not overmix. Roll dough out lightly into a 10x12-inch rectangle, about $\frac{1}{3}$ inch thick. Sprinkle blackberries on top, then add $\frac{1}{2}$ cup white sugar, the brown sugar, and nutmeg.

    Starting from the long edge, roll up dough like a jellyroll and transfer to a greased baking sheet, placing it seam-side-down. Pinch edges together and fold under. Pat roll into a tidy bundle and sprinkle remaining 2 tablespoons white sugar on top. Bake for 45 minutes or until the roll is golden brown. Slice and serve warm in bowls with cream. Serves 10.

Then 'til Now

Although blackberries were picked wild and processed for canning, few growers were interested in growing them commercially because of the thorns. In 1926, Philip Steffes of Sublimity, Oregon, found a thornless plant growing east of Stayton. When it was tested and found to be as productive as the thorny form, it quickly gained popularity and soon became the main blackberry sold in the United States, and grown extensively in Oregon.

Blackberry-Apple Crunch

Serve this warm dessert with frozen vanilla yogurt.

**4 cups sliced tart apples, such as
   Granny Smiths**
3/4 cup granulated sugar

**2 cups fresh or frozen blackberries
   (if using frozen berries, do not
   thaw)**

Preheat oven to 350°. In a large bowl, combine apples, sugar, and berries. Place into a greased 9x13-inch pan.

TOPPING:
**1/2–3/4 cup firmly packed
   brown sugar**
3/4 cup all-purpose flour
3/4 cup rolled oats

1/2 cup chopped walnuts
1/2 cup (1 stick) butter
1/2 teaspoon cinnamon or allspice

In a large bowl, combine brown sugar, flour, oats, walnuts, butter, and cinnamon and blend together. Sprinkle over top of fruit. Bake at 350° for approximately 1 hour, or until top is brown. Yields 12–15 servings.

From Portland's Palate

Pumpkin Crunch Dessert

1 (1-pound 13-ounce) can pumpkin
1 (13-ounce) can evaporated milk
1 cup sugar
3 eggs

1 teaspoon cinnamon
1 yellow pudding cake mix
1 cup chopped walnuts
1 1/2 sticks butter, melted

Mix together pumpkin, evaporated milk, sugar, eggs, and cinnamon and pour into 9x13-inch pan lined with waxed paper (bottom and sides). Sprinkle cake mix (dry) on top of mixture. Pat on chopped walnuts over this. Spoon melted butter over top. Bake at 350° for 60 minutes. Let cool completely in pan; invert onto cookie sheet or another 9x13-inch pan. Remove wax paper.

FROSTING:
**1 (8-ounce) package cream
   cheese, softened**

3/4 cup Cool Whip
1 cup powdered sugar

Mix cream cheese, Cool Whip, and powdered sugar together. Spread over cooled dessert. Cut into squares. Serves 12–16.

Grade A Recipes

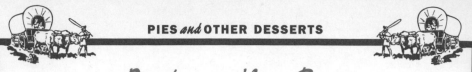

Pesche con Vino Rosso

(Peaches with Red Wine)

Just the right touch to top off the meal—not too heavy, not too sweet.

2 large, ripe peaches
1 cup red wine (a Chianti works
   very well)

1 tablespoon sugar
1 cinnamon stick

Dip peaches in boiling water for 1 minute. Remove with a slotted spoon and let cool. Peel. Cut peaches in half and remove pits.

   In a bowl, combine wine and sugar, stirring until sugar is dissolved. Add cinnamon stick and peach halves—stirring gently to coat. Cover bowl with plastic wrap and place in the refrigerator for 2–3 days. Serve cold—spooning a little of the wine over each peach half. Make 2–3 days in advance. Cover and chill. Yields 4 servings.

Nutritional Analysis: Serving Size: 1 peach half; Calories 59.6; % of Calories from Fat 1%; Total Fat .039g; Sat. Fat .005g; Prot. .393g; Carbo. 7.92g; Sod. 2.24mg; Chol. 0.0mg.

The Lighter Side of Italy

Four-Layer Torte

This dessert is sometimes called Watergate Dessert.

FIRST LAYER:
1 stick margarine, softened
1 cup flour

½ cup nuts

Mix and press into 9x13-inch pan. Bake at 350° for 15 minutes. Cool.

SECOND LAYER:
1 (8-ounce) package cream cheese,
   softened

½ (8-ounce) carton Cool Whip
1 cup powdered sugar

Mix and spread onto first layer.

THIRD LAYER:
2 (3-ounce) packages instant
   pudding (any flavor)

3 cups cold milk

Mix and spread on second layer.

FOURTH LAYER:
½ (8-ounce) carton Cool Whip

Chopped nuts (optional)

Spread Cool Whip on third layer; add nuts if desired. Chill several hours.

Heavenly Temptations

Heavenly Angel Dessert

2 eggs, separated
1 cup sugar
2 cups milk
1½ packages unflavored gelatin

5 tablespoons water
1 teaspoon vanilla
1 pint whipping cream
1 small plain angel food cake

Combine egg yolks, sugar, and milk. Mix and bring to a boil. Soften gelatin in water. Add to egg mixture and return to a boil. Let cool and add vanilla. Cool in refrigerator until mixture begins to congeal.

Beat egg whites until peaks form, but not dry. Whip cream. Fold egg whites and whipped cream into cooled cooked mixture. Scrape off exterior brown crumbs from angel food cake and then break cake into pieces. Stir pieces into whipped cream mixture and put in large round, lightly oiled ring mold or a square pan. Refrigerate.

Unmold and serve with fresh or frozen berry sauce (crushed berries with a little sugar). Festive to place fresh berries in stemmed serving dish and stand it in the middle of the ring.

Collection Extraordinaire

Ice Cream Pie

1 quart vanilla ice cream, softened
1 (6-ounce) can frozen lemonade

1 (9-inch) graham cracker crust

Add frozen concentrate to the softened ice cream. Mix with electric beater on low until well mixed and smooth. Pour into prepared crust and refreeze.

Oregon Cook Book

In 1858, the richest gold find in the Cascade Mountains was discovered in the Bohemia Mining District at Sharp's Creek near Cottage Grove.

Frozen Lemon Mousse

Light and lemony—one of Albertina's best.

CRUMB CRUST:

¼ cup butter, softened

2 tablespoons light brown sugar

½ cup flour

¼ cup chopped walnuts

Preheat oven to 400°. Mix together crust ingredients and put in a flat pan. Bake, stirring often until crumbs are brown. Cool. Press crumbs firmly into the bottom of an ungreased, 9-inch springform pan, reserving 2 tablespoons to sprinkle on top.

FILLING:

4 egg yolks, beaten (reserve whites)

½ cup fresh lemon juice

1½ tablespoons grated lemon rind

1 cup sugar, divided

4 egg whites

⅛ teaspoon cream of tartar

⅛ teaspoon salt

1½ cups whipping cream, whipped until stiff

Sweetened whipped cream and mint leaf for garnish

Combine egg yolks, lemon juice, rind, and ¼ cup sugar. Blend thoroughly. Beat egg whites until foamy. Add cream of tartar and salt. Beat until soft peaks form. Slowly add ¾ cup sugar, 2 tablespoons at a time, and beat until whites are stiff and shiny. Fold egg yolk mixture and whipped cream carefully into egg whites. Spoon into springform pan. Sprinkle with remaining crumbs. Cover and freeze.

Serve frozen with a dollop of whipped cream and a fresh mint leaf on each serving. Serves 10.

Albertina's Exceptional Recipes

Many of the 27,400 tons of cherries produced in Oregon each year are used to make maraschino cherries, which were developed in the 1920s by an Oregon State University food technologist.

Gone with the Wind Pudding

CRUST:

1 cup graham cracker crumbs

3 tablespoons butter, melted

3 tablespoons brown sugar

Pat ¾ of this mixture in a 8x8-inch baking dish; reserve the remainder for sprinkling on top of finished dessert.

CUSTARD:

2 eggs, separated

½ cup milk

1 cup sugar

1 envelope plain gelatin, soaked in
  ½ cup cold water

½ cup whipping cream

1 cup drained crushed pineapple

Maraschino cherries for garnish

Beat egg yolks and milk. Add sugar. Boil until mixture thickens. Add soaked gelatin and mix well. Cool.

Whip egg whites. Whip cream. Fold each into custard. Add drained pineapple. Pour into baking dish on top of cracker crumbs. Sprinkle remaining cracker crumbs on top of pudding. The pudding can also be layered with the crumb topping in pretty dessert dishes.

Cover with plastic wrap and refrigerate to set. Can be made several hours before serving. Cut in squares to serve and garnish with half a maraschino cherry.

Variation: Add ¼ cup chopped pecans or walnuts to crumb topping.

Potluck and Patchwork

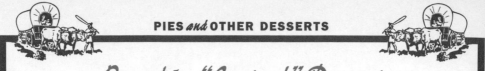
Pumpkin "Custard" Dessert

This tastes like pumpkin pie without the crust.

²/₃–¾ cup sugar
¼ cup flour
1 teaspoon baking powder
1 (13-ounce) can evaporated skim
   milk

½ cup egg substitute
1 (16-ounce) can pumpkin
1½ teaspoons pumpkin pie spice
2 teaspoons vanilla
2 tablespoons finely chopped walnuts

Preheat oven to 350°. Spray a 9x9-inch cake pan with nonstick cooking spray. Beat all ingredients, except walnuts, until smooth (1 minute in blender or 2 minutes on high with electric hand mixer). Pour into pan. Sprinkle nuts over top. Bake 50–55 minutes, or until knife inserted in center comes out clean. Serves 9.

Nutritional analysis per serving: Serving size 3-inch square; Calories 145; Fat 2g; Chol. 2mg; Prot. 6g; Carbo. 27g; Sod. 129mg.

Tastefully Oregon

Bread Pudding Deluxe

2 whole eggs
2 eggs, separated
2¾ cups milk, scalded
¾ cup plus 4 tablespoons sugar,
   divided
Dash of salt

½ teaspoon lemon extract
Dash of grated lemon rind
4 slices bread, torn
1 cup raisins
2 teaspoons vanilla
12 ounces strawberry preserves

Beat 2 whole eggs and 2 egg yolks (reserve whites); set aside. Heat milk in heavy saucepan. Add ¾ cup sugar and dash of salt to the beaten eggs. Add hot milk gradually, beating well. Add remaining ingredients except egg whites, preserves and 4 tablespoons sugar. Pour into a greased casserole and place in a pan of hot water and bake at 325° until almost set; cool 10 minutes. Spread top with strawberry preserves. Beat remaining egg whites and sweeten with 4 tablespoons sugar. Then spread meringue over preserves. Finish baking until meringue is browned on top and custard is set.

Favorite Recipes from the Kitchen of Alma Irey

Lime Chiffon Dessert

Plan ahead—needs to chill.

1½ cups crushed graham
   crackers (about 24 crackers)

⅓ cup sugar
½ cup butter or margarine, melted

Combine ingredients; set aside 3 tablespoons for topping. Press remaining crumbs onto the bottom of an ungreased 9x13x2-inch baking dish; set aside.

FILLING:

1 (3-ounce) package lime gelatin
1 cup boiling water
11 ounces cream cheese, softened
1 cup sugar

1 teaspoon vanilla
1 (16-ounce) carton frozen whipped
   topping, thawed

In a bowl, dissolve gelatin in boiling water; cool. In a mixing bowl, beat cream cheese and sugar. Add vanilla; mix well. Slowly add gelatin until combined. Fold in whipped topping. Spoon over crust; sprinkle with reserved crumbs. Cover and refrigerate for 3 hours or until set. Yields 12–15 servings.

Treasured Recipes

Norwegian Fruit Soup

1 cup prunes
1 cup raisins (or 2 cups mixed dried
   fruit)
4½ cups boiling water
Dash salt
½ lemon

1 stick cinnamon
2½ tablespoons tapioca
   (quick-cooking)
¾ cup sugar
½ tablespoon vinegar

Rinse fruit several times and drain. Place in saucepan and add boiling water and salt. Soak several hours or overnight. Slice lemon in thin slices. Break cinnamon stick in half. Add lemon and cinnamon to fruit and boil about 5 minutes. Add tapioca and cook 10 minutes more. Add sugar and cook another 10 minutes. Add vinegar. Serves 8.

Favorite Recipes from the Kitchen of Alma Irey

Poached Pears with Orange Sauce and Mascarpone

These delicate pears are a refreshing conclusion to a Christmas feast.

½ cup apple cider
½ cup water
1½ cups sugar
Finely minced or grated zest of
  2 oranges
Finely minced or grated zest of
  1 lemon

3 tablespoons fresh lemon juice
6 firm pears such as Comice or Bosc
1 cup fresh orange juice
¾ cup mascarpone cheese
6 tablespoons minced crystallized
  ginger, divided

In a saucepan large enough to hold upright pears without crowding, combine apple cider, water, sugar, orange and lemon zests, and lemon juice. Place over medium heat and cook, stirring often, until sugar dissolves and mixture comes to a boil. Remove from heat and set aside.

Peel pears, leaving stems attached. If necessary, cut a thin sliver off the bottoms so they will stand upright. Place pears upright in pan. With bulb baster or spoon, drizzle each pear with syrup. Cover and bring to a simmer over medium-high heat. Cook, basting frequently with syrup, until pears can be easily pierced with tip of a sharp knife, 20–25 minutes. Remove from the heat. With a slotted spoon, transfer pears to a shallow serving platter.

Pour poaching syrup through a fine-mesh sieve placed over a pitcher. Reserve zest to use as garnish. Measure 1 cup syrup and pour it into a small saucepan. (Reserve and chill remaining syrup for use in other recipes.) Add orange juice and stir to mix. Place over medium heat, bring to a gentle boil, and boil until reduced to a thick syrup, about 20 minutes. Remove from heat and let cool until warm. Drizzle 1 tablespoon of warm sauce over each pear.

To serve, arrange pears on individual plates. Place a spoonful of mascarpone next to each pear and spoon the remaining sauce over each pear. Garnish each pear with some of the reserved zest. Garnish each spoonful of mascarpone with 1 tablespoon of minced ginger and a few flecks of remaining zest. Serve immediately. Serves 6.

Christmastime Treats

Fruit Pizza for a Crowd

I get lots of compliments when I make this because it looks so impressive. The secret is arranging the fruit in an attractive pattern. I often use a combination of strawberries, raspberries, blueberries, and kiwi fruit. Light whipped topping can also be added.

1 (20-ounce) package sugar cookie dough
1 large (1.4-ounce) box sugar-free vanilla instant pudding
3 cups skim milk

6 ounces ($\frac{1}{2}$ of a 12-ounce tub) light cream cheese, room temperature
1 quart strawberries, washed and hulled (or other fresh fruit)

Preheat oven to 350°. Spray a 16-inch pizza pan with a nonstick spray. Slice cookie dough into $\frac{1}{4}$-inch-thick slices. Arrange slices on pizza pan so that they are $\frac{1}{2}$ to 1 inch apart. Bake for 18–20 minutes or until golden and set. Cool. In small mixing bowl, combine pudding mix and milk. Beat on low to mix. Add cream cheese and beat until smooth and thickened. Pour over cooled cookie crust. Arrange fruit on top. Yields 18 servings.

Serving size: $\frac{1}{18}$ of the pie; Calories 185; Carbo. 24g; Prot. 5g; Fat 8g; Exchanges 1$\frac{1}{2}$ starch, 1$\frac{1}{2}$ fat.

Note: People with diabetes should limit the use of this recipe because it contains significant amounts of sugar.

Quick & Healthy Recipes and Ideas (ScaleDown)

Because of the fertile volcanic soil, the Hood River Valley is one of the most prolific fruit producing valleys in the world, producing over 30% of the nation's winter pears including Anjou, Comice (pronounced cumees) and Bosc.

Coffee Pecan Sauce

Wonderful over ice cream!

1 cup finely chopped pecans
¼ cup instant coffee granules
3 tablespoons cornstarch

2 cups water
2 cups light corn syrup
1 teaspoon vanilla

Lightly toast pecans on pan in 350° oven (watch closely; don't burn); set aside. Mix coffee granules and cornstarch. Gradually stir in water. Stir in corn syrup. Bring to a boil; cook for 1 minute. Remove from heat; stir in pecans and then vanilla; cool. Store covered in refrigerator.

Great Recipes from Redeemer's Fellowship

Chocolate Espresso Sorbet with Fresh Berries

The following recipe comes from Portland Farmers' Market, Chef in the Market series, where every year chefs from local restaurants give cooking demonstrations that include farm fresh produce.

2 cups sugar
1 cup cocoa
1 teaspoon cinnamon
Pinch of salt
4 cups water
½ cup espresso or strong coffee

1 tablespoon coffee liqueur or
hazelnut liqueur (optional)
Garnish: 1 cup mixed fresh berries
or cherries, mint sprigs, and
chopped toasted hazelnuts

In a large saucepan, stir together all ingredients and bring to a boil, stirring constantly. Cool in the refrigerator until thoroughly cold. Freeze in an ice cream machine according to manufacturer's instructions. To serve, scoop into a bowl and garnish with fruit, mint, and toasted hazelnuts.

Recipe by Mark Gould, executive chef, Red Star Tavern and Roast House, Portland
Oregon Farmers' Markets Cookbook and Guide

Contributing Cookbooks

The Oregon Pioneer statue stands high atop the capitol in Salem. Because the 22-foot tall statue is gilded in gold leaf, it is more popularly known as the Golden Pioneer. This heroic figure represents the spirit of Oregon's early settlers.

Catalog
of
Contributing Cookbooks

All recipes in this book have been selected from the cookbooks shown on the following pages. Individuals who wish to obtain a copy of any particular book may do so by sending a check or money order to the address listed by each cookbook. Please note the postage and handling charges that are required. Prices and addresses are subject to change, and the books may sell out and become unavailable. Retailers are invited to call or write to same address for discount information.

ALBERTINA'S EXCEPTIONAL RECIPES

Albertina's   Phone 503-231-3909
424 NE 22nd Avenue
Portland, OR 97232

Albertina's Exceptional Recipes is a collection of outstanding recipes served at Albertina's Restaurant which is associated with the shops at Albertina Kerr. Albertina's is staffed and managed by volunteers with the proceeds going to help support the programs of Albertina Kerr Centers.

$ 20.00   Retail price
$ 4.50   Postage and handling

Make check payable to Albertina's
ISBN 0-9654691-0-7

ALL ABOUT CRAB: THE CRAB LOVER'S GUIDE TO DUNGENESS

by Nancy Brannon
ConAmore Publishing   Phone 541-997-4050
68 Spyglass Lane   Fax 503-218-8986
Florence, OR 97439   conamorepub@starband.net

Everything you ever wanted to know about Oregon's favorite—Dungeness Crab! How to catch, determine the sex (only males allowed!), and clean a Dungeness—then 50 great recipes (some fairly traditional, most all new) for Dungeness—truly the "royalty" of the Pacific Northwest!

$ 6.95   Retail price
$ 2.00   Postage and handling

Make check payable to ConAmore Publishing
ISBN 0-9623036-6-6

BEGGED, BORROWED AND STÖLLEN RECIPES
by Jean Ritter Smith
Eugene, OR

After years of begging, my notebook overflowed with often used best recipes served to us. I began copying choice recipe collections as beginner cookbooks for dearest girls. Many of our happiest hours have been spent sharing good conversation over fine food. My recipes are for creating warm times to remember. Currently out of print.

"CATE"RING TO SHRIMP
by Carol Cate
C. R. Bears   Phone 541-673-4248
P. O. Box 795
Winchester, OR 97495

Shrimp, one of the most popular shellfish, is so versatile and available everywhere. Delicious as appetizers, in salads, or entrées—all can be found in this little book of delicious recipes. 108 pages, spiralbound.

$ 5.00   Retail price

Make check payable to C. R. Bears

CAVEMAN CLASSIC CUISINE
Grants Pass-Josephine County
Chamber of Commerce   Phone 541-476-7717
P. O. Box 970   Fax 541-476-9574
Grants Pass, OR 97528   gpcoc@grantspasschamber.org

A 96-page souvenir cookbook of Grants Pass, Oregon, dedicated to the Caveman and to you. Recipes from local businesses, restaurants, river guides, and our Chamber/Visitor Center volunteers.

$ 6.00   Retail price   Visa/MC accepted (if ordering two or more)
$ 1.50   Postage and handling

Make check payable to Chamber of Commerce

CHRISTIAN BAKERS COOKBOOK
Christian Church of Burns   Phone 541-573-2216
125 S. Buena Vista
Burns, OR 97720-2213

The *Christian Bakers Cookbook* is a collection of family favorite recipes that are tried-and-true. Included are cooking tips, herbs and spices, equivalency charts and even napkin folding charts. This 152-page book is a must for your bookshelf.

$ 12.50   Retail Price
$ 3.00   Postage and handling

Make check payable to Christian Church of Burns

CHRISTMASTIME TREATS
by Sara Perry
Chronicle Books   www.chronbooks.com
85 Second Street/Sixth Floor
San Francisco, CA 94105

Craft manual, recipe book, and family frolic guide all in one, turning the hectic, commercial side of the holidays into handmade, heart-cherished fun. Sara Perry, columnist for the *Oregonian,* offers holiday cheer for the whole family in this delightful 96-page volume of more than 50 new traditions.

$ 14.95 Retail price
$ 3.00 Postage and handling

Make check payable to Chronicle Books

ISBN 0-8118-2491-8

CLAM DISHES AND ROCK FISHES
by Carol Cate
C. R. Bears   Phone 541-673-4248
P. O. Box 795
Winchester, OR 97495

On the Pacific coast, the most common species of clams are the butter, littleneck, razor and pizmo. Often served in chowders, there are a variety of excellent ways to cook them. Rockfish, including red cod, perch, sea bass, and red snapper, can be prepared in many delicious dishes. 108 pages, spiralbound.

$ 5.00 Retail price

Make check payable to C. R. Bears

COASTAL FLAVORS
American Association of University Women, Seaside Branch
P. O. Box 693   Phone 503-738-8285
Seaside, OR 97138-0693   counbun@pacifier.com

All of the proceeds from this 256-page cookbook, featuring the favorite recipes of friends and supporters of AAUW, will be used to promote education and equity for women and girls. Local scenery of the North Oregon coast and exceptional recipes make this a must for any collection.

$ 18.00 Retail price
$ 2.00   Postage and handling

Make check payable to AAUW

ISBN 0-9669545-0-5

COLLECTION EXTRAORDINAIRE
Assistance League of Eugene   Phone 541-485-3721
1149 Willamette Street
Eugene, OR 97401

Collection Extraordinaire consists of 195 pages of favorite recipes presented by our members. These recipes are divided into seven groups: appetizers, breakfast, brunch and breads, soups, salads, side dishes, entrées, and desserts.

$ 12.95 Retail price
$ 2.50 Postage and handling

Make check payable to Assistance League of Eugene

COOKIN' WITH CAPITAL PRESS

Capital Press Agriculture Weekly
P. O. Box 2048
Salem, OR 97308-2048

Phone 800-882-6789
Fax 503-370-4383
granderson@capitalpress.com

Cookin' with Capital Press is a compilation of recipes from the "What's Cookin'" pages of *Capital Press*, an agricultural newspaper headquartered in Salem, Oregon. The book includes over 600 recipes, including staff favorites and a special sourdough section. Profits support Newspapers in Education, which places newspapers in classrooms for use as a learning tool.

$ 10.50 Retail price
$ 3.50 Postage and handling

Visa/MC accepted

Make check payable to Capital Press

COOKING FROM THE COAST TO THE CASCADES

Junior League of Eugene, Oregon
2839 Willamette Street
Eugene, OR 97405

Phone 800-364-4031
Fax 541-345-8823
jlecookbook@mindspring.com

This cookbook offers an abundance of fresh recipes from picturesque Oregon with over 200 selections for elegant dining, outdoor entertaining, and quick weeknight meals. You will also find scenic photographs and references to Oregon's award-winning wines. Proceeds are returned to the community by the Junior League of Eugene.

$ 24.95 Retail price
$ 5.00 Postage and handling

Visa/MC accepted

Make check payable to *A Taste of Oregon*
ISBN 0-9607976-2-9

COOKING ITALIAN

by Joe Bianco
Avellino Press
P. O. Box 8454
Portland, OR 97207

Phone 503-223-6737
Fax 503-827-0653
jrbmedia@hevanet.com

Cooking Italian is a trip down memory lane and the foods that went with it. The book is softcover, perfectbound with 82 pages plus cover. Originally published in 1977 by the former Touchstone Press, Beaverton, Oregon, and subsequently re-published by new owner and reviewed by the media.

$ 9.95 Retail price
$ 1.50 Postage and handling

Make check payable to Bianco Publishing/Avellino Press
ISBN 0-9643408-4-4

COOKING WITH LOVE

Diana Bishop
Glide Garden Club
2749 Whistlers Park Road
Roseburg, OR 97470

Phone 541-673-0498
ddbishop@internetcds.com

A collection of 250 delicious recipes from Glide Garden Club members and friends, the book is a community favorite here in the Cascade foothills on the North Umpqua River. Sales help fund two $500 scholarships the club gives annually to Glide High School graduates.

$ 6.50 Retail price
$ 2.00 Postage and handling

Make check payable to Glide Garden Club

DILLEY FAMILY FAVORITES

Bible Church of Dilley   Phone 503-359-1327
4225 SW Dilley Road
Forest Grove, OR 97116

A collection of recipes by members past and present of Dilley Bible Church. Beautifully bound in a hardcover, three-ring binder for easy use. 126 pages of recipes.

$ 10.00 Retail price
$ 3.00 Postage and handling
Make check payable to Bible Church of Dilley

DUNGENESS CRABS AND BLACKBERRY COBBLERS:
THE NORTHWEST HERITAGE COOKBOOK

by Janie Hibler   www.randomhouse.com

Janie Hibler weaves fascinating pieces of lore, history, geography, and personal reminiscences of the Northwest into her collection of 212 recipes. The dishes blend old with new in delectable combinations which feature all the delights that the Northwest has to offer. A James Beard Award Nominee.

$ 18.00 Retail price

Available at bookstores or through www.randomhouse.com

ISBN 0-394-57745-0

FAVORITE RECIPES COOKBOOK

First Presbyterian Church   Phone 541-673-5559
823 S. E. Lane
Roseburg, OR 97470

Favorite recipes of wonderful cooks from Roseburg First Presbyterian Church. This 273-page spiralbound cookbook includes many delicious recipes that you are sure to enjoy.

$ 7.00 Retail price
$ 2.50 Postage and handling
Make check payable to First Presbyterian Church Women's Association

FAVORITE RECIPES FROM RURALITE READERS

Ruralite Services, Inc.   Phone 503-357-2105 ext 3002
P. O. Box 558   Fax 503-357-8615
Forest Grove, OR 97116   info@ruralite.org

Grandma's secret recipes. Old family favorites. The best of the West. Those are just a few ways to describe the culinary delights found in *Favorite Recipes from Ruralite Readers,* a 133-page cookbook featuring more than 600 tried-and-true recipes that appeared in *Ruralite Magazine* during the 1960s to late 1970s.

$ 12.00 Retail price   Visa/MC accepted

Make check payable to *Favorite Recipes*

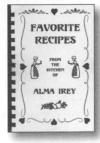

FAVORITE RECIPES FROM THE KITCHEN OF ALMA IREY

St. Paul's Ladies' Guild   Phone 541-476-2565
865 NW 5th Street
Grants Pass, OR 97526

Favorite Recipes . . . shares recipes of this wonderful cook who shared her recipes and food with everyone she met. Her personal comments and tips are interwoven with 150 old and new favorites in this 76-page book. All proceeds benefit Project Comfort for quilts to keep God's people of the world warm.

$ 6.00 Retail price
$ 2.00 Postage and handling

Make check payable to St. Paul's Ladies' Guild

FAVORITE RECIPES, SECOND EDITION

Buckeroo Square & Round Dance Club   Phone 541-459-7710
2661 Grayfox Drive
Sutherlin, OR 97479

The Buckeroo book is unique in that all the divider pages give the very interesting history of the "barn," or dance hall, and the club which will be 50 years old in April 2002. Square dancers have lots of potlucks and our recipes were always requested. The first edition sold out so we created the second, a 154-page collection.

$ 10.00 Retail price
$ 3.00 Postage and handling

Make check payable to Buckeroo Square & Round Dance Club

FEASTING IN THE FOREST

by Nancy Brannon
ConAmore Publishing   Phone 541-997-4050
68 Spyglass Lane   Fax 503-218-8986
Florence, OR 97439   conamorepub@starband.net

Now residing in the coastal town of Florence, Oregon, this husband and wife duo tells the love story of their years of owning and operating a gourmet Italian feast place in the Rocky Mountains. (100 recipes included.)

$ 10.95 Retail price   Visa/MC/AmEx
$ 2.00 Postage and handling

Make check payable to ConAmore Publishing
ISBN 0-9623036-0-7

FIDDLIN' IN THE KITCHEN

The Chamber Music Society of Oregon   Phone 503-287-2175
1935 NE 59th Avenue   delorenzoh@earthlink.net
Portland, OR 97213-4117

A 217-page cookbook from appetizers to desserts. This collection of recipes from members, family, and friends of the Chamber Music Society of Oregon is sure to please the most particular palate. Enjoy.

$ 5.95 Retail price
$ 1.00 Postage and handling (per copy)

Make check payable to CMSO

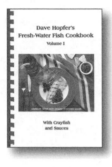

FLAVOR IT GREEK!

Philoptochos Society of Holy Trinity
  Greek Orthodox Church
3131 NE Glisan Street
Portland, OR 97232

Phone 503-234-0468
Fax 503-236-8379
elenistrat@aol.com

This exciting 338-page cookbook is jampacked with 300 time-honored recipes from three generations of Portland, Oregon's Greek community. Sun-drenched flavors of the Mediterranean, from appetizers to delectable desserts, are featured and include ingredients plentiful to the Northwest.

$ 27.95 Retail price   Visa/MC accepted
$ 4.00 Postage and handling

Make check payable to Philoptochos Cookbook
ISBN 0-9673935-0-7

FRESH-WATER FISH COOKBOOK

by Dave Hopfer   www.cookbooksmenusandbytes.biz
P. O. Box 511
Turner, OR 97392

There are 16 types of fresh-water fish, crayfish and sauces, with 20 recipes cooking with wine. Everything from bass to walleye, just about any fish caught in rivers, lakes, ponds and streams. Indexed, combbound, 300 recipes, 116 pages.

$ 12.95 Retail price
$ 3.95 Postage and handling

Make check payable to Dave Hopfer Enterprises
ISBN 0-9621207-0-7

FROM PORTLAND'S PALATE

Junior League of Portland
4838 SW Scholls Ferry Road
Portland, OR 97225

Phone 503-297-6364
Fax 503-297-8234
jlofp@teleport.com

From Portland's Palate is a collection of recipes that was lovingly compiled by the women of the Junior League of Portland. Popular since its first printing in 1992, its 272 pages of recipes were carefully culled to present Portland's unique blend of cosmopolitan flair and small-city friendliness.

$ 24.95 Retail price   Visa/MC accepted
$ 5.00 Postage and handling

Make check payable to Junior League of Portland
ISBN 0-9632525-1-8

THE FRUIT LOOP COOKBOOK

Hood River Fruit Loop
2665 Reed Road
Hood River, OR 97031

Phone 541-386-7697
Fax 541-386-7315
jamqueen@aol.com

The Fruit Loop Cookbook profiles the farms located in the Hood River Valley. Each farm provided their family's favorite recipes. Over 130 recipes featuring apples, pears, cherries, blueberries, chestnuts, and other products grown in our valley. 137 pages.

$ 12.95 Retail price
$ 2.50 Postage and handling

Make check payable to Fruit Loop

GEMS FROM THE KITCHEN

by Beverly Thielbar, C.G.   Phone 541-476-6553
1920 Southgate Way
Grants Pass, OR 97527

An exceptional collection of recipes spanning over 50 years. As a former home economics teacher, I made it a life-long project of collecting the best of recipes. This book contains 550 recipes on 203 pages—assorted unusual, old family, quick & easy, and prize winners.

$ 10.00 Retail price
$ 3.00 Postage and handling

Make check payable to Beverly Thielbar

GET COOKIN' WITH SOUND CONSTRUCTION

Sound Construction, Inc.   Phone 541-382-1879
413 NW Hill Street   Fax 541-382-2132
Bend, OR 97701   sconst@callatg.com

Get Cookin' with Sound Construction is an 84-page cookbook of 60+ family-loved recipes and "words of wisdom" from Sound Construction homeowners and employees. All money raised (100%) is donated to two local aid organizations: Grandma's House of Central Oregon and the Humane Society of Central Oregon. So far, over $3,000 has been donated.

$ 15.00 Retail price
$ 3.00 Postage and handling

Make check payable to Sound Construction Cookbook Fund

GLORIOUS SOUPS AND BREADS!

by Nancy Brannon
ConAmore Publishing   Phone 541-997-4050
68 Spyglass Lane   Fax 503-218-8986
Florence, OR 97439   conamorepub@starband.net

An international collection of soups, stews, breads and spreads. Contains nutritional information for each recipe.

$ 12.95 Retail price   Visa/MC/AmEx
$ 2.00 Postage and handling

Make check payable to ConAmore Publishing

ISBN 0-9623036-4-X

GRADE A RECIPES

Christ Lutheran School   Phone 541-267-3851
1835 North 15th   chlucs@msn.com
Coos Bay, OR 97420

This cookbook originated with several people in our parent/teacher league swapping recipes. A proposal was made to compile a cookbook of favorite recipes from school families. Many of the recipes contain fish (a major industry in Coos Bay) and berries (very plentiful here).

$ 10.00 Retail price
$ 4.00 Postage and handling

Make check payable to Christ Lutheran School

GRANDMA JEAN'S RAINY DAY RECIPES

Kristina Y. McMorris   Fax 503-284-0004
8338 NE Alderwood Road, Suite 200
Portland, OR 97220

Featured on television programs throughout the Northwest! Originally printed as a surprise Christmas gift from her granddaughter, *Grandma Jean's Rainy Day Recipes* offers more than 400 down-home-cooking recipes to warm the hearts and fill the bellies of food lovers everywhere. All proceeds benefit the Food Bank.

$ 15.00 Retail price
$ 2.50 Postage and handling

Make check payable to Grandma Jean

GREAT RECIPES FROM REDEEMER'S FELLOWSHIP

Redeemer's Fellowship   Phone 541-672-0230
729 SE Jackson Street
Roseburg, OR 97470

"Being a great cook is largely a matter of confidence—you can do it if you think you can!" So begins *Great Recipes from Redeemer's Fellowship*, a collection of over 365 terrific recipes from great cooks—all tried-and-true favorites! Hardcover; 3 ring binder. Wonderful gift or addition to your collection.

$ 10.00 Suggested Donation
$ 4.00 Postage and handling

Make check payable to Redeemer's Fellowship

HAZELNUTS & MORE COOKBOOK

by Lucy Gerspacher, CCP
Graphic Arts Center Publishing   Phone 503-678-6823
21595-A Dolores Way NE   Fax 503-678-6823
Aurora, OR 97002   hazelnut@oregonhazelnuts.org

Each recipe contains prep time and sidebars highlighting unique features, unusual ingredients, special techniques, low-fat tips or helpful shortcuts. Gerspacher's 20 years of culinary experience includes consultant, recipe developer, food stylist and teacher with the Oregon Hazelnut Marketing Board.

$ 24.95 Retail price
$ 2.00 Postage and handling

Make check payable to Hazelnut Marketing Board

ISBN 1-55868-203-1

HEAVENLY TEMPTATIONS

St. Anne's Catholic School
c/o M. Schlumpberger   Phone 541-476-5602
2736 Fish Hatchery Road   Fax 541-472-1872
Grants Pass, OR 97527   bschlump@msn.com

Our rural southern Oregon city has many good cooks and our 166 pages of favorite recipes show how good our potlucks really are!

$ 7.50 Retail price
$ 2.50 Postage and handling

Make check payable to St. Anne's Catholic School

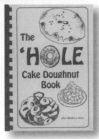

THE 'HOLE CAKE DOUGHNUT BOOK

by Alice Mathews Jones   Phone 541-269-1534
973 D. Street
Coos Bay, OR 97420

A book of doughnuts leavened with baking powder, soda or eggs collected from many sources over 50 years. Covers historical recipe writing, doughnuts, baked and drop doughnuts, crullers, foreign, and some fritters and miscellaneous fried breads. 224 pages, 240 recipes, some never published before.

$ 15.00 Retail price
$ 3.00 Postage and handling
Make check payable to Alice M. Jones

HUCKLEBERRIES AND CRABMEAT

by Carol Cate
C. R. Bears   Phone 541-673-4248
P. O. Box 795
Winchester, OR 97495

You will delight in this 110-page, 153-recipe cookbook with emphasis on Dungeness crab and wild huckleberries. Spiralbound for easy use.

$ 5.00 Retail price
Make check payable to C. R. Bears

KING ESTATE NEW AMERICAN CUISINE PINOT GRIS COOKBOOK

King Estate Winery   Phone 800-884-4441
80854 Territorial Road   Fax 541-942-9867
Eugene, OR 97405

King Estate is dedicated to developing food and wine pairings emphasizing Northwest wines and seasonal organic ingredients. To carry their pairing education deeper into the public, King Estate created the *New American Cuisine Pinot Gris Cookbook*, featuring 22 of America's most respected and innovative chefs.

$ 16.95 Retail price   Visa/MC/AmEx accepted
$ 4.00 Postage and handling, each additional add $1.00
Make check payable to King Estate Winery
ISBN 0-9645500-1-6

THE LIGHTER SIDE OF ITALY

by Nancy Brannon
ConAmore Publishing   Phone 541-997-4050
68 Spyglass Lane   Fax 503-218-8986
Florence, OR 97439   conamorepub@starband.net

A fabulous collection of authentic Italian recipes that just happen to be low in fat, low in cholesterol and heart healthy! (No substitutions; no fake cheese; no skim milk.) Nutritional information included for each recipe.

$ 14.95 Retail price Visa/MC/AmEx
$ 2.00 Postage and handling
Make check payable to ConAmore Publishing
ISBN 0-9623036-5-8

LOOK WHAT'S COOKING

Oregon Farm Bureau Federation
Women's Advisory Council
3415 Commercial Street SE, Suite 117
Salem, OR 97302-5169

Phone 503-399-1701
Fax 503-399-8082
jessica@oregonfb.org

From our membership to you, *Look What's Cooking* is a compilation of favorite recipes submitted by County Farm Bureaus throughout the state of Oregon. The Oregon Farm Bureau Women's Advisory Council sponsored the publication of this cookbook in 1993 and it has been well loved by friends and families throughout the years.

$ 10.00 Retail price
$ 2.00 Postage and handling

Make check payable to Oregon Farm Bureau Federation

MANNA BY THE SEA

St Peter the Fisherman Lutheran Women's Missionary League
P. O. Box 169
Lincoln City, OR 97367

Phone 541-994-2007
lutheranchurchlc@hotmail.com

Dedicated to all cooks, this 3-ring cookbook reflects the love of good cooking by using 420 treasured family recipes from a variety of nationalities. The *Manna by the Sea* cover depicts the Christian symbolism of a fish, identifying the membership and location of St. Peter the Fisherman Lutheran Church.

$ 10.00 Retail price
$ 6.00 Postage and handling

Make check payable to Lutheran Women's Missionary League (or LWML)

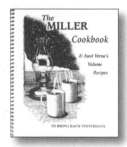

THE MILLER COOKBOOK

Carrie Gingerich
31982 Boston Mill Road
Shedd, OR 97377

Phone 541-369-2968

The Miller Cookbook has 500 recipes from 200 people. Contributors include many of Carrie Gingerich's 64 first cousins. Aunt Verna's volume recipes feature cooking for large crowds. A delightful collection of her family-style recipes.

$ 8.00 Retail price
$ 2.00 Postage and handling

Make check payable to Carrie Gingerich

MULTNOMAH FALLS LODGE COOK BOOK

Multnomah Falls Lodge Company
P. O. Box 367
Troutdale, OR 97060

Phone 503-695-2376
mflterri@yahoo.com

In our 48-page cookbook, not only will you discover unique recipes, you will find enchanting photographs of the Columbia River Gorge—home to Multnomah Falls Lodge.

$ 6.99 Retail price
$ 4.00 Postage and handling

Make check payable to Multnomah Falls Lodge Company

THE NEW AMERICAN DIET COOKBOOK
by Sonja L. Connor, M.S., and William E. Connor, M.D.
NAD Press
2600 SW Sherwood Place
Portland, OR 97201

The New American Diet Cookbook contains more than 250 new well-tested, great-tasting recipes gathered from a broad spectrum of cultures. It shows an easy and delicious way to move to an exciting and more healthful way of eating to help prevent heart disease and other chronic diseases. 344 pages.

$ 18.95 Retail price
$ 3.00 Postage and handling
Make check payable to NAD Press
ISBN 0-9678960-0-2

THE NEW COMPLETE COFFEE BOOK
by Sara Perry
Chronicle Books   www.chronbooks.com
85 Second Street/Sixth Floor
San Francisco, CA 94105

Author Sara Perry offers up-to-the-minute information and recipes from the world's favorite brewed beverage. Whether it's a perfect shot of espresso or a classic cup of joe, *The New Complete Coffee Book* is the essential guidebook to the modern world of coffee. Softcover, 120 pages.

$ 16.95 Retail price
$ 3.00 Postage and handling
Make check payable to Chronicle Books
ISBN 0-8118-2867-0

THE NEW TEA BOOK
by Sara Perry
Chronicle Books   www.chronbooks.com
85 Second Street/Sixth Floor
San Francisco, CA 94105

Cookbook author, columnist and radio commentator Sara Perry, revisits the world of tea in her completely revised and updated *The New Tea Book: A Guide to Black, Green, Herbal, and Chai Tea.* Softcover, 120 pages.

$ 16.95 Retail price
$ 3.00 Postage and handling
Make check payable to Chronicle Books
ISBN 0-8118-3053-5

OREGON COOK BOOK
by Janet Walker
Golden West Publishers   Phone 800-658-5830
4113 North Longview Avenue   Fax 602-279-6901
Phoenix, AZ 85014-4949   goldwest1@mindspring.com

Featuring favorite recipes from Oregon's finest restaurants, bed and breakfasts, homemakers, dignitaries and chefs. More than 200 tasty recipes! Featuring apples, berries, nuts, pears, seafood and more. Now you can bring the flavors of Oregon to your table.

$ 6.95 Retail price   Visa/MC accepted
$ 3.00 Postage and handling
Make check payable to Golden West Publishers
ISBN 1-885590-03-2

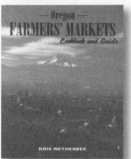

OREGON FARMERS' MARKETS COOKBOOK AND GUIDE

by Kris Wetherbee
Maverick Publications, Inc.   Phone 541-849-2838
4290 Rice Valley Road   kwether@jeffnet.org
Oakland, OR 97462

Oregon Farmers' Markets contains 192 pages of earthly delights found at the state's farmers' markets. Interspersed among an irresistible collection of over 200 recipes and market information are dozens of tips on growing, picking, storing, and preparing foods, plus interesting facts about foods.

$ 14.95 Retail price
$ 2.00 Postage and handling

Make check payable to Kris Wetherbee

ISBN 0-89288-278-6

OREGON: THE OTHER SIDE

Beta Omicron Chapter - ESA
Cookbook, P. O. Box 441
Hines, OR 97738

This 602-recipe collection has been compiled by a group of women from the high desert side of Oregon. It includes family recipes handed down from pioneer ranchers and homesteaders and also from the many Basque people who came here with the sheep industry. This diverse recipe collection has been featured in *Good Housekeeping* magazine.

$ 10.00 Retail price
$ 2.00 Postage and handling

Make check payable to Beta Omicron

OREGON TRAIL COOKING

by Mary Gunderson
Blue Earth Books/Capstone Press   Phone 800-747-4992
151 Good Counsel Drive   Fax 888-262-0705
Mankato, MN 56001   www.capstone-press.com

Bring interest in history to a rolling boil with this simple recipe book! By making foods popular on the Oregon Trail, readers get a taste of life on the wagon train. Simple text and interesting photographs present foods of the period, plus customs, family roles, everyday life and important celebrations. A veritable feast of information and valuable resource for children and adults.

Visit web for current pricing   Visa/MC accepted

Make check payable to Capstone Press

ISBN 0-7368-0355-6

OUR FAVORITE RECIPES

Elliott Prairie Community Church   Phone 503-982-9202
13023 Elliott Prairie Road   Fax 503-634-2627
Woodburn, OR 97071

Enjoy just good eating? *Our Favorite Recipes* contains 78 pages of good food from the best cooks in Oregon's farm country. The Elliott Prairie Church was built in 1892 to fulfill the religious needs of an Oregon Farm Community. We round out our recipe collection with bible verses and helpful hints.

$ 5.00 Retail price
$ 2.00 Postage and handling

Make check payable to Elliott Prairie Church

"PACIFIC"ALLY SALMON
by Carol Cate
C. R. Bears   Phone 541-673-4248
P. O. Box 795
Winchester, OR 97495

Totally salmon, this collection offers first courses, salads, main dishes, sandwiches and sauces. 108 pages, 155 recipes, spiralbound for easy use.

$ 5.00 Retail price

Make check payable to C. R. Bears

PIG OUT
White Eagle Grange # 683   Phone 541-276-3778
P. O. Box 803   rgwilson@oregontrail.net
Pilot Rock, OR 97868

Pig Out with White Eagle Grange and Friends in 316 pages of down-home recipes like Grandma used to make. Lots of helpful hints, a dash of fun, and a bunch of good eats. The Grange is well known for their potlucks, and most of the recipes have been tried out at the potluck suppers. You should be able to find something for everyone in these fun-filled pages.

$ 12.00 Retail price
$ 5.00 Postage and handling

Make check payable to White Eagle Grange

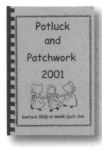

POTLUCK AND PATCHWORK
Skip-a-Week Quilt Club   Phone 503-630-5000
35935 SE Bowman Road   tradbh@aol.com
Estacada, OR 97023

Trading recipes at our once-a-month potlucks has encouraged our members to produce this cookbook. Within these 154 pages, you'll find taste-tempting delights enhanced with delightful illustrations. Enjoy.

$ 10.00 Retail price
$ 3.00 Postage and handling

Make check payable to Skip-a-Week

QUICK & HEALTHY RECIPES AND IDEAS
by Brenda J. Ponichtera, Registered Dietitian
Scaledown Publishing, Inc.   Phone 541-296-5859
1519 Hermits Way   Fax 541-296-1875
The Dalles, OR 97058   scaledwn@gorge.net

Targets people who want good-tasting food but have little time to cook. Includes 180 low-fat recipes, time-saving ideas, 50 weight loss tips, menus, grocery lists, nutrient analysis and diabetes exchanges. "Well-organized, well-thought-out, takes into account how busy most of us really are."—*Miami Herald*

$ 16.95 Retail price   Visa/MC accepted
$ 3.50 Postage and handling, each add'l add $2.00

Make check payable to ScaleDown Publishing, Inc.

ISBN 0-9629160-0-5

QUICK & HEALTHY VOLUME II

by Brenda J. Ponichtera, Registered Dietitian
Scaledown Publishing, Inc.
1519 Hermits Way
The Dalles, OR 97058

Phone 541-296-5859
Fax 541-296-1875
scaledwn@gorge.net

This award-winning cookbook features 190 low-fat quick-to-prepare recipes that appeal to the entire family. Includes weekly menus with grocery lists, tips for trimming fat from your diet, nutritional analysis, and diabetes exchanges. "Healthful cooking for busy people who live in the real world."— *Post Crescent*

$ 16.95 Retail price   Visa/MC accepted
$ 3.50 Postage and handling, each add'l add $2.00

Make check payable to ScaleDown Publishing, Inc.

ISBN 0-9629160-1-3

RAINY DAY TREATS AND SUNNY TEMPTATIONS

Medical Faculty Auxiliary of the Oregon Health and Science University
Nancy Cutler   Phone 503-494-4088
7030 SW Canyon Drive   (voice mail at OHSU-MFA)
Portland, OR 97225

Presented here are 200 pages of classic recipes by the members of our group. The cover is an original watercolor by a former employee at Oregon Health Sciences University.

$ 10.00 Retail price
$ 2.00 Postage and handling

Make check payable to M.F.A. at OHSU

RECIPES AND REMEMBERING

by Dorothy J. O'Neal   Phone 541-688-3292
3459 Hawthorne Avenue   lanerecipes@aol.com
Eugene, OR 97402

A 45-year collection of 507 taste-tested family recipes dating back to 1907. There are a few short memories of Dorothy's Great Depression childhood on a rural ranch.

$ 12.00 Retail price
$ 2.00 Postage and handling

Make check payable to Food for Thought

RECIPES FOR THE WEEKEND GOURMET

by Sallie Anne Simpson   Phone 541-776-7729
2090 Waters Creek Road
Wilderville, OR 97543

This cookbook is for those who love to cook and receive joy from cooking. It is a collection of recipes from family, friends, and cookbooks over the last 25 years.

$ 5.95 Retail price   Visa/MC/Discover accepted
$ 3.00 Postage and handling

Make check payable to Sallie Simpson

RECIPES FROM THE KITCHENS OF FAMILY & FRIENDS

Bahari Court #104, Ladies Oriental Shrine of North America
461 Dawson Drive   Phone 541-784-3849
Winston, OR 97496-9609

This 120-page book was compiled from favorite recipes from several different members that belong to the many organizations within our Masonic Fraternal Family. Some of the recipes are treasured family keepsakes and some are new; however, they all reflect the love of good cooking.

$ 12.50 Retail price
$ 2.50 Postage and handling

Make check payable to Bahari Court #104 LOSNA

RECIPES, RECIPES, RECIPES!

Easter Seals Oregon   Phone 541-344-2247
3575 Donald Street   Fax 541-344-7082
Eugene, OR 97404

This 304-page collection of recipes from clients and staff of the Easter Seals Aquatic Center is a tasty sampling of Oregon's cuisine. Sure to please your palate.

$ 10.00 Retail price
$ 2.95 Postage and handling

Make check payable to Easter Seals Oregon

ROGUE RIVER RENDEZVOUS

Junior League of Jackson County   Phone 541-779-5020
P. O. Box 1504
Medford, OR 97501

Winner of the prestigious Tabasco Cookbook Award in 1992, this hardback book of 222 pages is a delight to encounter. Enjoy the savory tastes of recipes indigenous to the Pacific Northwest. This is a region where berries, pears, nuts and apples are grown in abundance and wildlife flourishes.

$ 19.95 Retail price
$ 3.00 Postage and handling

Make check payable to Rogue River Rendezvous

ISBN 0-9632671-0-8

SAGEBRUSH SURPRISES COOKBOOK

Oregon Trail Shop   Phone 541-523-1844
P. O. Box 987   Fax 541-523-1855
Baker City, OR 97814   nhotic@or.blm.gov

Sagebrush Surprises is the combined effort of Trail Tender members and personnel at the National Historic Oregon Trail Interpretive Center. Recipes—old and new—have changed with the times, the people, and the country, but all reflect the resourceful, independent tradition of people in Eastern Oregon.

$ 12.95 Retail price   Visa/MC accepted
$ 5.95 Postage and handling

Make check payable to Oregon Trail Shop

SAVOR THE FLAVOR

Portland Adventist Community Services
11020 NE Halsey
Portland, OR 97220

Phone 503-252-8500
Fax 503-257-2884
rhondaw@pdxacs.com

Savor the Flavor is a vegetarian cookbook put together as a cooperative effort of volunteers. Over 216 cooks have contributed the nearly 600 recipes found within the 266 pages of this book. Proceeds from the sale of this book support our agency in providing emergency food, clothing, and medical care for poverty-level individuals.

$ 11.99 Retail price
$ 2.00 Postage and handling

Visa/MC accepted

Make check payable to Portland Adventist Community Services (PACS)

SAVOR THE FLAVOR OF OREGON

Junior League of Eugene
2839 Willamette Street
Eugene, OR 97405

Phone 800-364-4031
Fax 541-345-8823
jlecookbook@mindspring.com

Features 500 recipes from around the world—from appetizers and salads to entrées and desserts—with a special emphasis on foods of the Pacific Northwest. Also includes full-color food photography throughout.

$ 19.95 Retail price
$ 5.50 Postage and handling

Visa/MC accepted

Make check payable to *A Taste of Oregon*

ISBN 0-9607976-1-0

SCALLOPS AND SOLE FOOD

by Carol Cates
C. R. Bears
P. O. Box 795
Winchester, OR 97495

Phone 541-673-4248

This collection of recipes is sure to please anyone who enjoys seafood delicacies such as scallops and sole. Spiralbound, 108 pages.

$ 5.00 Retail price

Make check payable to C. R. Bears

SEASONED WITH WORDS

Oregon Writers Colony
c/o Marlene Howard
4140 SE 37th Avenue, Apt 10
Portland, OR 97202

Phone 503-771-0428
marlenehow@attbi.com

A smorgasbord of storytelling and poetry related to food. Members and friends of Oregon Writers Colony wrote vignettes and recipes: *New York Times* best-selling authors, regional and national award winners, and writers whose time is yet to come are represented here. A good read for people who like writing and food.

$ 22.00 Retail price
$ 3.00 Postage and handling

Visa/MC accepted

Make check payable to Oregon Writers Colony

ISBN 1-891535-01-3

SERVING UP OREGON

Atkinson Graduate School of Management/Willamette University
Cindy Koch   Phone 503-581-9623
685 Court Street   Fax 503-581-9626
Salem, OR 97301   cindykymca@aol.com

Serving Up Oregon takes you on a unique journey throughout our beautiful state of Oregon. Along the way, you will pause and discover entertaining stories and facts while sampling local dishes from native Oregonians. The sales proceeds benefit the Salem Family YMCA.

$ 15.00 Retail price
$ 3.95 Postage and handling

Make check payable to YMCA

SUMMERTIME TREATS

by Sara Perry
Chronicle Books   www.chronbooks.com
85 Second Street/Sixth Floor
San Francisco, CA 94105

What better time to bond with your kids, whipping up delicious treats or dabbling in easy-to-make arts and crafts, indoors and out? Illustrated with color photographs throughout, this 96-page handbook by Sara Perry, columnist for the *Oregonian,* is the ultimate guide to creating a terrific season.

$ 14.95 Retail price
$ 3.00 Postage and handling

Make check payable to Chronicle Books
ISBN 0-8118-2323-7

A TASTE OF OREGON

Junior League of Eugene   Phone 800-364-4031
2839 Willamette Street   Fax 541-345-8823
Eugene, OR 97405   jlecookbook@mindspring.com

Winner of the Walter S. McIlhenny Hall of Fame and Southern Living Hall of Fame. Sold over 360,000 copies. This collection of 600 recipes also includes anecdotes from early pioneer days.

$ 19.95 Retail price   Visa/MC accepted
$ 5.50 Postage and handling

Make check payable to *A Taste of Oregon*
ISBN 0-9607976-0-2

A TASTE OF TILLAMOOK

Tillamook Chamber of Commerce   Phone 503-842-7525
3705 Hwy 101 N   Fax 503-842-7526
Tillamook, OR 97141   tillchamber@wcn.net

A special collection of rave review foods for everyday eating or special occasions. There are 300 favorite recipes from the good cooks of Tillamook County.

$ 10.00 Retail price   Visa/MC accepted
$ 3.50 Postage and handling

Make check payable to Tillamook Chamber of Commerce

TASTEFULLY OREGON

Oregon Dietetic Association
P. O. Box 6497
Portland, OR 97228-6497

Tastefully Oregon successfully bridges the gap between taste and health with a wealth of delicious recipes that not only reflect Northwest cuisine, but also meet nutrition goals. In 292 pages, there are 241 recipes with full nutritional analysis. All recipes meet USDA Dietary Guidelines. Full-color, glossy, stain-resistant cover, plastic binder, lays flat.

$ 15.95   Retail price

Make check payable to Oregon Dietetic Association

ISBN 0-9650697-0-2

THEN 'TIL NOW

by Dorothy J. O'Neal   Phone 541-688-3292
3459 Hawthorne Avenue   lanerecipes@aol.com
Eugene, OR 97402

Four hundred and thirty farm-ranch-type recipes with several short stories about Dorothy's childhood during the Great Depression.

$ 12.00   Retail price
$ 2.00   Postage and handling

Make check payable to Food for Thought

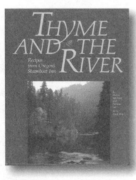

THYME AND THE RIVER

by Patricia Lee & Sharon Van Loan: Steamboat Inn
Graphic Arts Center Publishing Company   Phone 541-498-2230
P. O. Box 207   Fax 541-498-2411
Idleyld Park, OR 97447   stmbtinn@rosenet.net

Original recipes from southern Oregon's celebrated Steamboat Inn, located high above the North Umpqua River. From Zucchini and Three-Pepper Stir-Fry to Filbert Roulade, there's something here for everyone. Also includes cooking tips by the authors and photographs and history of the area.

$ 22.95   Retail price   Visa/MC accepted
$ 3.00   Postage and handling

Make check payable to *Thyme and the River* Publications

ISBN 1-55868-479-4

THYME & THE RIVER, TOO

by Patricia Lee & Sharon Van Loan: Steamboat Inn
Graphic Arts Center Publishing Company   Phone 541-498-2230
P. O. Box 207   Fax 541-498-2411
Idleyld Park, OR 97447   stmbtinn@rosenet.net

This book focuses on the abundance and diversity of ingredients native to the Pacific Northwest. Whether planning for a Sunday brunch or a full dinner party, you can find what you are looking for. Over 100 recipes, along with color photographs and historical notations.

$ 22.95   Retail price   Visa/MC accepted
$ 3.00   Postage and handling

Make check payable to *Thyme and the River* Publications

ISBN 1-55868-155-8

TREASURED RECIPES

Western Welcome Newcomers   Phone 541-955-8830
4545 Azalea Drive   bobpat@magick.net
Grants Pass, OR 97526

Selected recipes from Western Welcome Newcomers new to the Grants Pass, Oregon area, a nonprofit social organization to help people meet, make new friends and become acquainted with the locale. This is a 6x9-inch ringbound, illustrated, indexed, 248-page, 700-recipe cookbook with nutritional information and many helpful cooking hints.

$ 10.00 Retail price
$ 2.00 Postage and handling
Make check payable to Western Welcome Newcomers

WEST COAST SEAFOOD RECIPES

by Blaine Freer   Phone 800-541-9498
Frank Amato Publications, Inc.   Fax 503-653-2766
P. O. Box 82112   sales@amatobooks.com
Portland, OR 97282   www.amatobooks.com

Spicy, curried shrimp, grilled salmon, calamari, tuna casserole—the fantastic meals that can be created from the delights of the sea are endless. With its easily obtained ingredients, simple directions, calorie and fat counts, this book is all you need to create an incredible seafood meal for two!

$ 14.95 Retail price   Visa/MC accepted
$ 3.00 Postage and handling
Make check payable to Frank Amato Publications, Inc.
ISBN 1-57188-046-1

WHAT'S COOKING??

St. Gerard Guild
General Publishing and Binding, Inc.   Phone 503-644-4534
Mrs. Donna Schuetze
4820 SW 141st Avenue
Beaverton, OR 97005

A wonderful and delightful all-around cookbook full of tested recipes to delight anyone's tastes. Especially nice is the "Helpful Hints" in the back of the 150-page cookbook, which contains over 400 exciting recipes.

$ 5.00 Retail price
$ 3.00 Postage and handling
Make check payable to St. Gerard Guild

WHAT'S COOKING IN SISTERS

Friends of the Sisters Library   Phone 541-549-9780
P. O. Box 1378   eclarke610@coinet.com
Sisters, OR 97759

Sisters is a small town at the foot of the Three Sisters Mountains, a beautiful sight; Faith, Hope and Charity, thus the name. The artwork in the book portrays areas in Sisters and its surroundings. 191 pages of recipes plus index.

$ 15.00 Retail price
$ 3.00 Postage and handling
Make check payable to Friends of the Sisters Library

WHAT'S FOR DINNER?

by Brenda Abelein & Kelly Wilkerson
P. O. Box 33991
Portland, OR 97292

Phone 503-760-7205
abz@integrity.com

Does five o'clock roll around and you don't know what's for dinner? We outline a process of cooking dinners ahead for the freezer (including 63 of our favorite recipes). We cook and freeze about 60 meals every time we cook ahead and so can you!

$ 15.00 Retail price
$ 3.00 Postage and handling

Make check payable to Brenda Abelein

Wreckage of the ship "Peter Iredale" can be seen at low tide near the mouth of the Columbia River in Fort Smith State Park. Bound for Portland, the ship was struck by a heavy squall, and grounded in October 1906 with no loss of life.